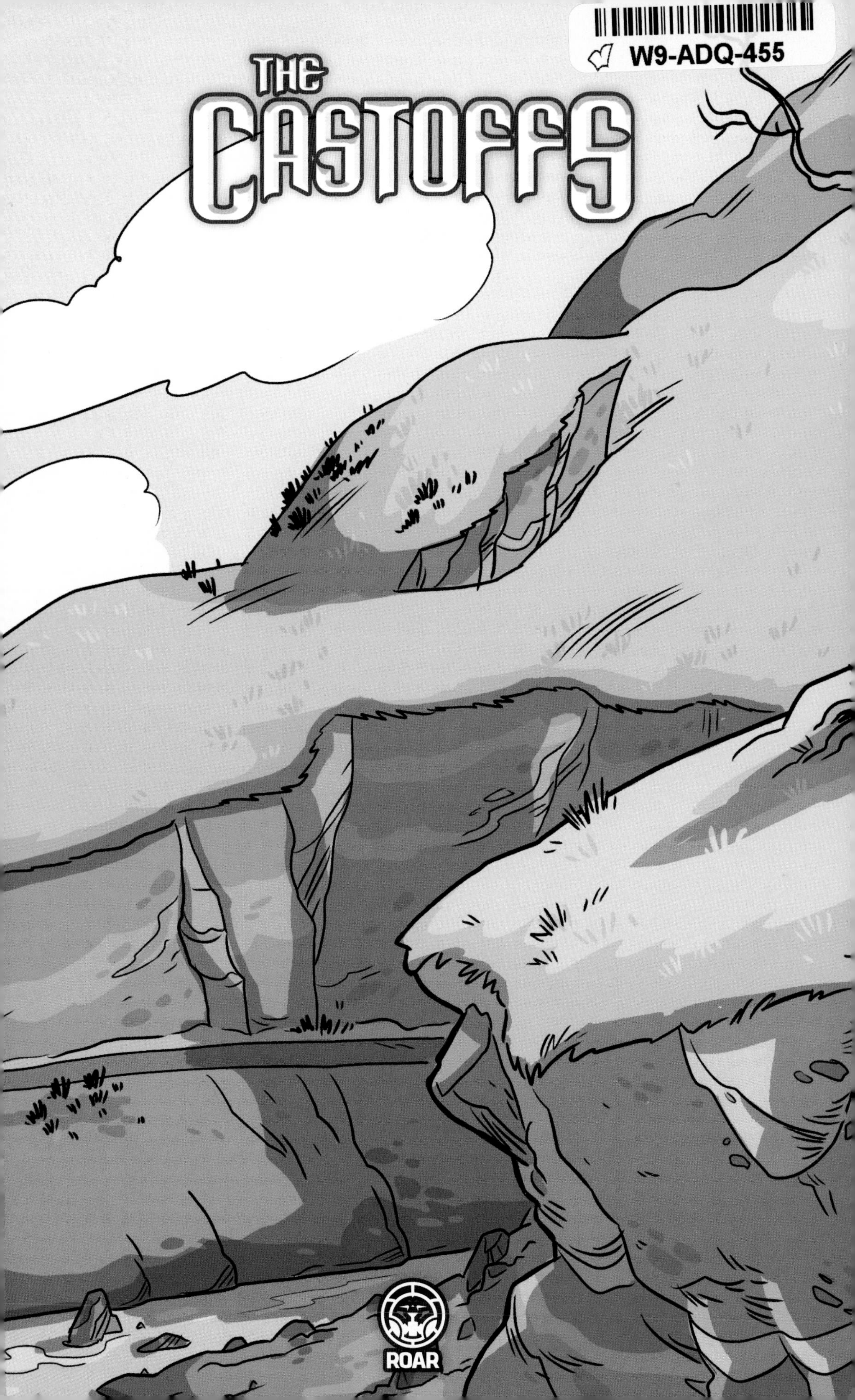
THE
CASTOFFS
ROAR

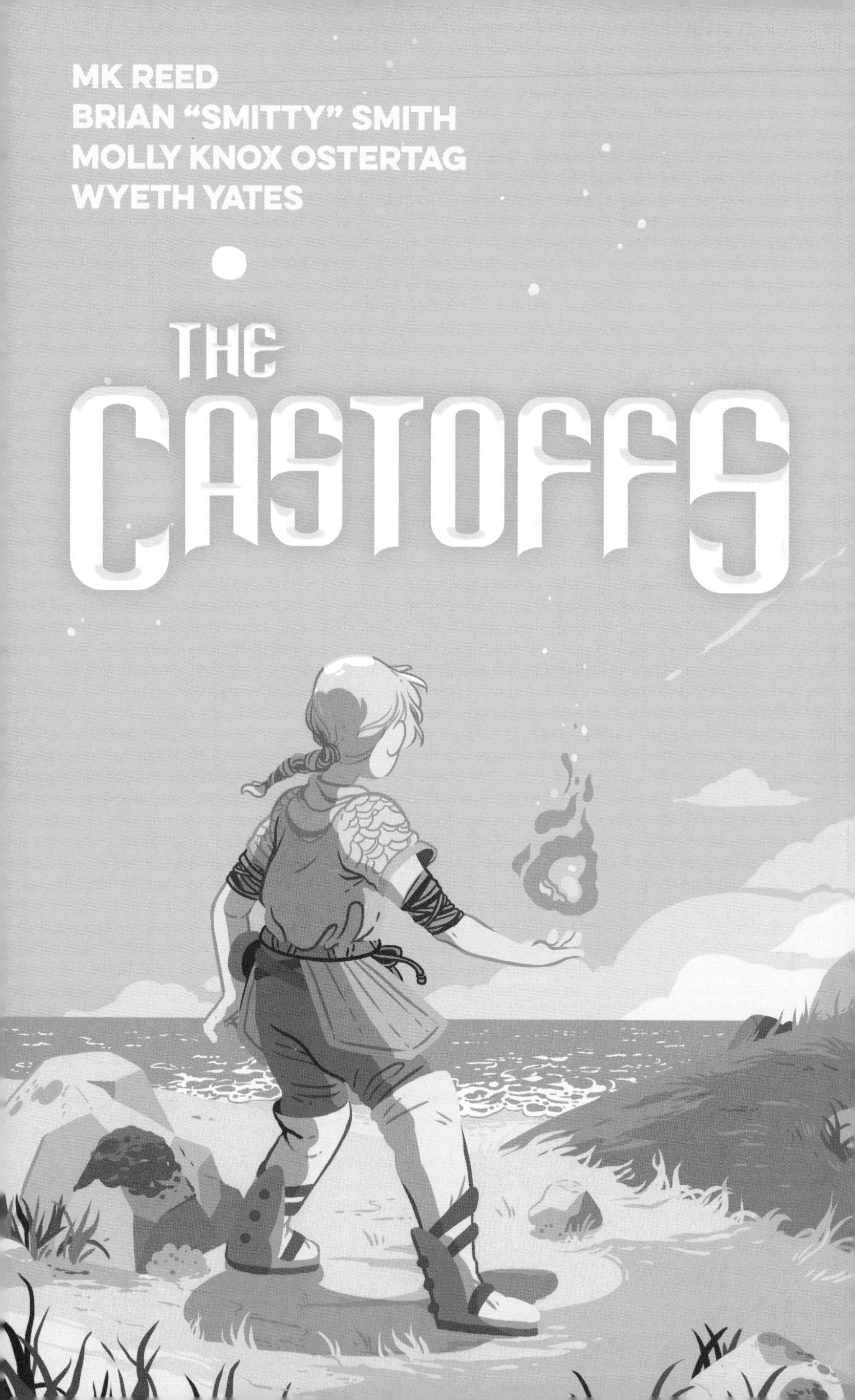
MK REED
BRIAN "SMITTY" SMITH
MOLLY KNOX OSTERTAG
WYETH YATES
THE CASTOFFS

THE CASTOFFS

MK REED & BRIAN "SMITTY" SMITH *WRITERS*

MOLLY KNOX OSTERTAG *ARTIST, Issues 1-4, Covers*

WYETH YATES *ARTIST, Prologue*

MOLLY KNOX OSTERTAG *COLORIST, Issues 1-2, Covers*

BRIAN "SMITTY" SMITH *COLORIST, Prologue, Issues 3-4*

AW'S D.C. HOPKINS
LETTERER

ROSEMARY VALERO O'CONNELL
TITLE SPREAD ILLUSTRATION

SLOANE LEONG
BACKUP ILLUSTRATION

ANDREA COLVIN
EDITOR

HAZEL NEWLEVANT
ASSISTANT EDITOR

ANDWORLD DESIGN
DESIGNER

PUBLISHER'S CATALOGING-IN-PUBLICATION DATA

(PREPARED BY THE DONOHUE GROUP, INC.)

Names: Reed, M. K., author. | Smith, Brian (Comic book writer), author, colorist. | Ostertag, Molly, illustrator, colorist. | Yates, Wyeth, illustrator. | Hopkins, D. C., letterer. | Valero-O'Connell, Rosemary, illustrator. | Leong, Sloane, illustrator. | Colvin, Andrea, editor. | Newlevant, Hazel, editor.

Title: The Castoffs. Vol.1, Mage against the machine / MK Reed & Brian "Smitty" Smith, writers ; Molly Knox Ostertag, artist, Issues 1-4, covers ; Wyeth Yates, artist, Prologue ; Molly Know Ostertag, colorist, Issues 1-2, covers ; Brian "Smitty" Smith, colorist, Prologue, Issues 3-4 ; AW's D.C. Hopkins, letterer ; Rosemary Valero O'Connell, title spread illustration ; Sloane Leong, backup illustration ; Andrea Colvin, editor ; Hazel Newlevant, assistant editor ; Andworld Design, designer.

Description: [St. Louis, Missouri] : The Lion Forge, LLC, 2017. | Interest age level: 12 and up. | "Roar." | "Portions of this book were previously published in The Castoffs, Vol. 1, digital issues 1-4 and The Castoffs, Vol. 1, print issues 1-4." | Summary: "In the aftermath of the Great Mage Machine War three young magic-users are sent on a short mission through a ravaged land. But their purpose is not what they think and their future is anything but simple. Twenty years ago, mages fought for their survival against the Surrogate, a hive-minded robot army that consumed everything in its path. Now, a trio of apprentice mages must cross the ruined landscape to deliver a magical cure to a remote town. But the would-be heroes aren't exactly of the same mind: Charris is a hotheaded fighter with elemental powers; Trinh is a shy mage who can literally turn invisible; and Ursa is a healer with more power than she lets on. Can our mages stop bickering long enough accomplish their task? And is the Surrogate really defeated?"-- Provided by publisher.

Identifiers: ISBN 978-1-941302-27-9

Subjects: LCSH: Teenagers--Comic books, strips, etc. | Magic--Comic books, strips, etc. | Robots--Comic books, strips, etc. | Good and evil--Comic books, strips, etc. | LCGFT: Graphic novels. | Science fiction.

Classification: LCC PN6728 .C37 2017 | DDC 741.5973 [Fic]--dc23

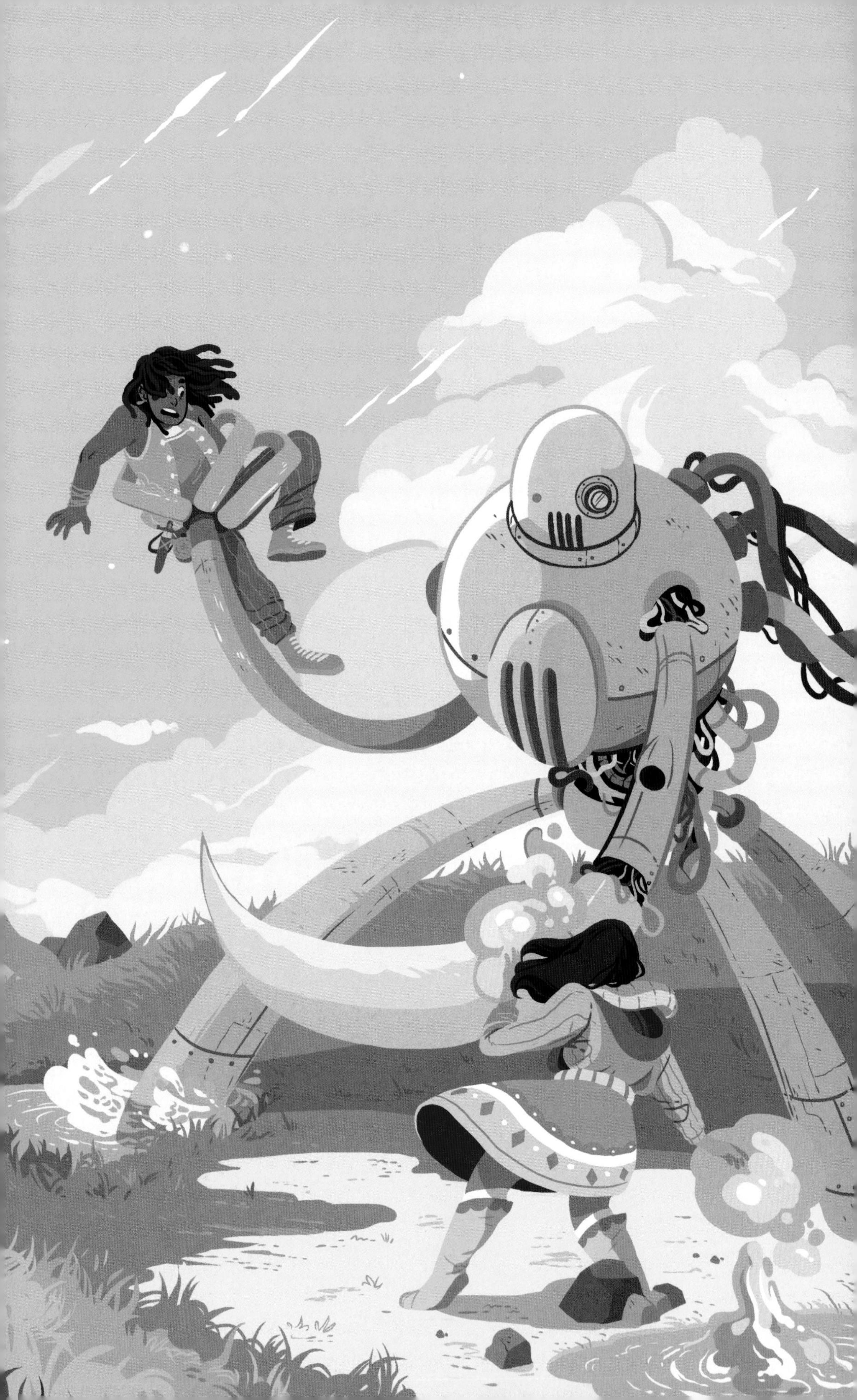

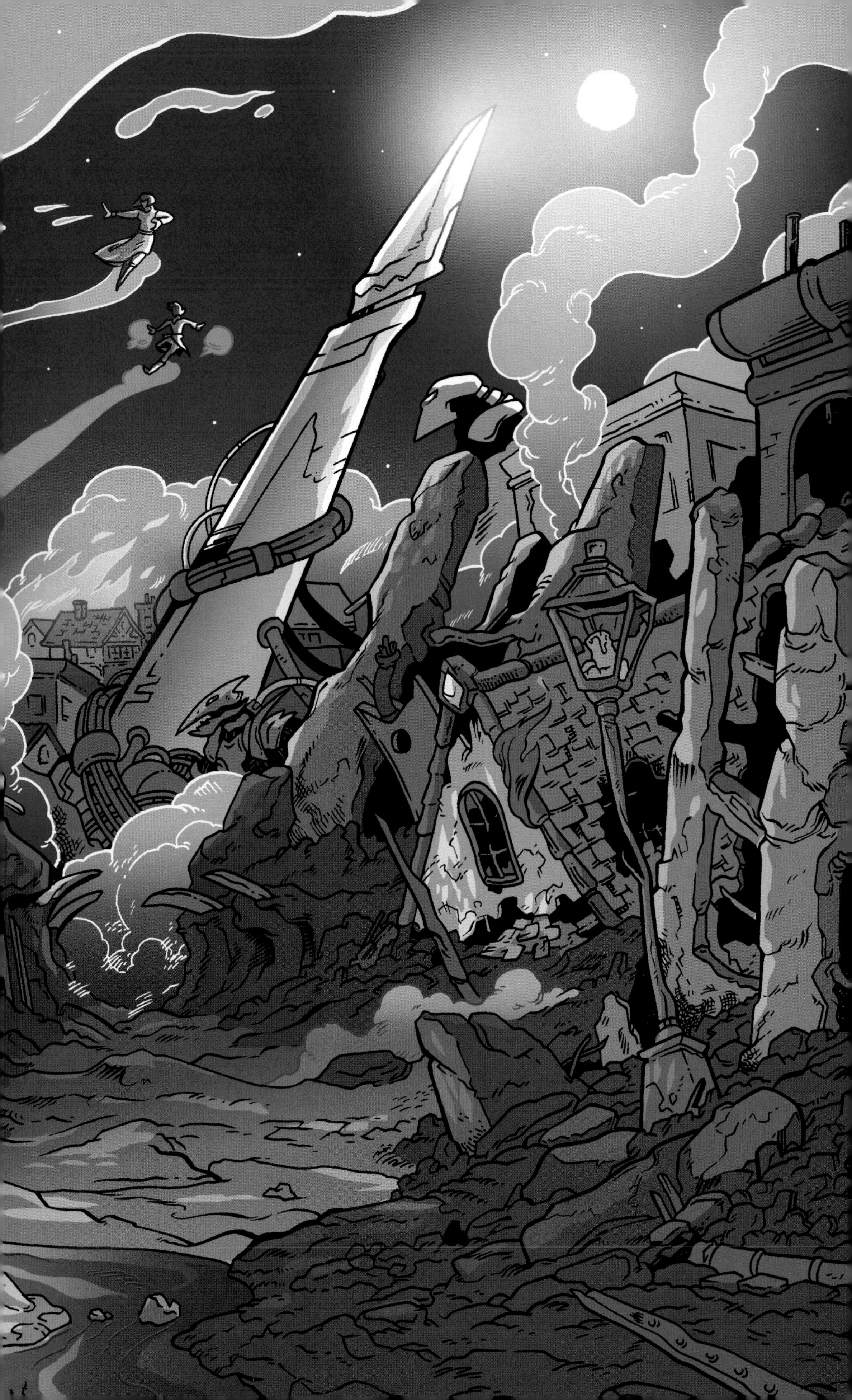

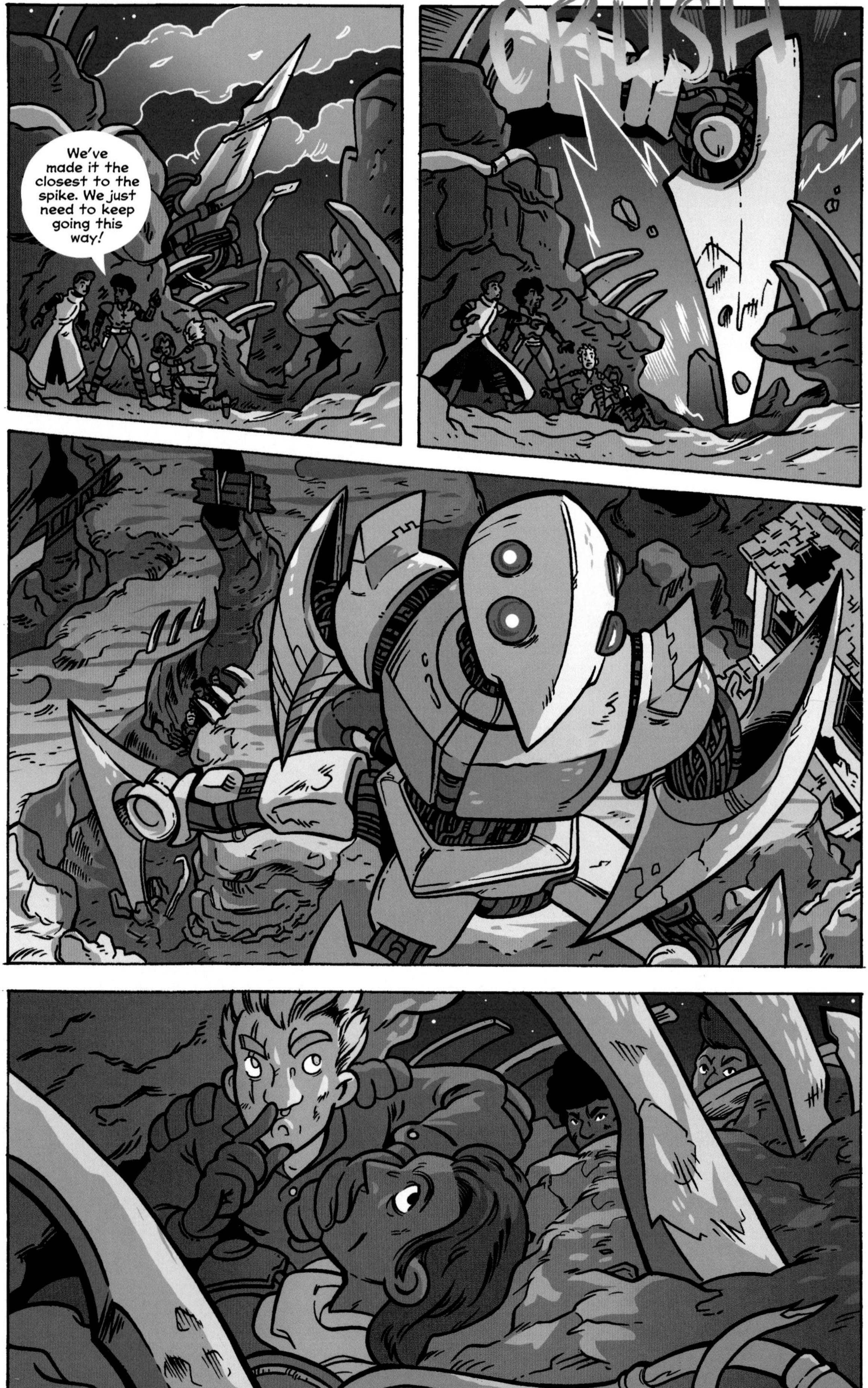
We've made it the closest to the spike. We just need to keep going this way!
CRUSH

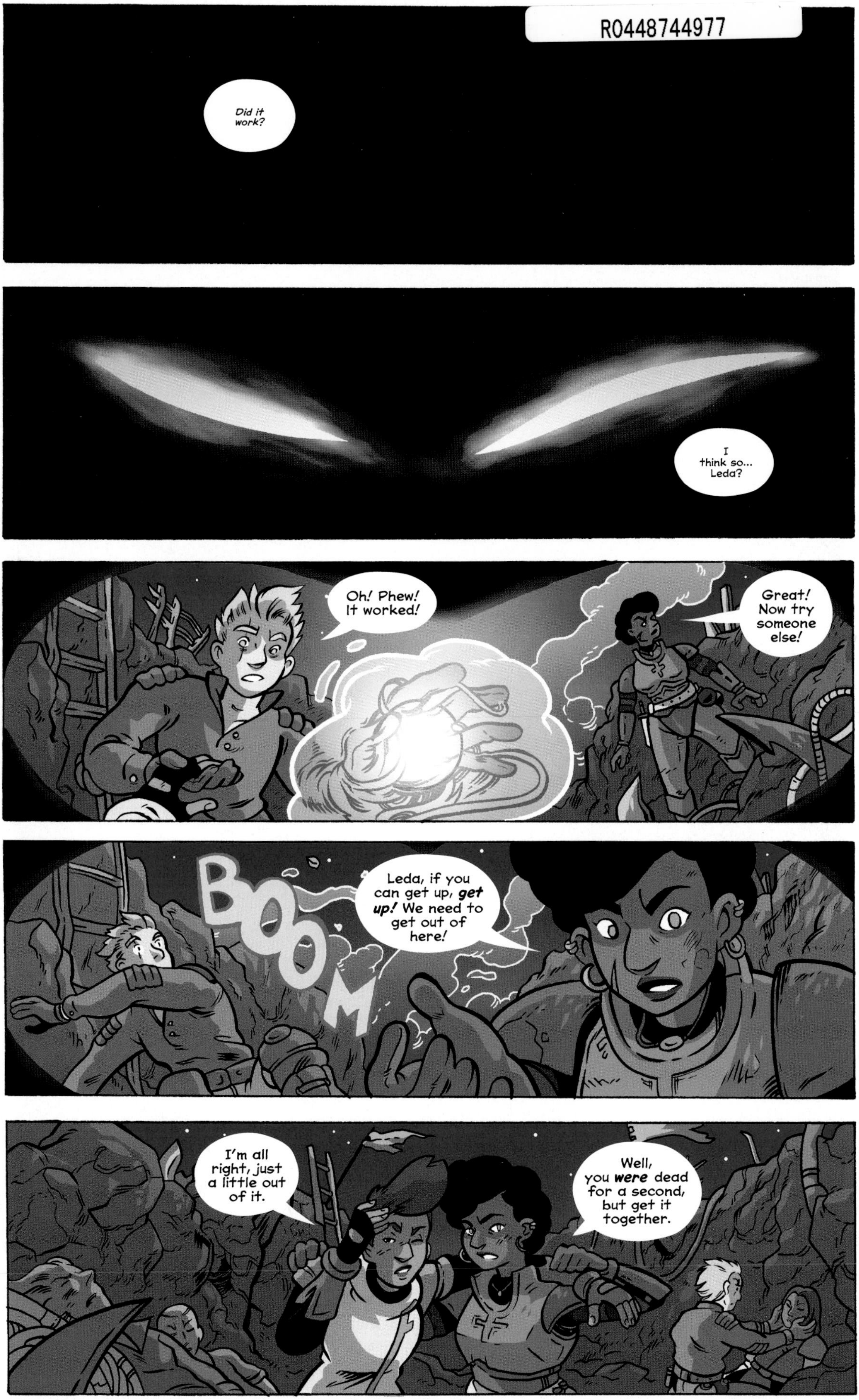
Did it work?
I think so... Leda?
Oh! Phew! It worked!
Great! Now try someone else!
BOOM
Leda, if you can get up, *get up!* We need to get out of here!
I'm all right, just a little out of it.
Well, you *were* dead for a second, but get it together.

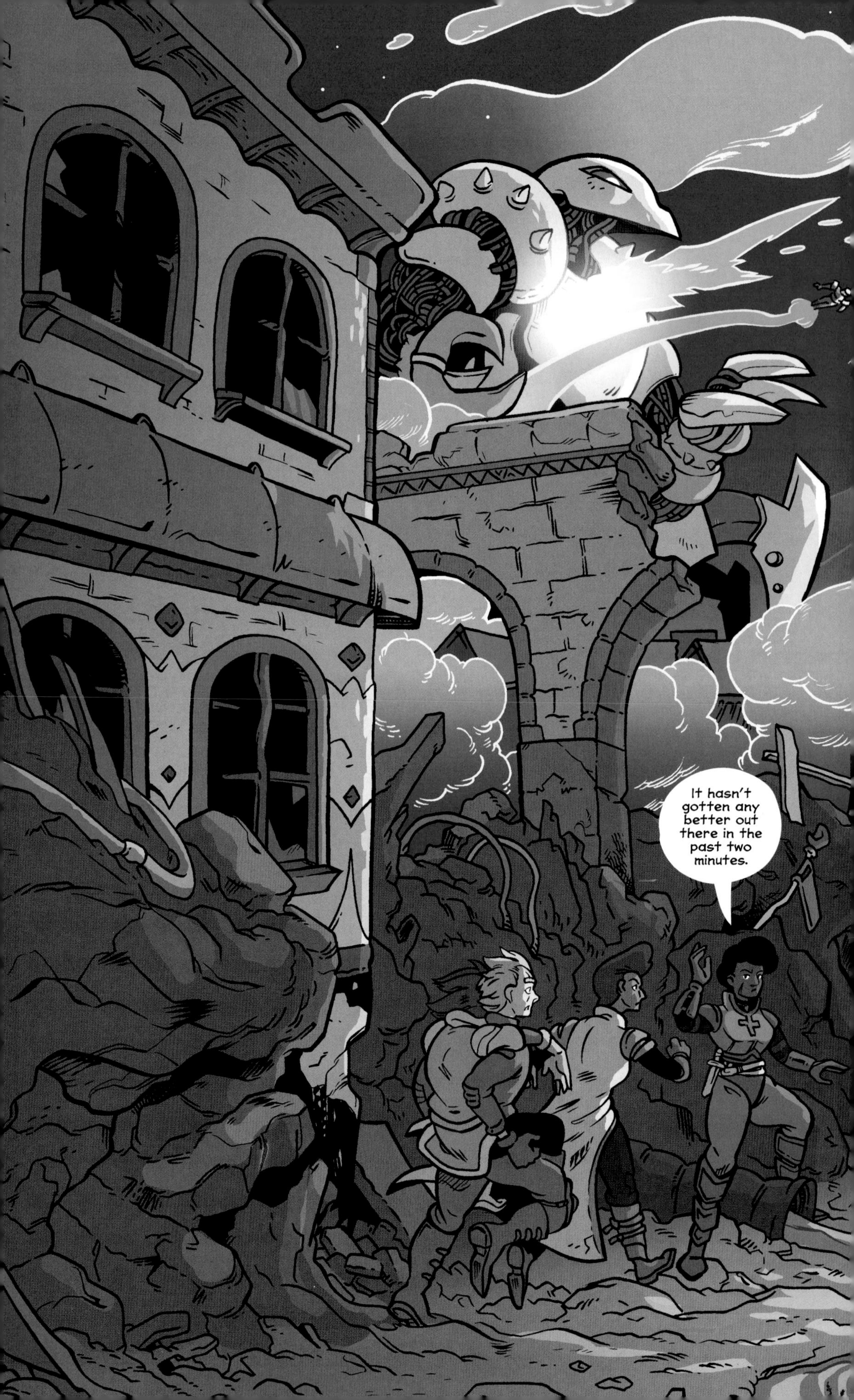
It hasn't gotten any better out there in the past two minutes.

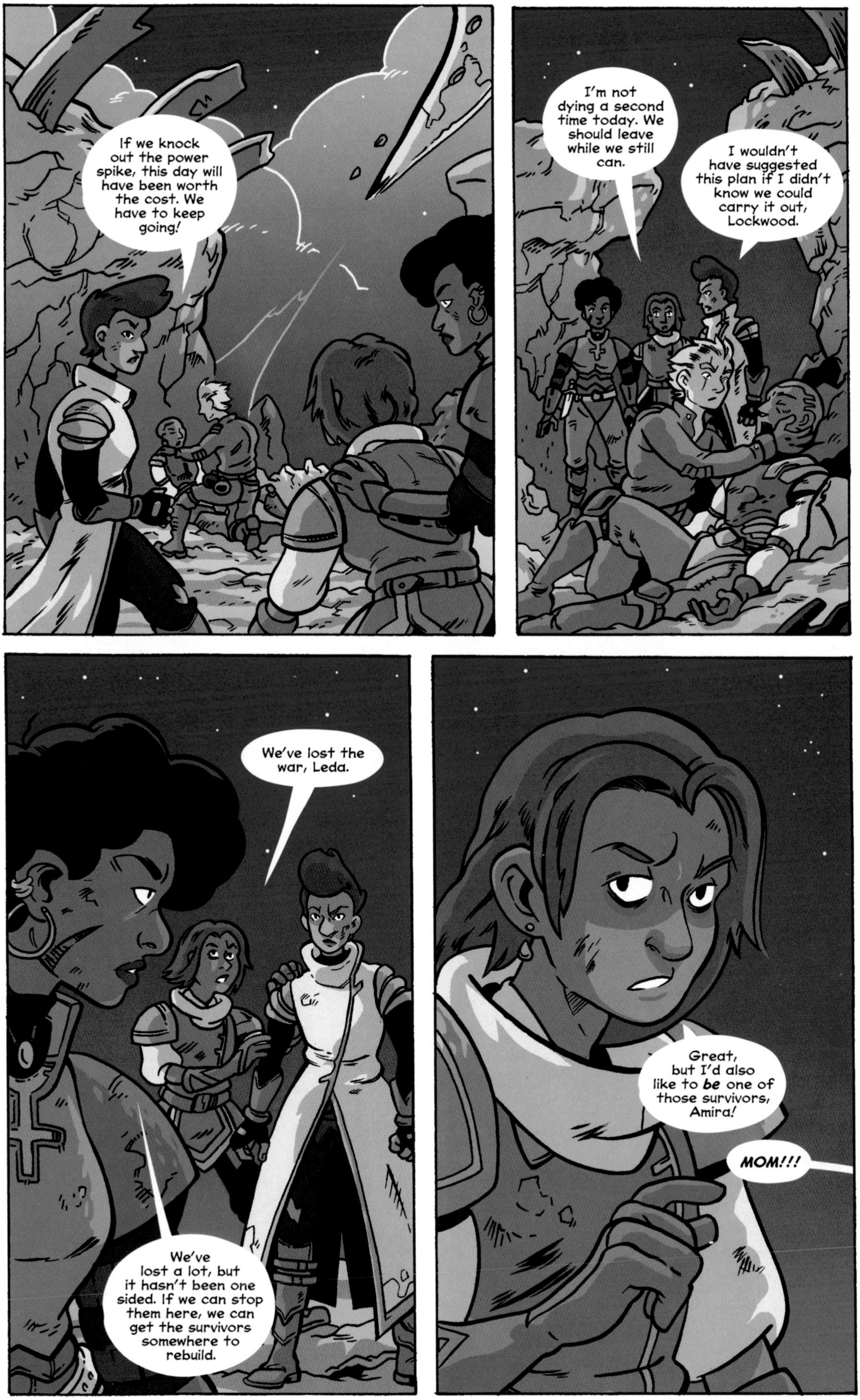
If we knock out the power spike, this day will have been worth the cost. We have to keep going!
I'm not dying a second time today. We should leave while we still can.
I wouldn't have suggested this plan if I didn't know we could carry it out, Lockwood.
We've lost the war, Leda.
We've lost a lot, but it hasn't been one sided. If we can stop them here, we can get the survivors somewhere to rebuild.
Great, but I'd also like to *be* one of those survivors, Amira!
MOM!!!

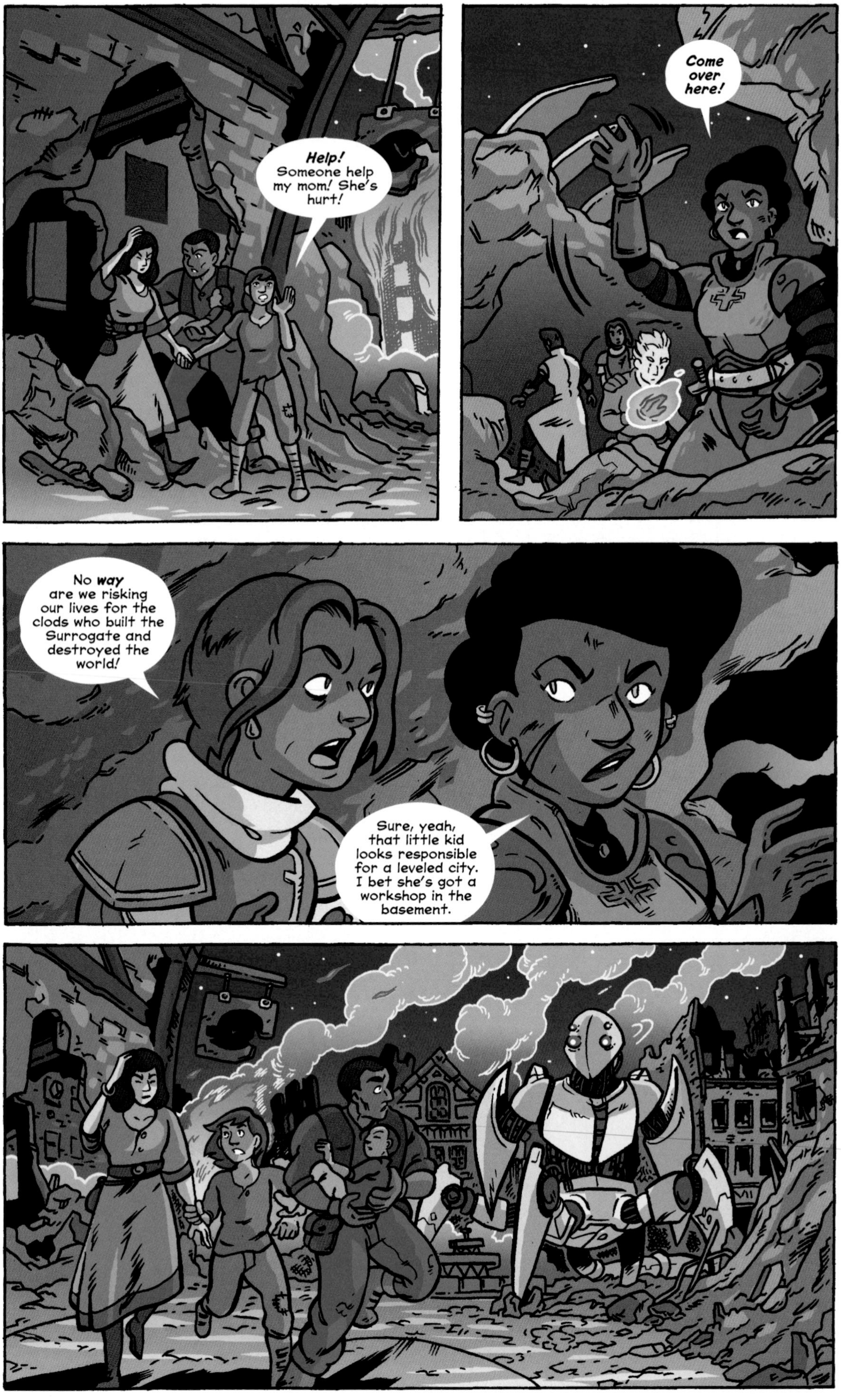

Help! Someone help my mom! She's hurt!
Come over here!
No ***way*** are we risking our lives for the clods who built the Surrogate and destroyed the world!
Sure, yeah, that little kid looks responsible for a leveled city. I bet she's got a workshop in the basement.

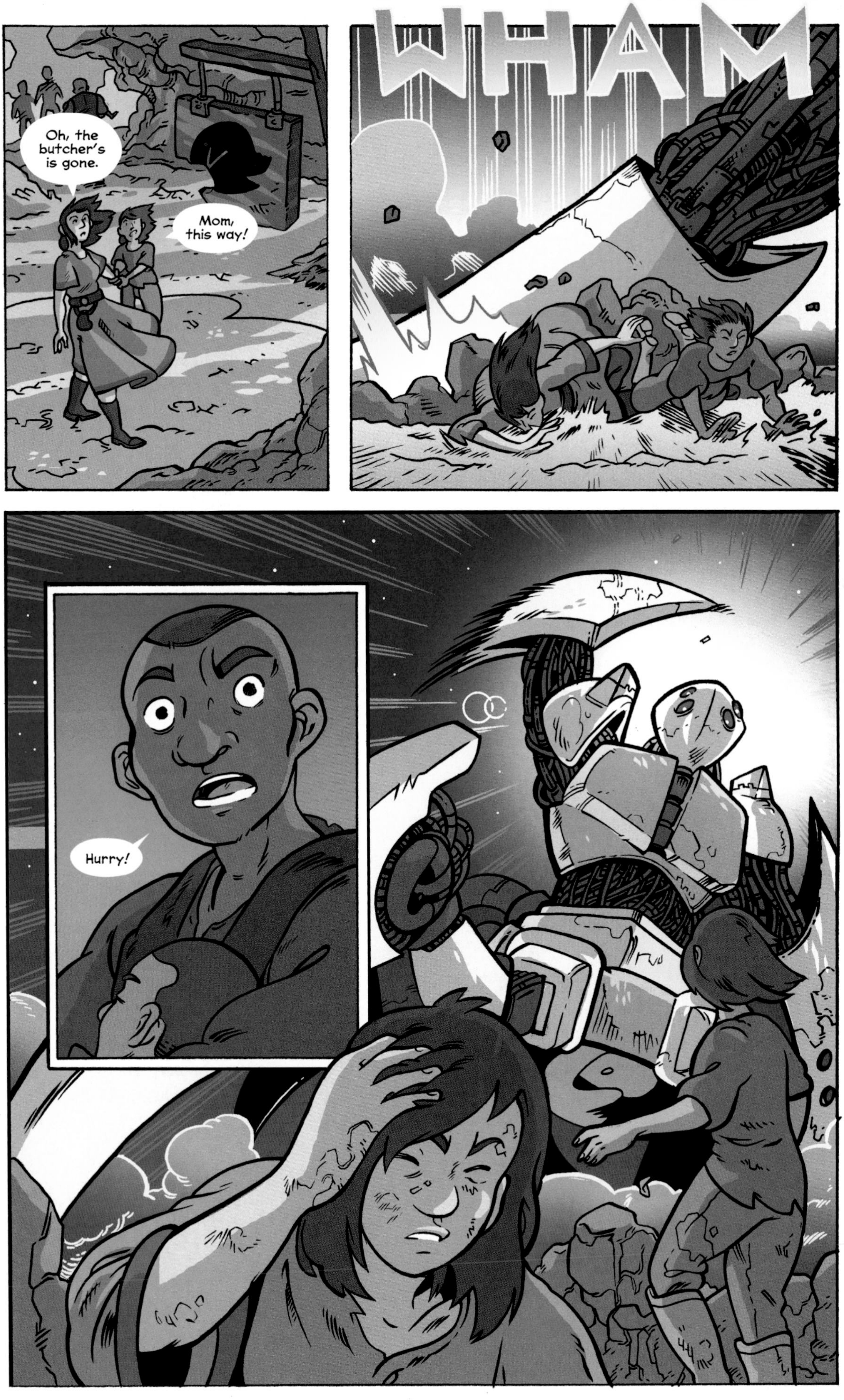
Oh, the butcher's is gone.
Mom, this way!
WHAM
Hurry!

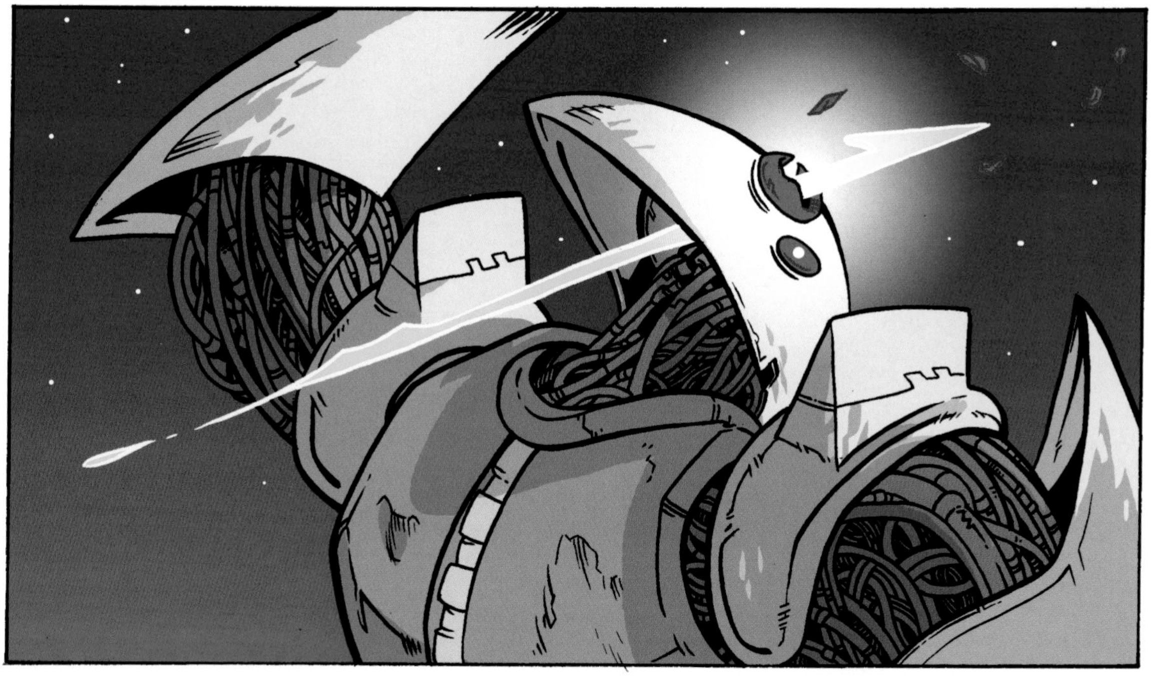
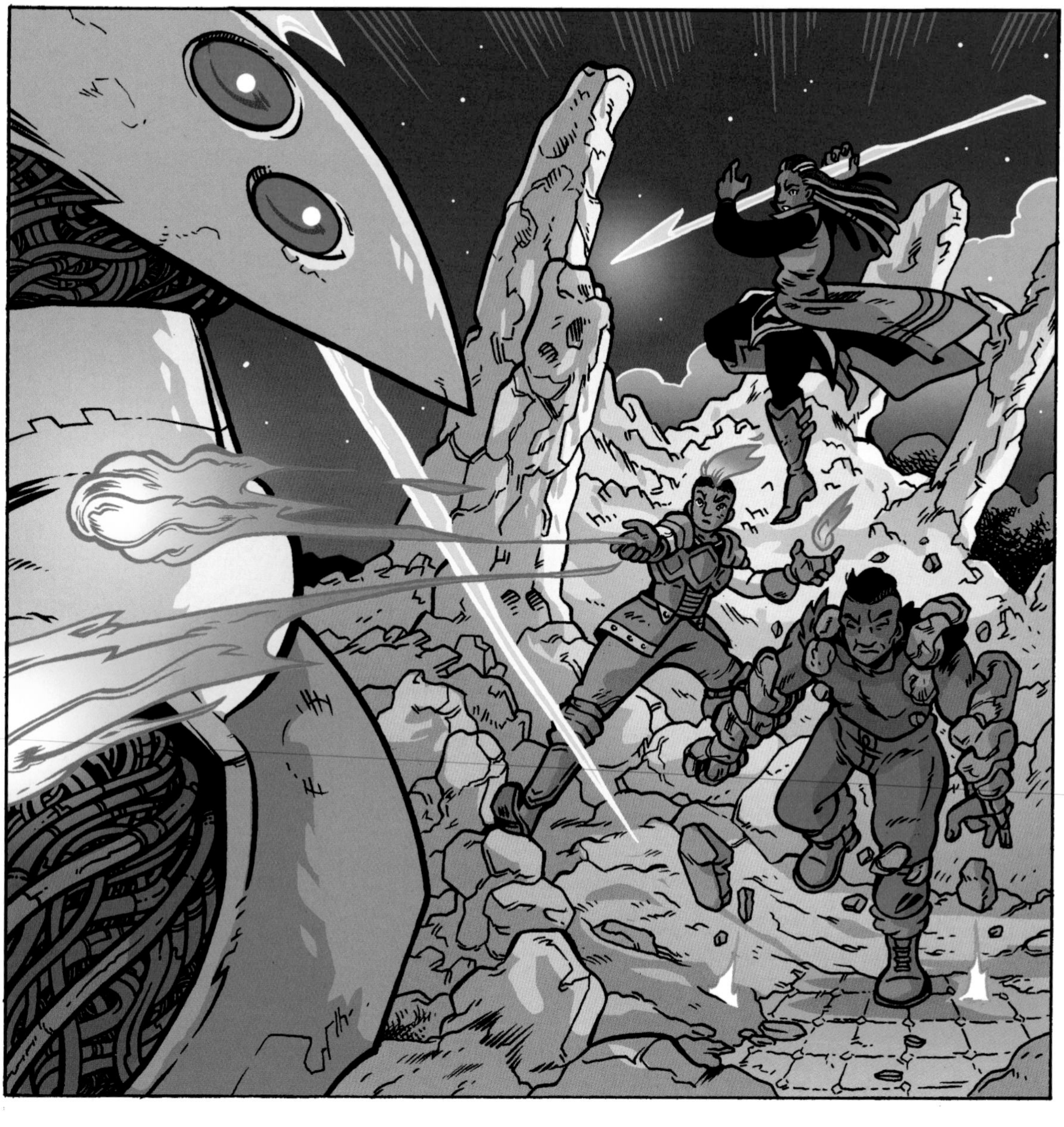

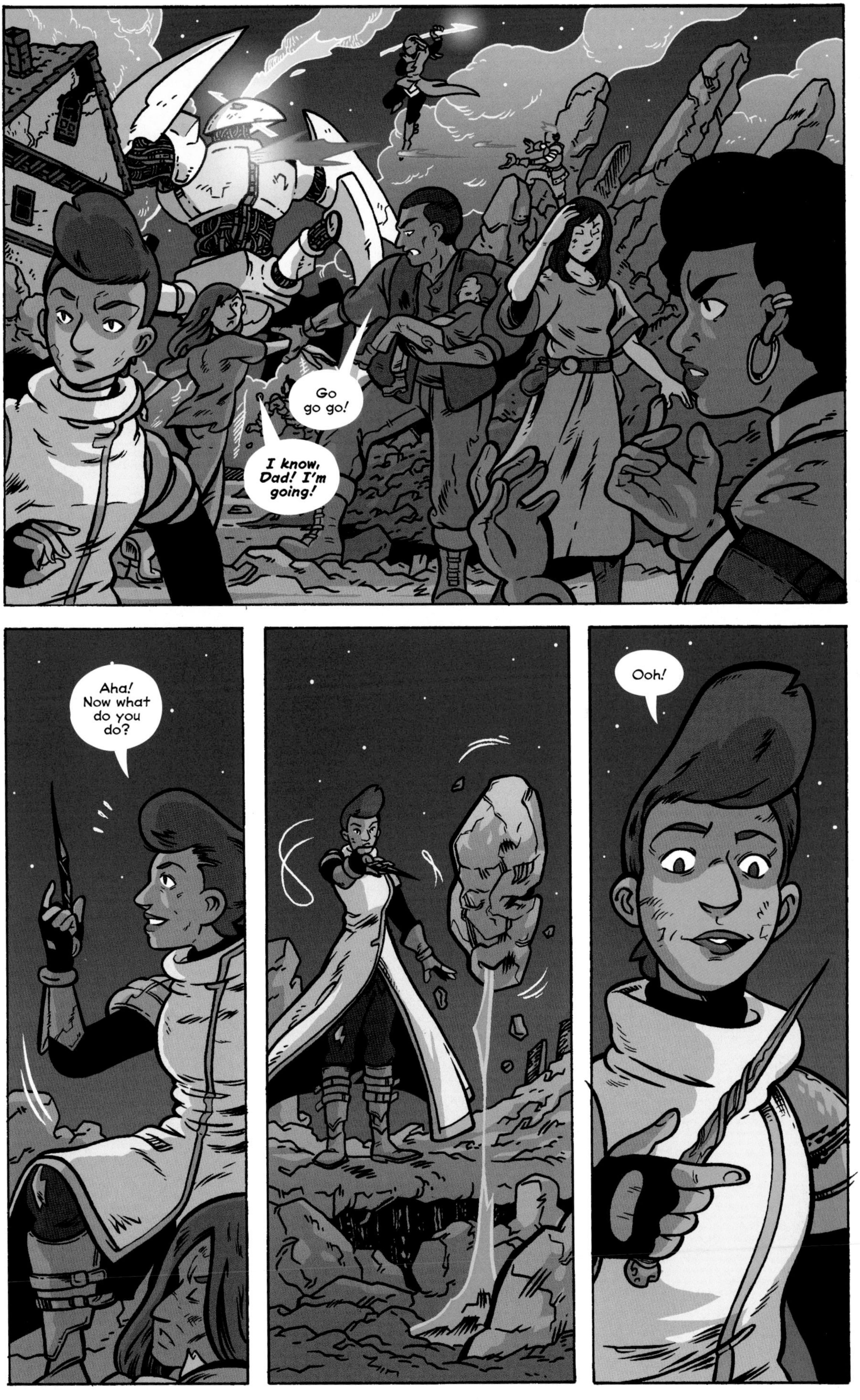
Go go go!
I know, Dad! I'm going!
Aha! Now what do you do?
Ooh!

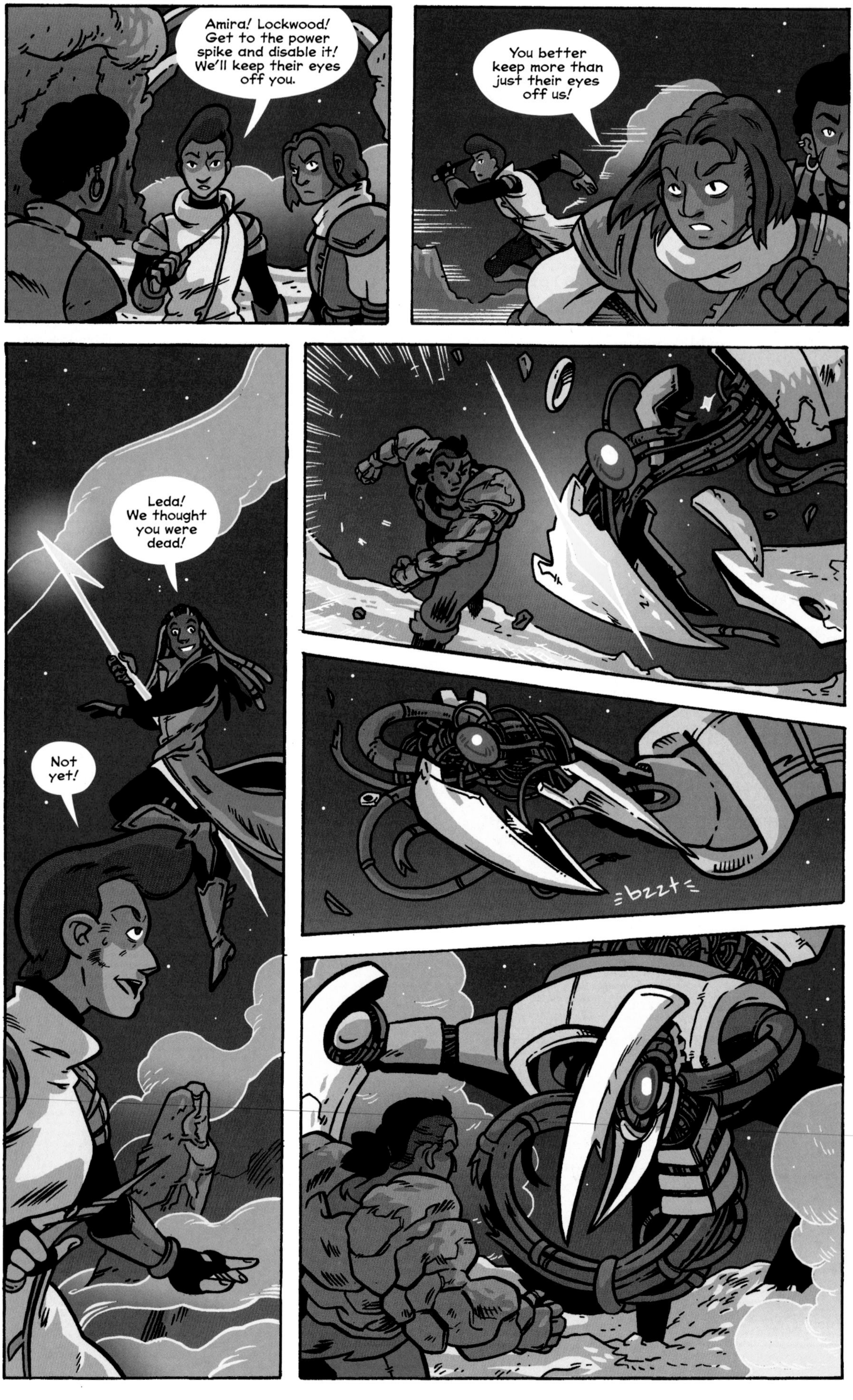
Amira! Lockwood! Get to the power spike and disable it! We'll keep their eyes off you.
You better keep more than just their eyes off us!
Leda! We thought you were dead!
Not yet!
bzzt

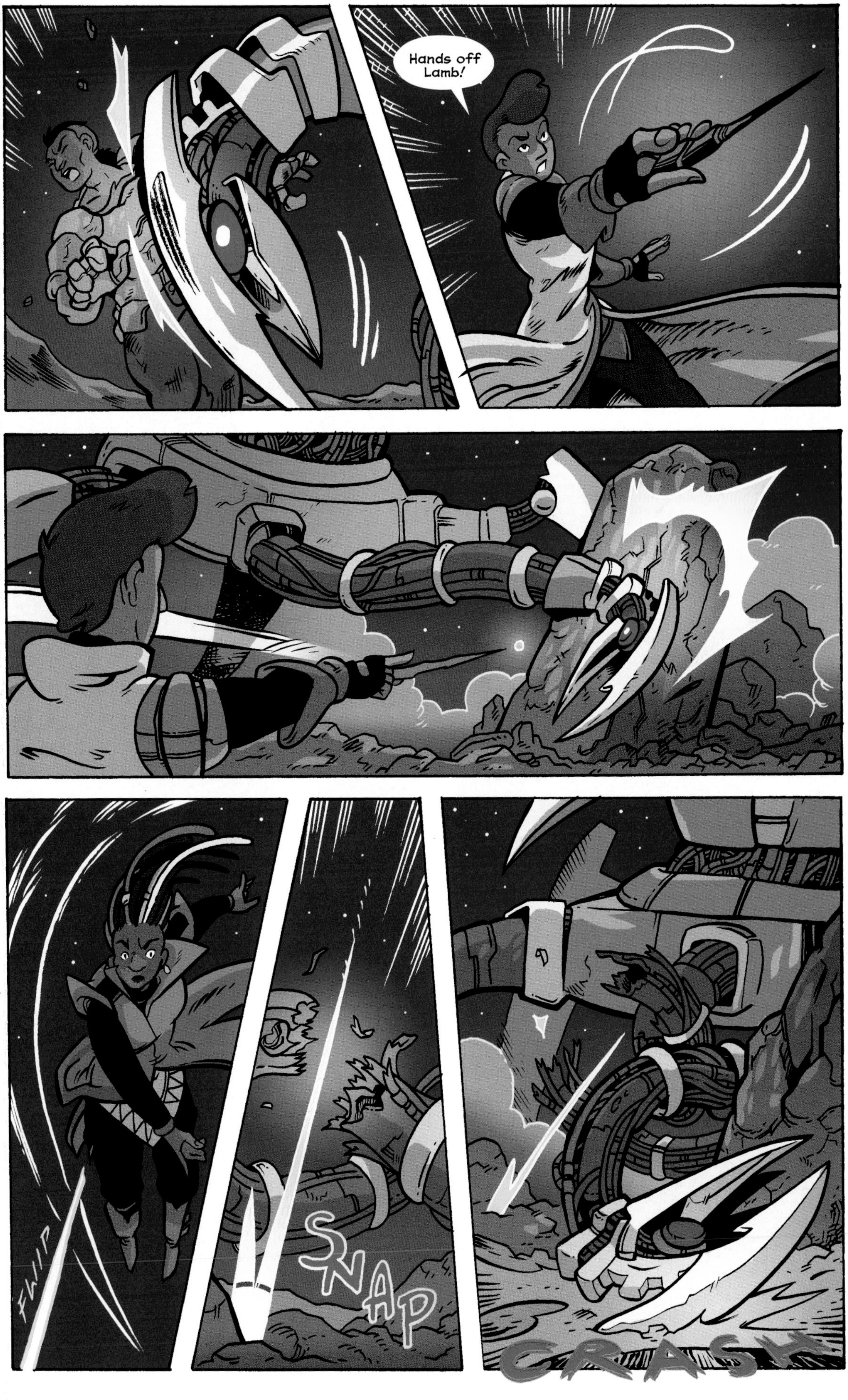
Hands off Lamb!
FWIP
SNAP
CRASH

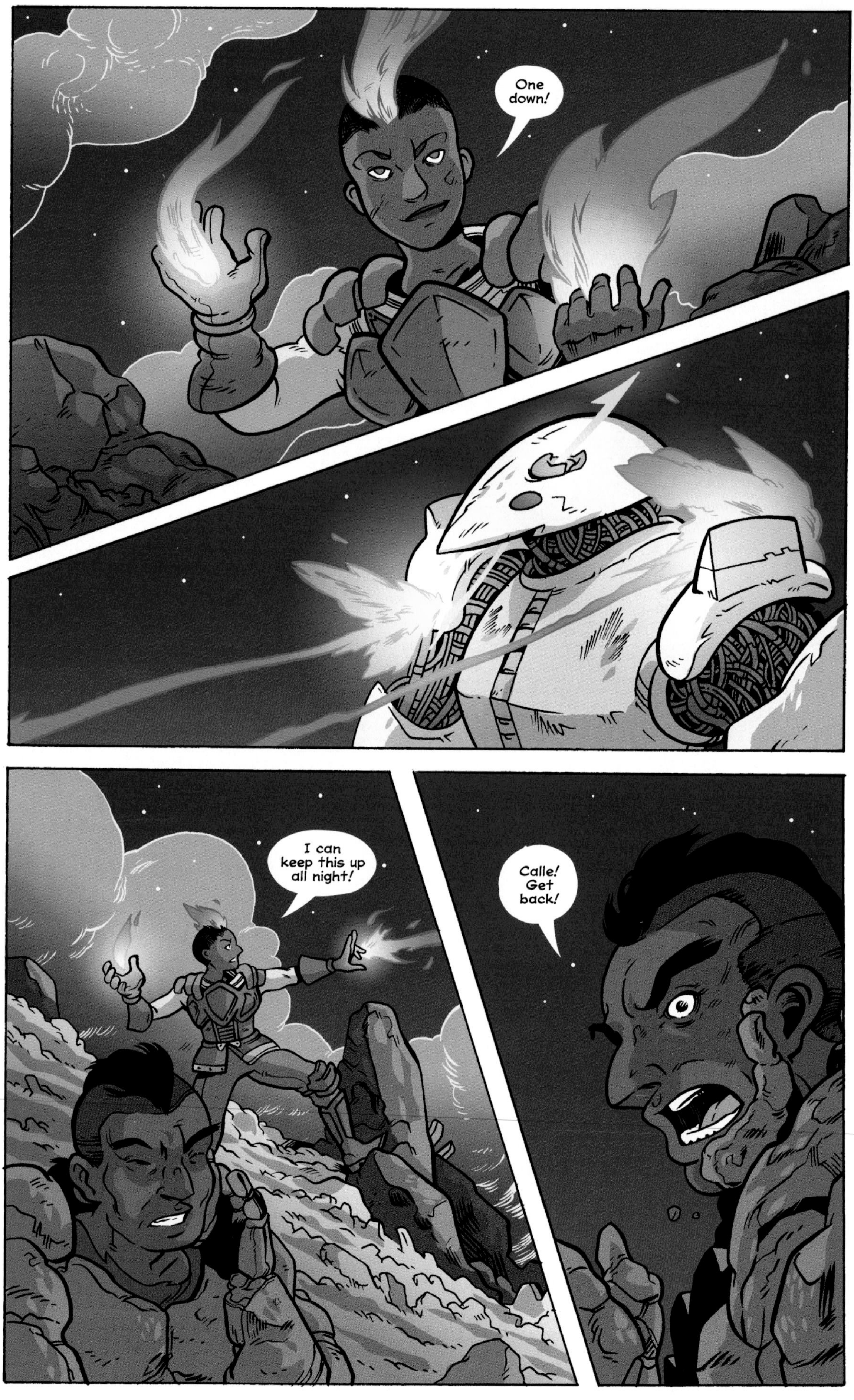
One down!
I can keep this up all night!
Calle! Get back!

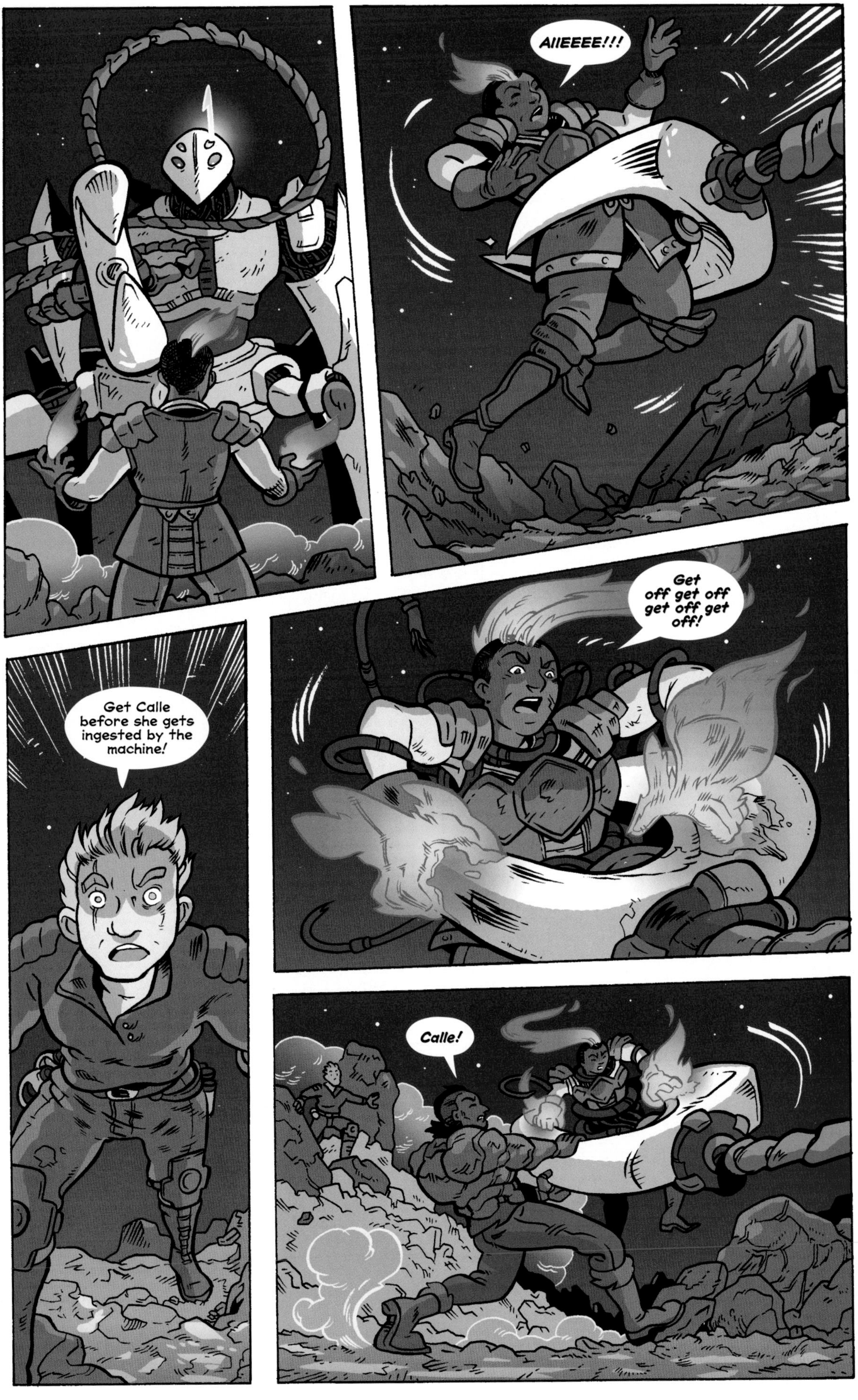
AIIEEEE!!!
Get off get off get off get off!
Get Calle before she gets ingested by the machine!
Calle!

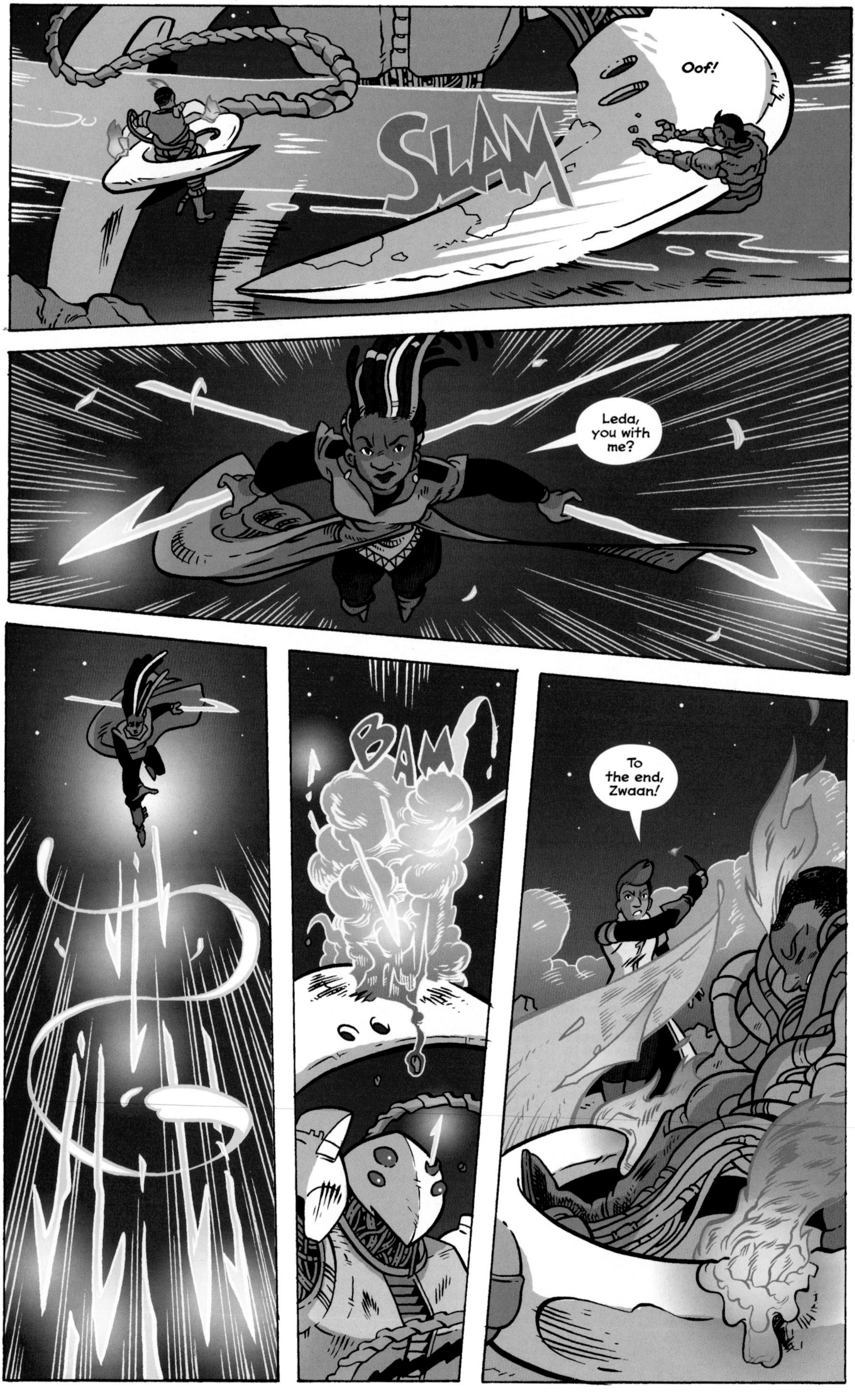
SLAM
Oof!
Leda, you with me?
BAM
To the end, Zwaan!

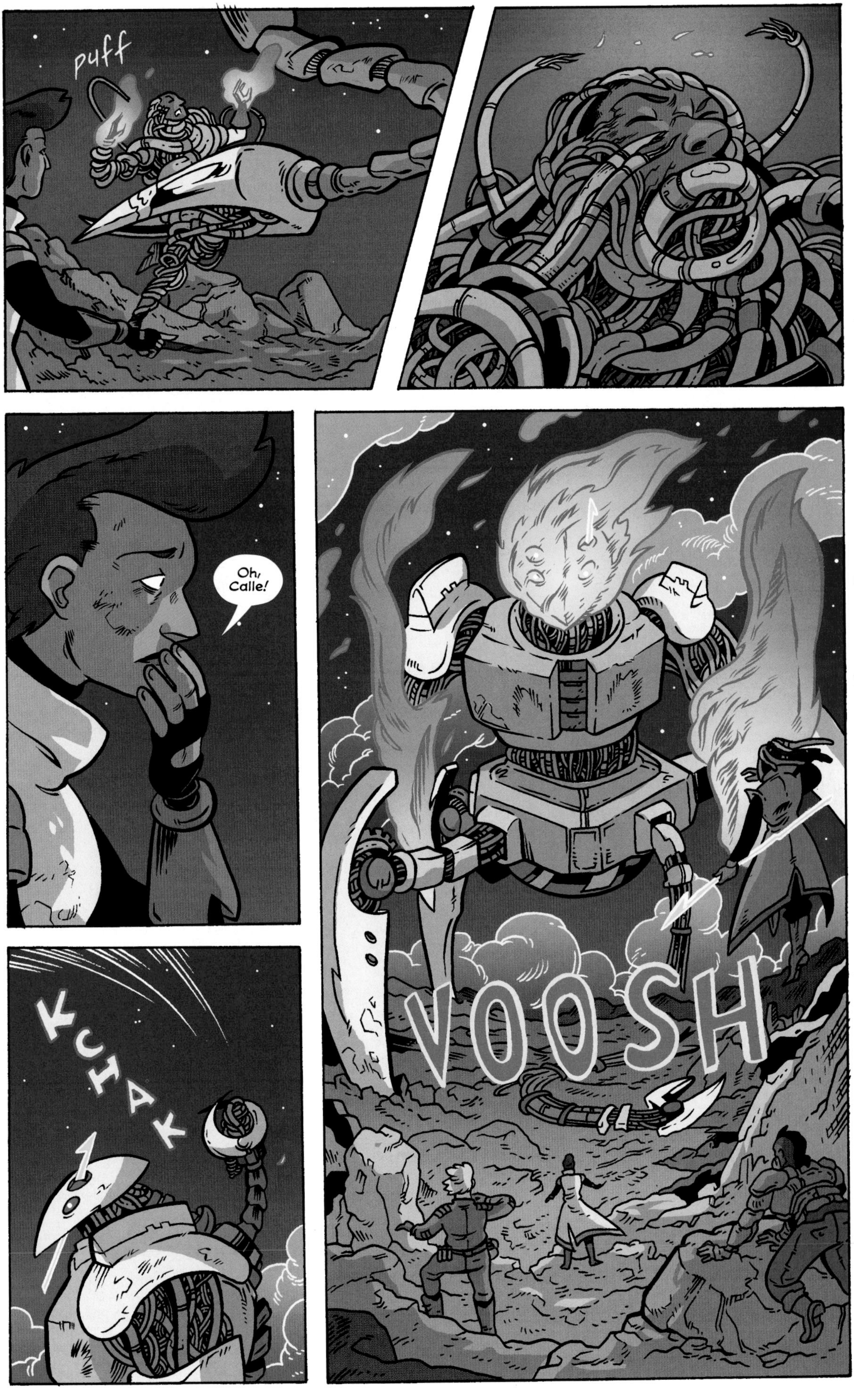

puff
Oh, Calle!
KCHAK
VOOSH

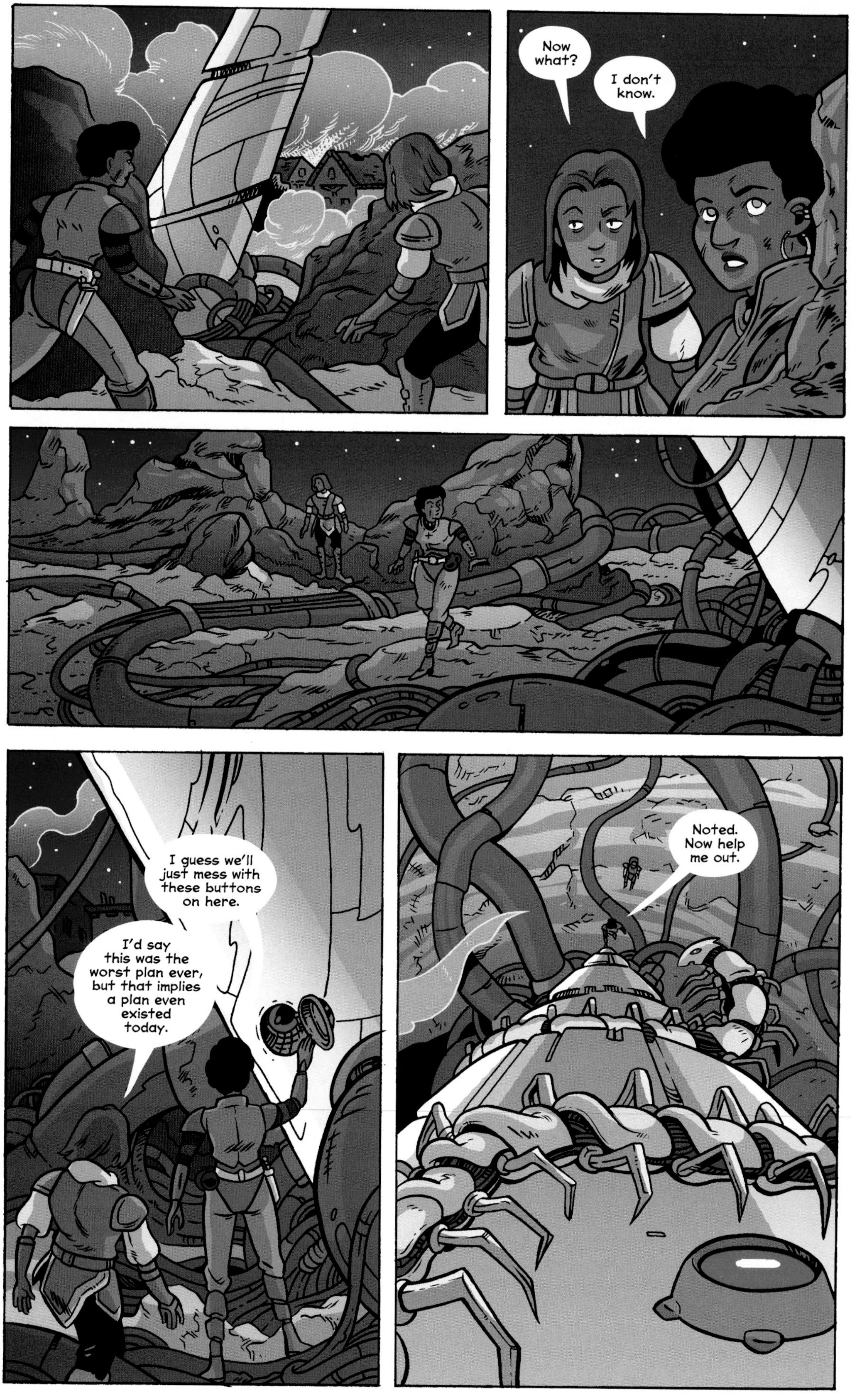
Now what?
I don't know.
I guess we'll just mess with these buttons on here.
I'd say this was the worst plan ever, but that implies a plan even existed today.
Noted. Now help me out.

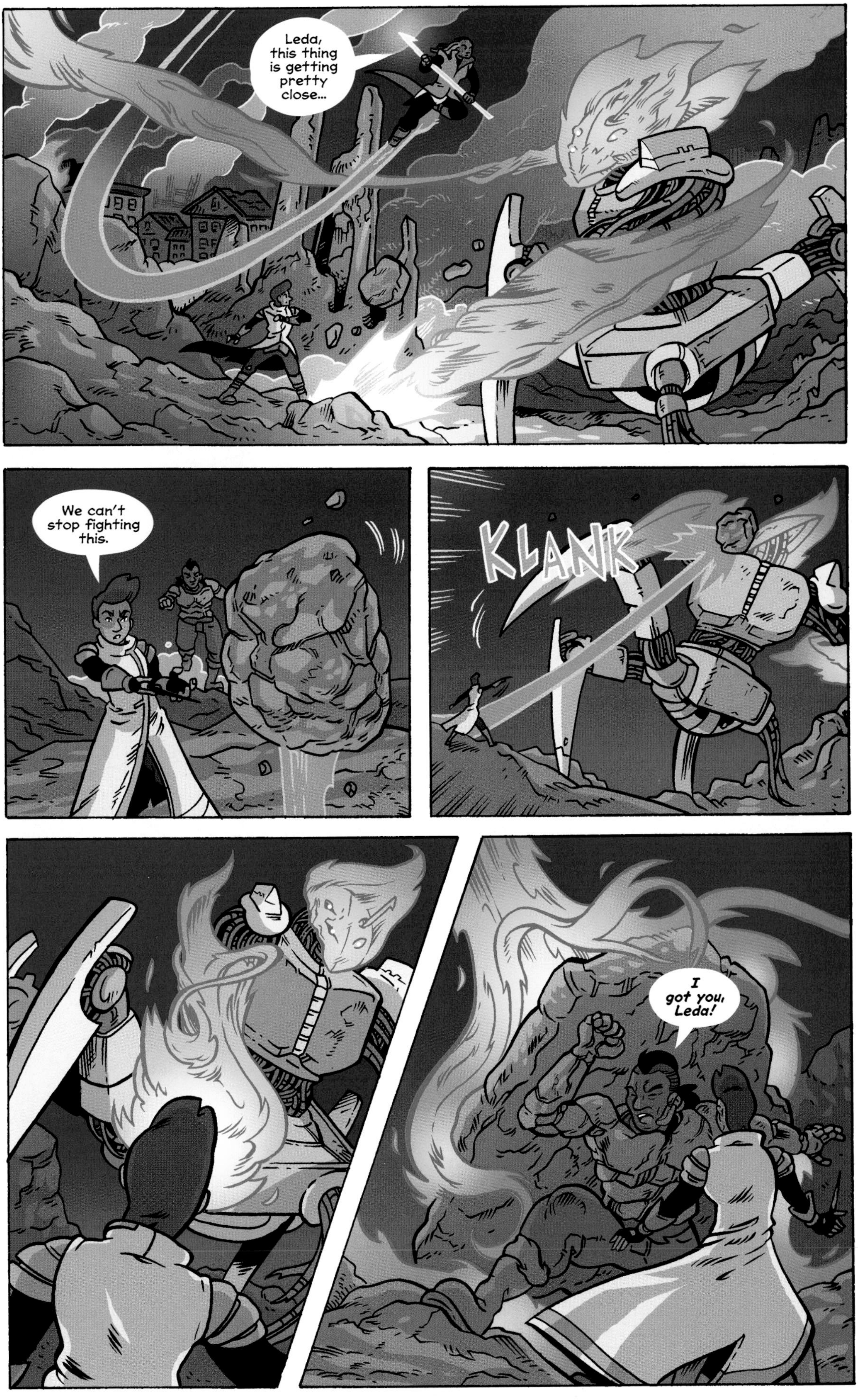
Leda, this thing is getting pretty close...
We can't stop fighting this.
KLANK
I got you, Leda!

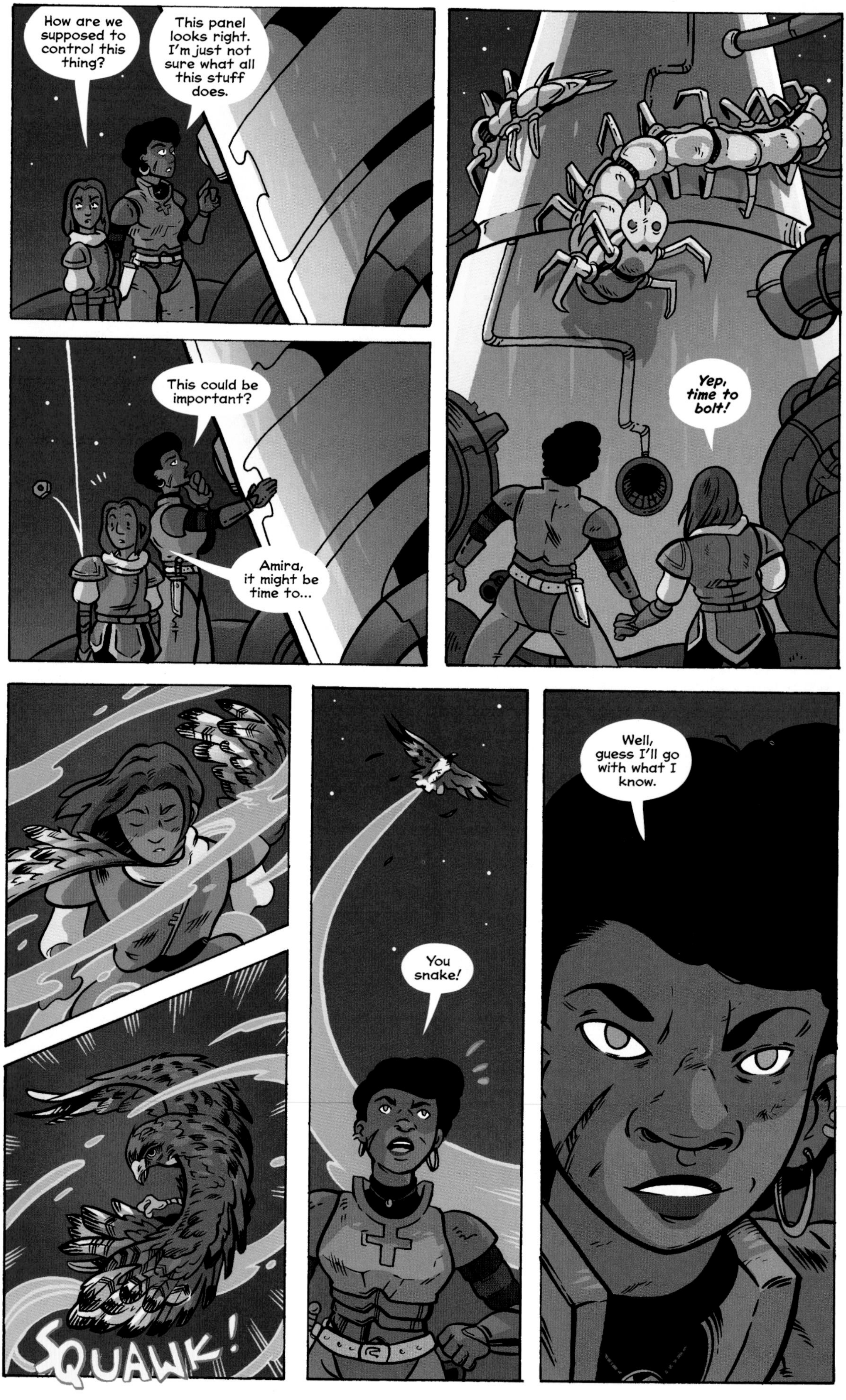
How are we supposed to control this thing?
This panel looks right. I'm just not sure what all this stuff does.
This could be important?
Amira, it might be time to...
Yep, time to bolt!
SQUAWK!
You snake!
Well, guess I'll go with what I know.

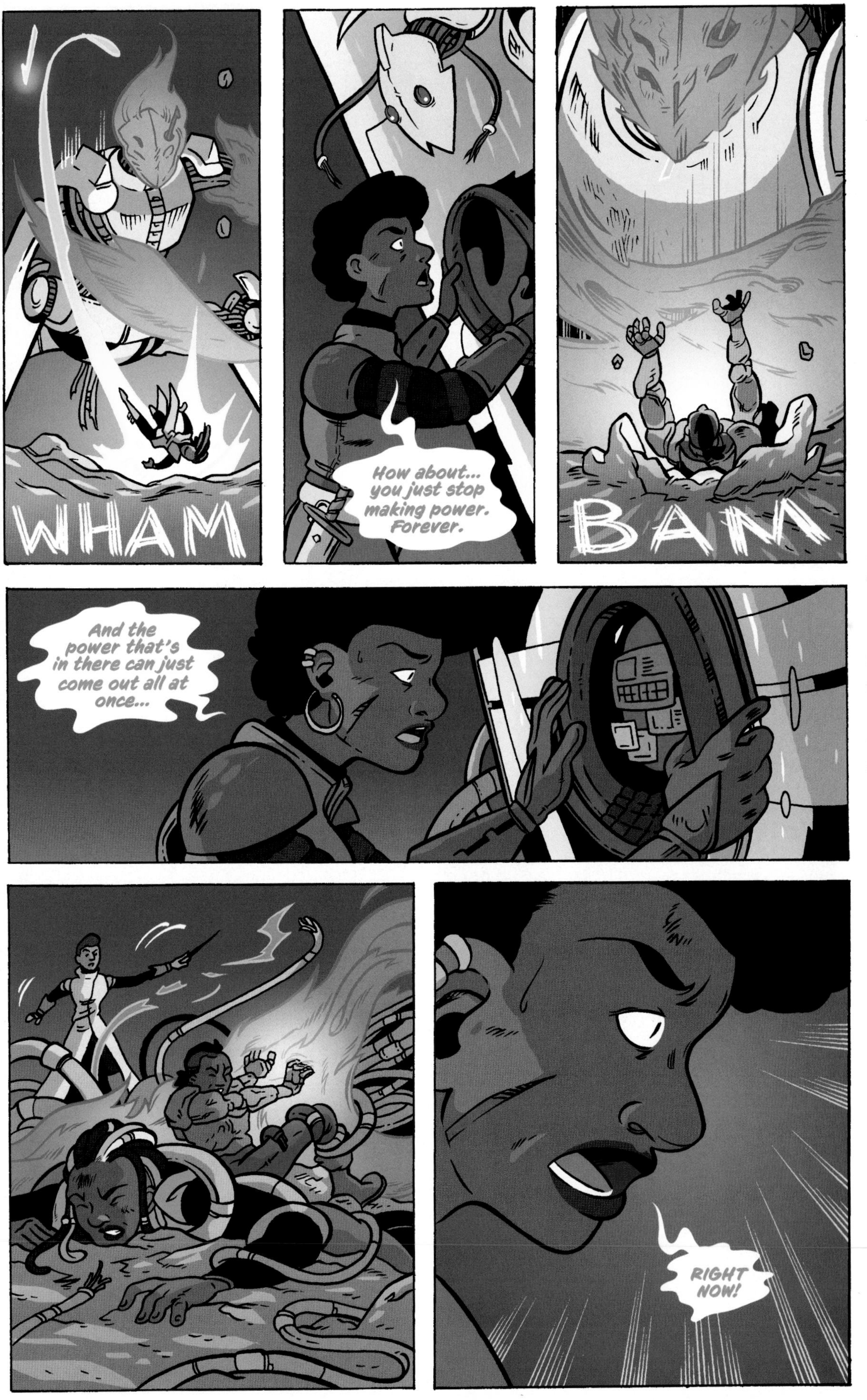
WHAM
How about... you just stop making power. Forever.
BAM
And the power that's in there can just come out all at once...
RIGHT NOW!

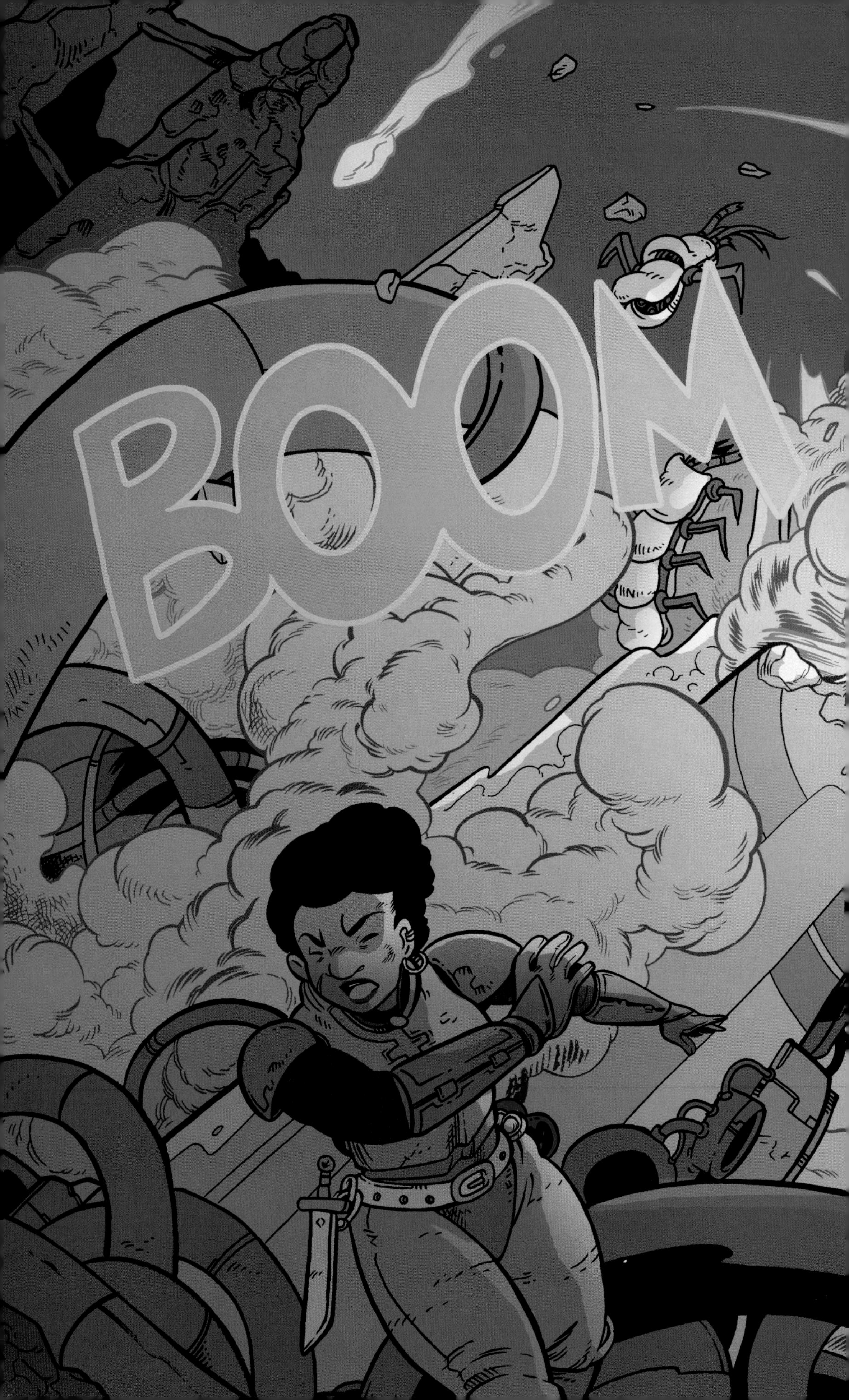
BOOM

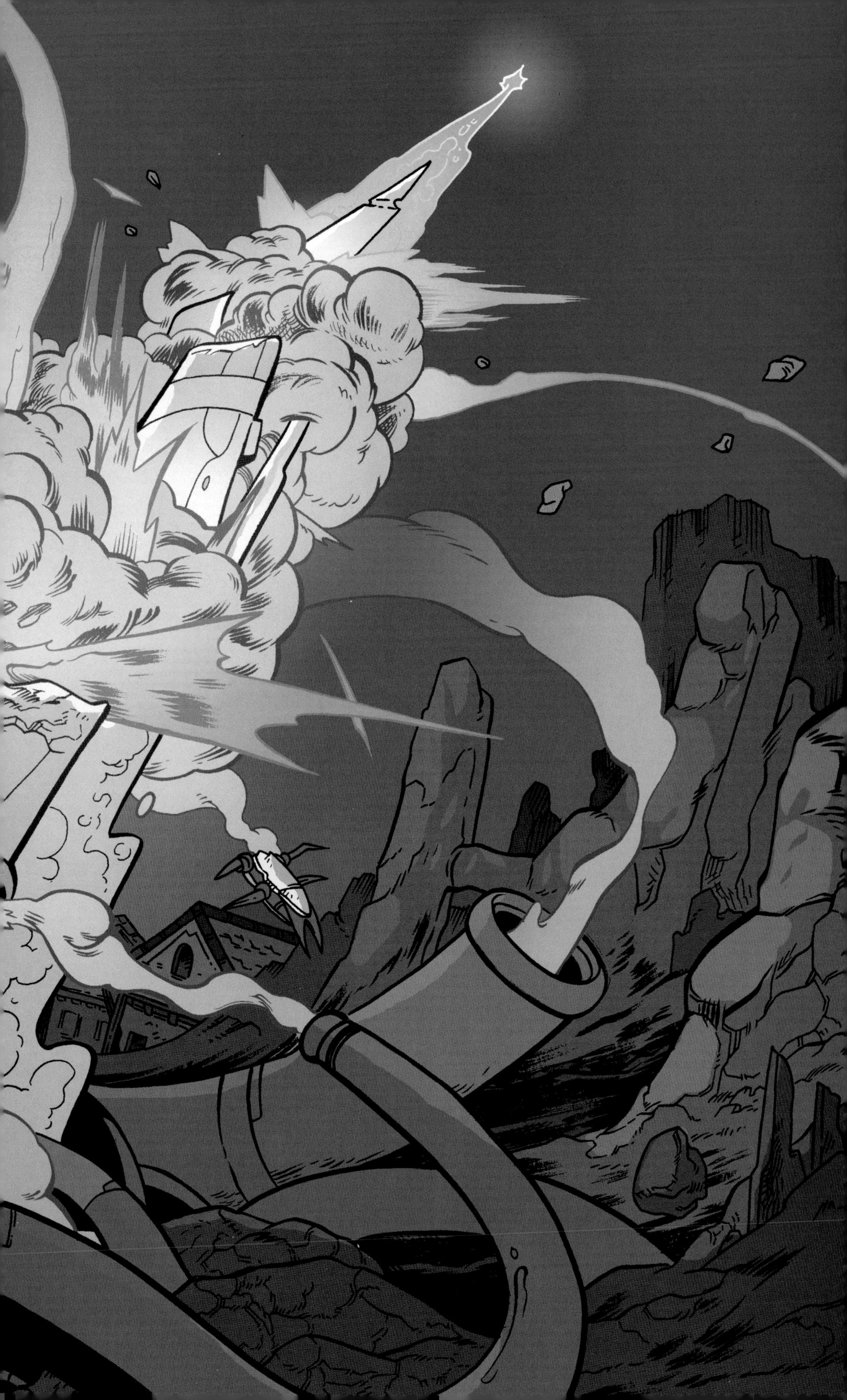

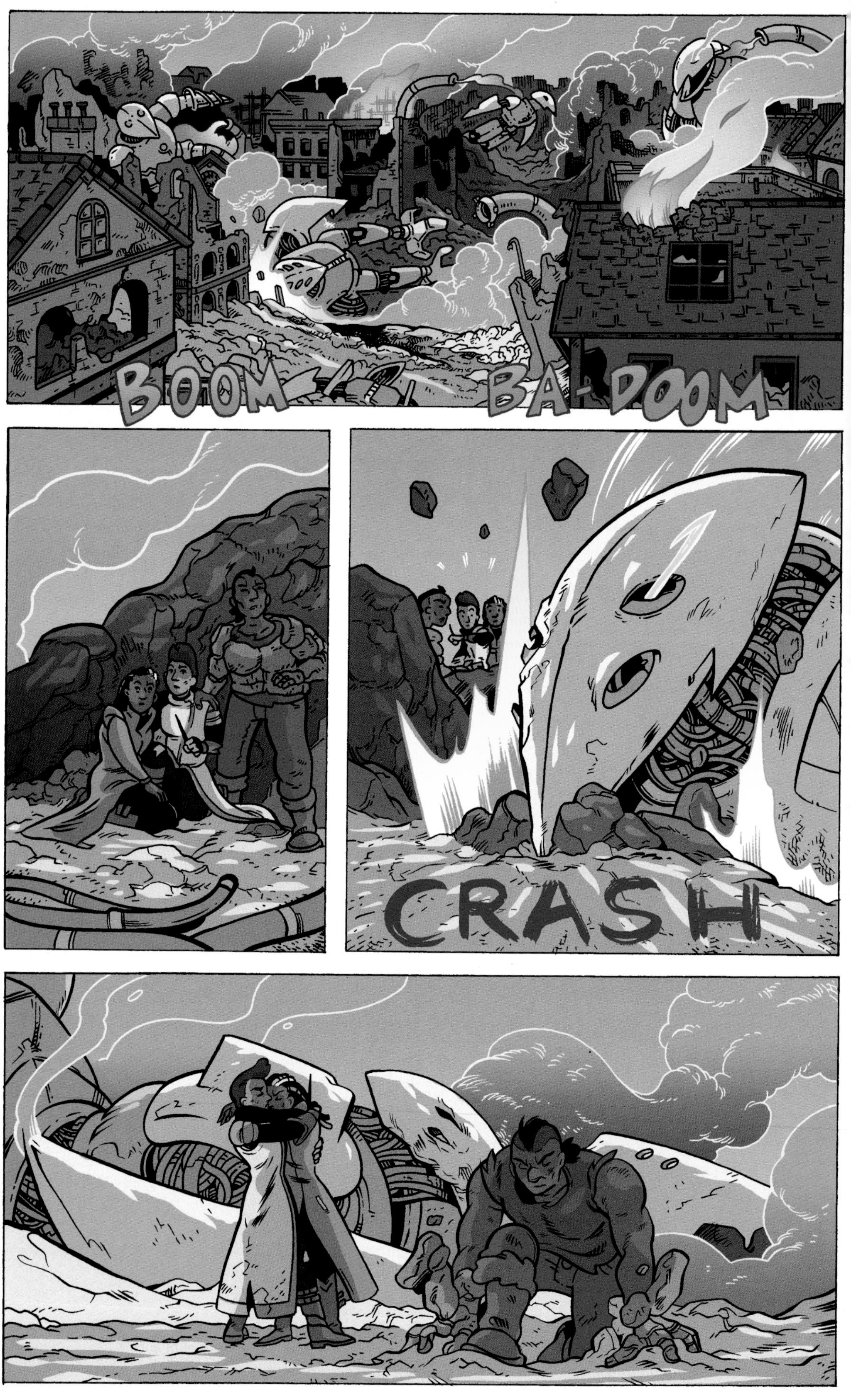
BOOM
BA-DOOM
CRASH

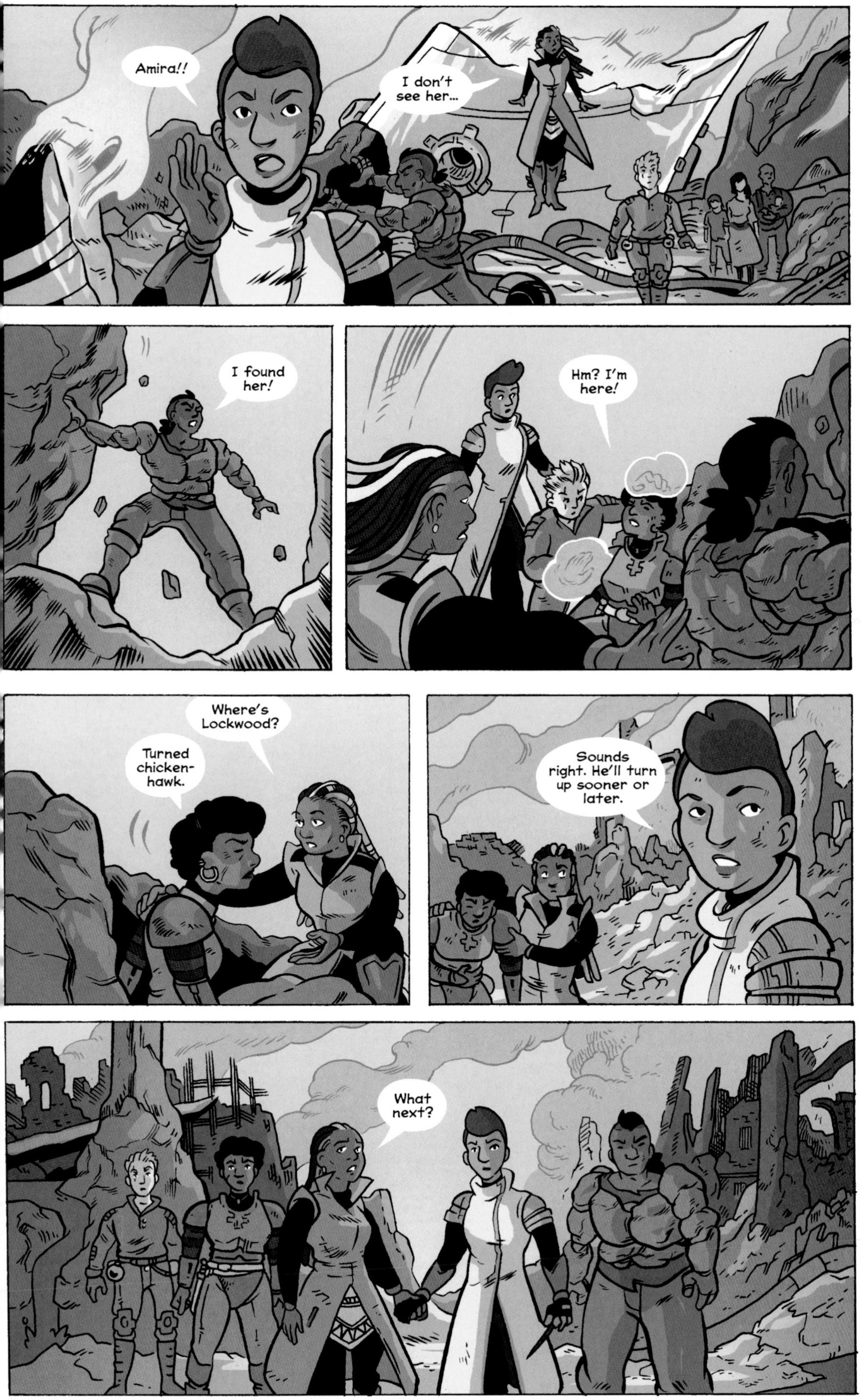
Amira!!
I don't see her...
I found her!
Hm? I'm here!
Where's Lockwood?
Turned chicken-hawk.
Sounds right. He'll turn up sooner or later.
What next?

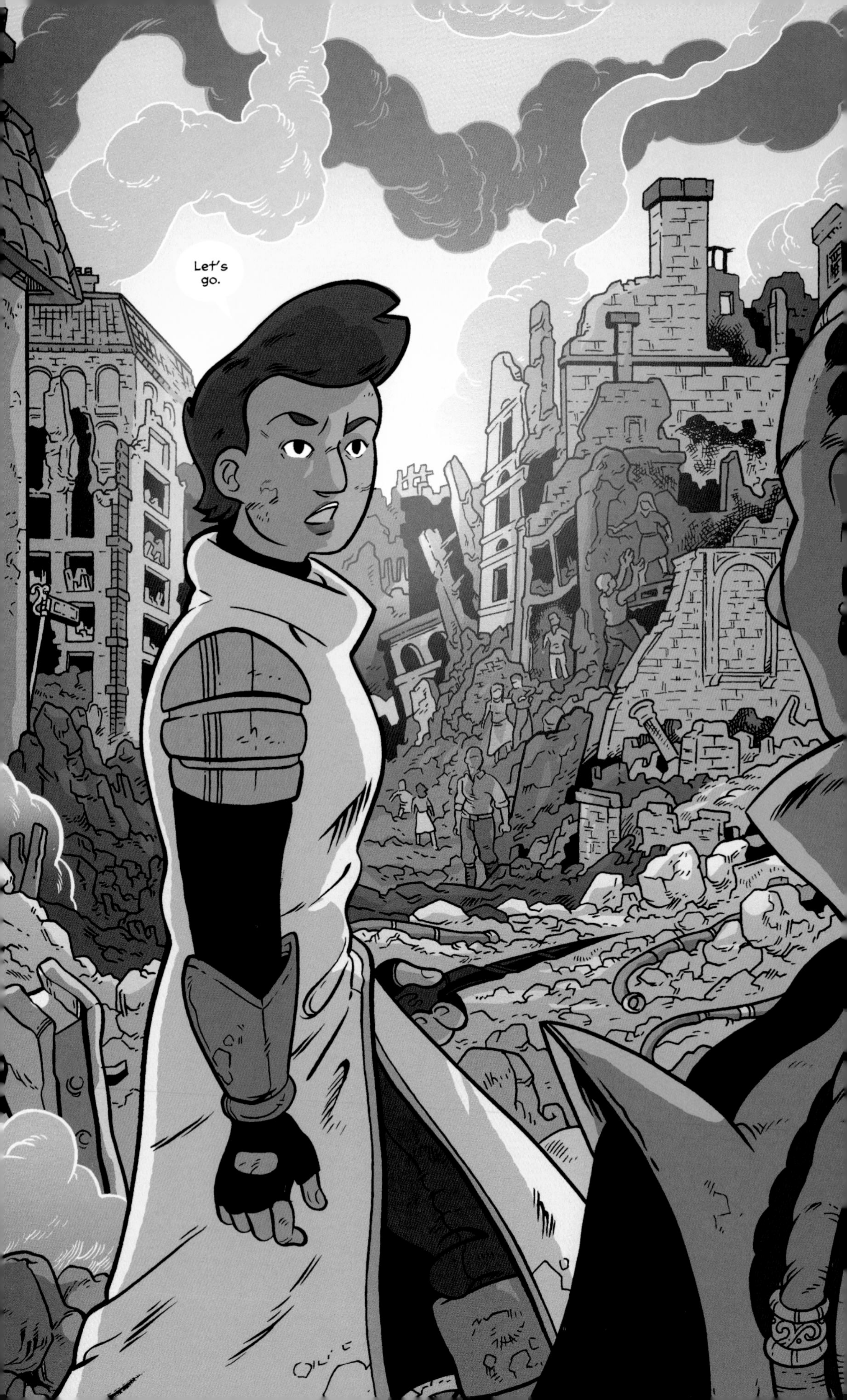
Let's go.

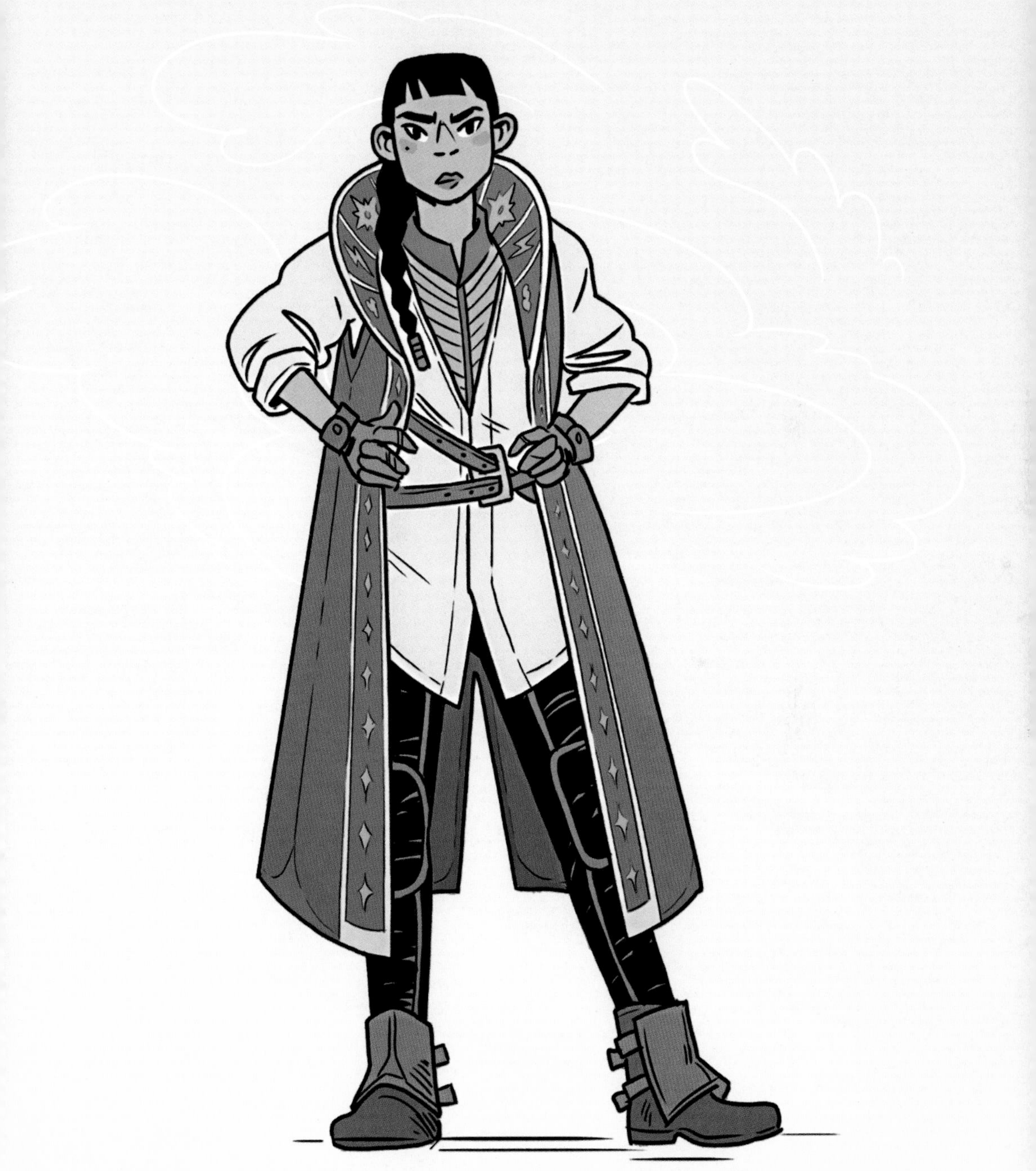

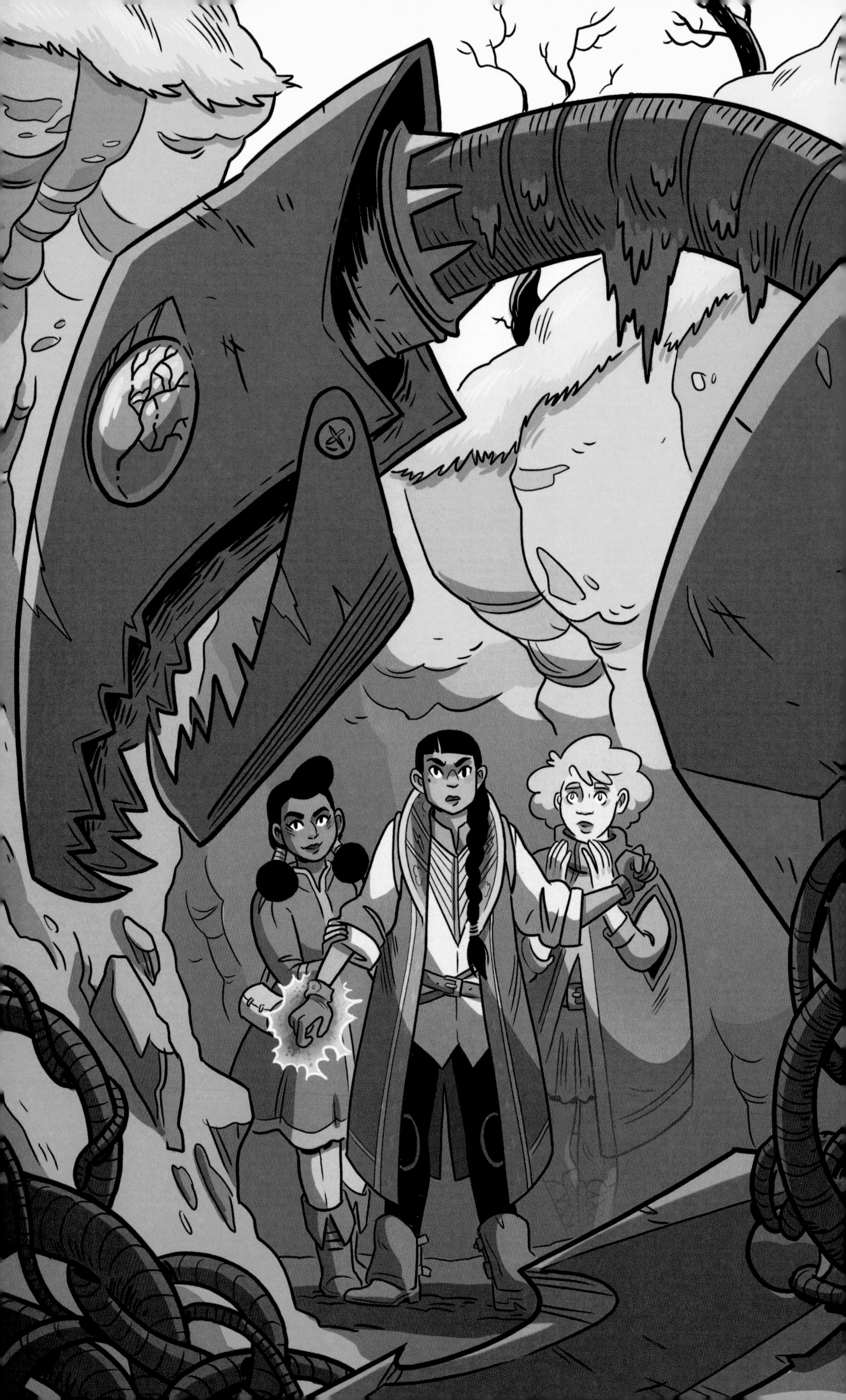

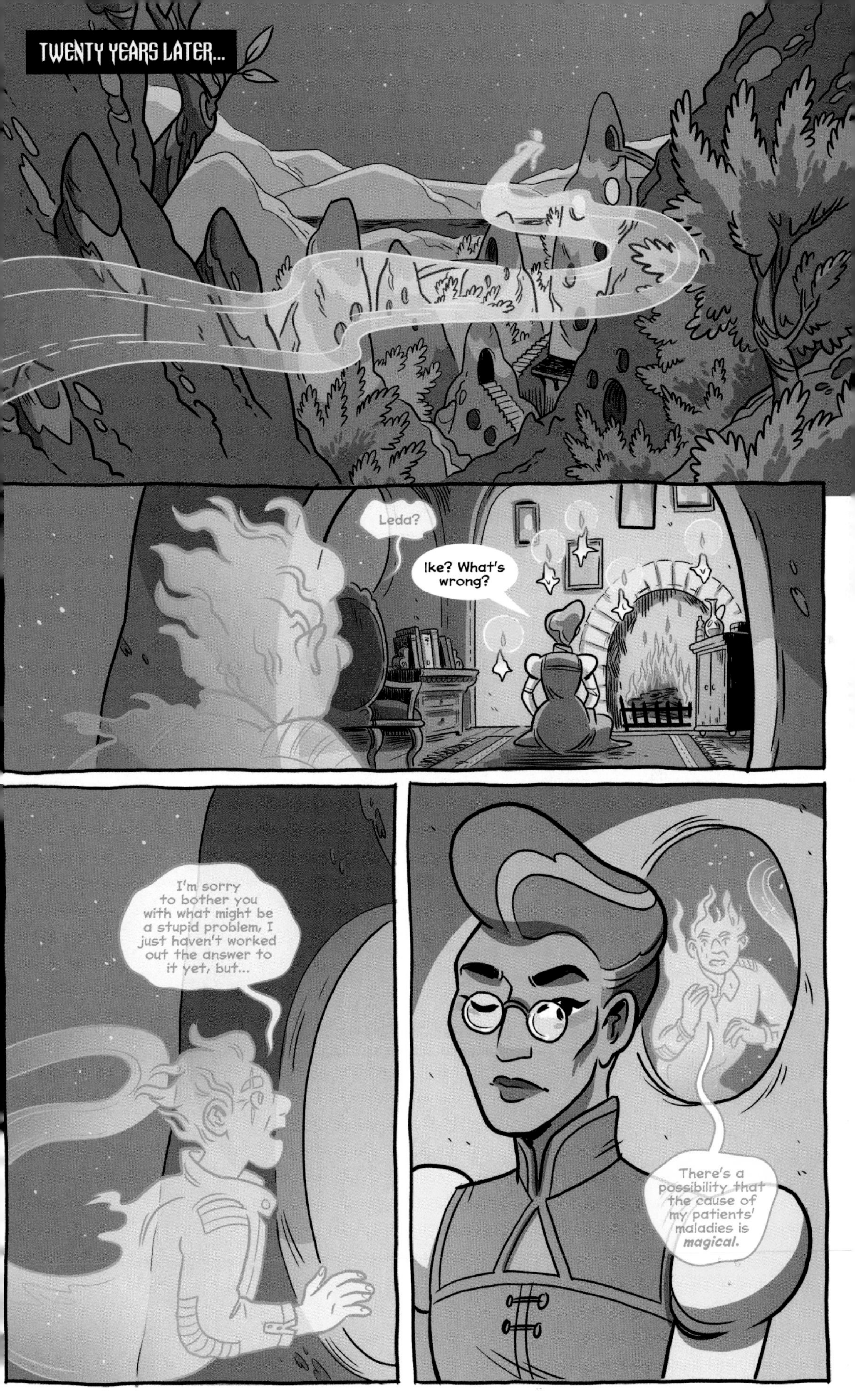
TWENTY YEARS LATER...
Leda?
Ike? What's wrong?
I'm sorry to bother you with what might be a stupid problem, I just haven't worked out the answer to it yet, but...
There's a possibility that the cause of my patients' maladies is *magical.*

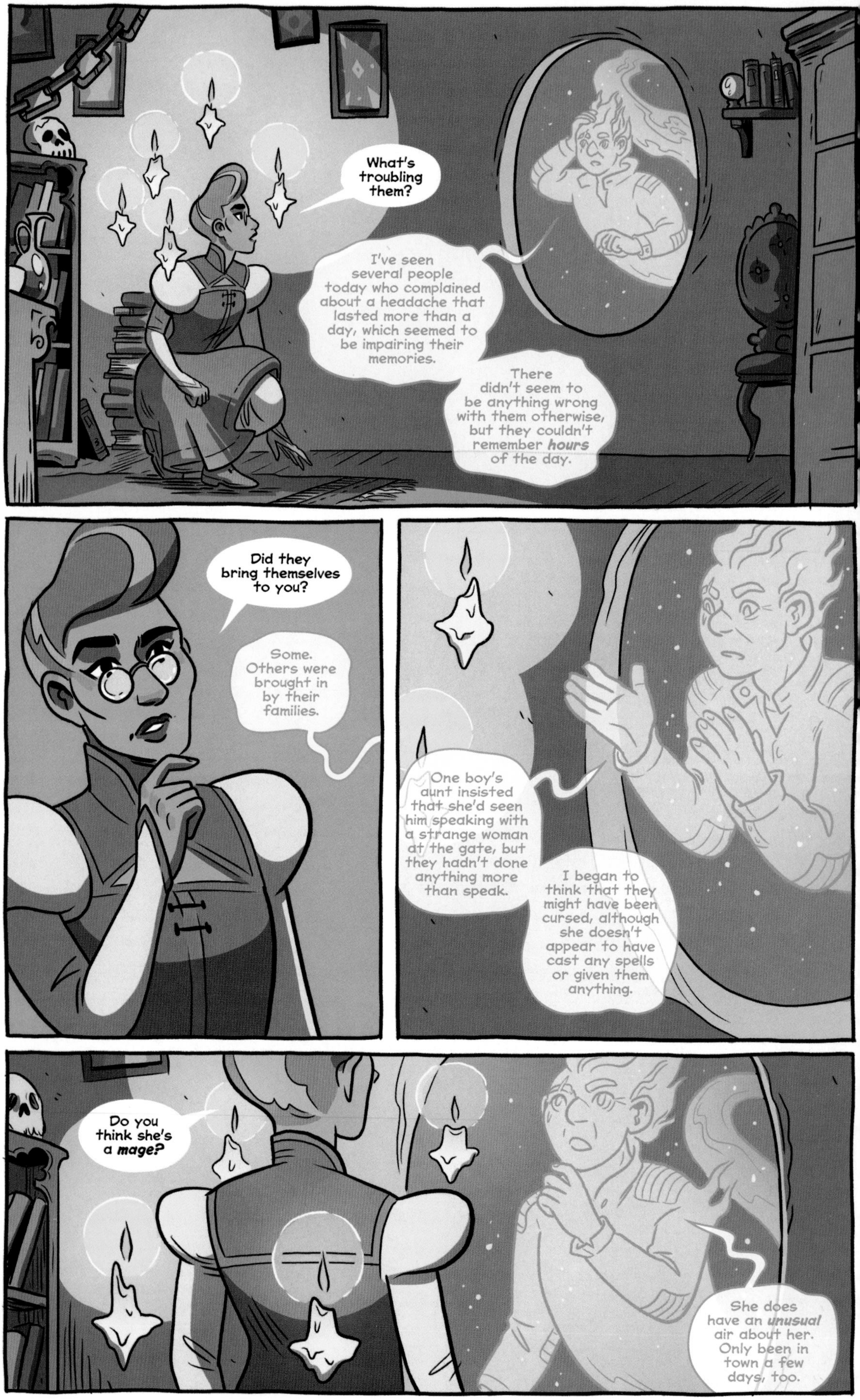
What's troubling them?
I've seen several people today who complained about a headache that lasted more than a day, which seemed to be impairing their memories.
There didn't seem to be anything wrong with them otherwise, but they couldn't remember *hours* of the day.
Did they bring themselves to you?
Some. Others were brought in by their families.
One boy's aunt insisted that she'd seen him speaking with a strange woman at the gate, but they hadn't done anything more than speak.
I began to think that they might have been cursed, although she doesn't appear to have cast any spells or given them anything.
Do you think she's a *mage?*
She does have an *unusual* air about her. Only been in town a few days, too.

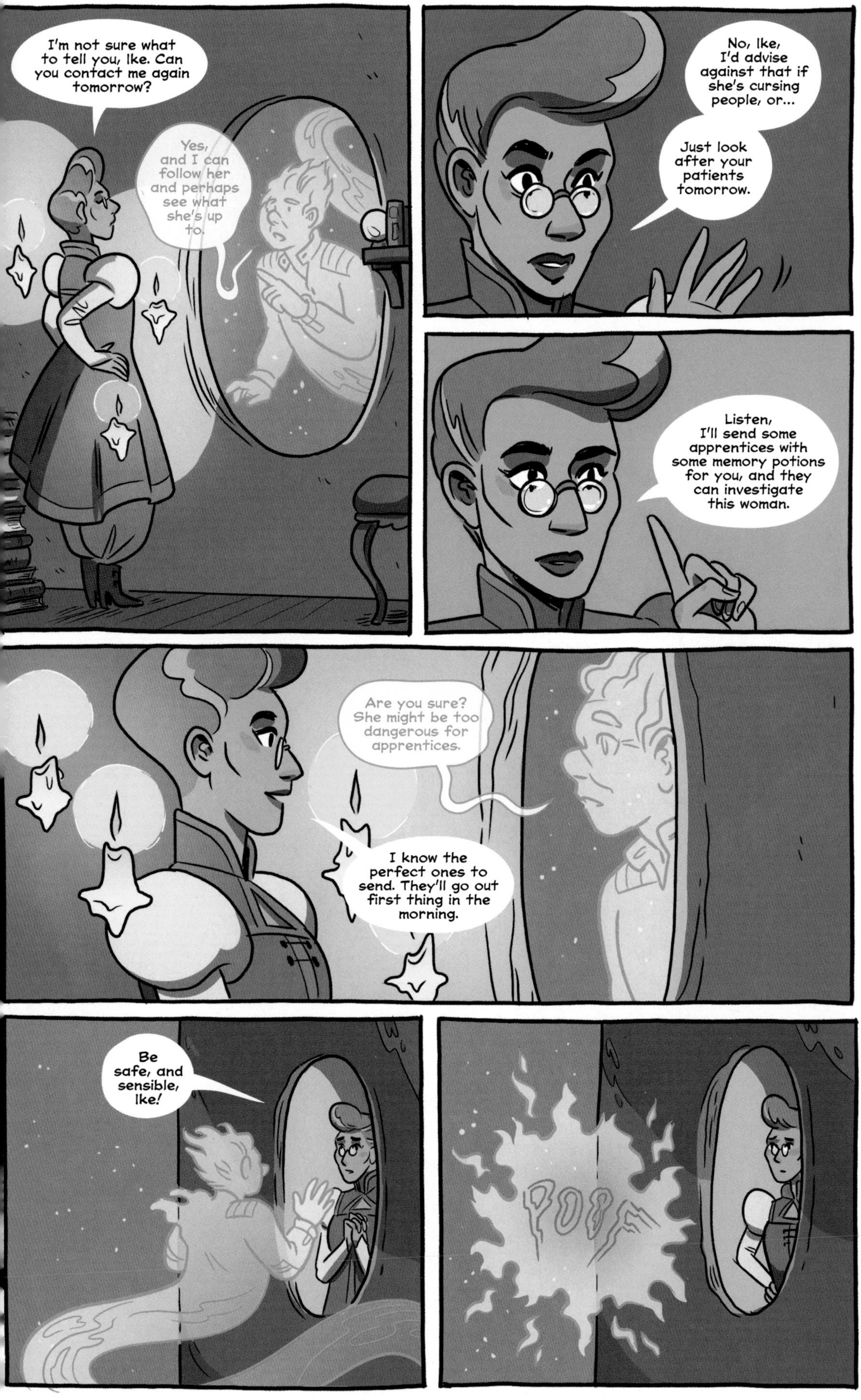
I'm not sure what to tell you, Ike. Can you contact me again tomorrow?
Yes, and I can follow her and perhaps see what she's up to.
No, Ike, I'd advise against that if she's cursing people, or...
Just look after your patients tomorrow.
Listen, I'll send some apprentices with some memory potions for you, and they can investigate this woman.
Are you sure? She might be too dangerous for apprentices.
I know the perfect ones to send. They'll go out first thing in the morning.
Be safe, and sensible, Ike!
POOF

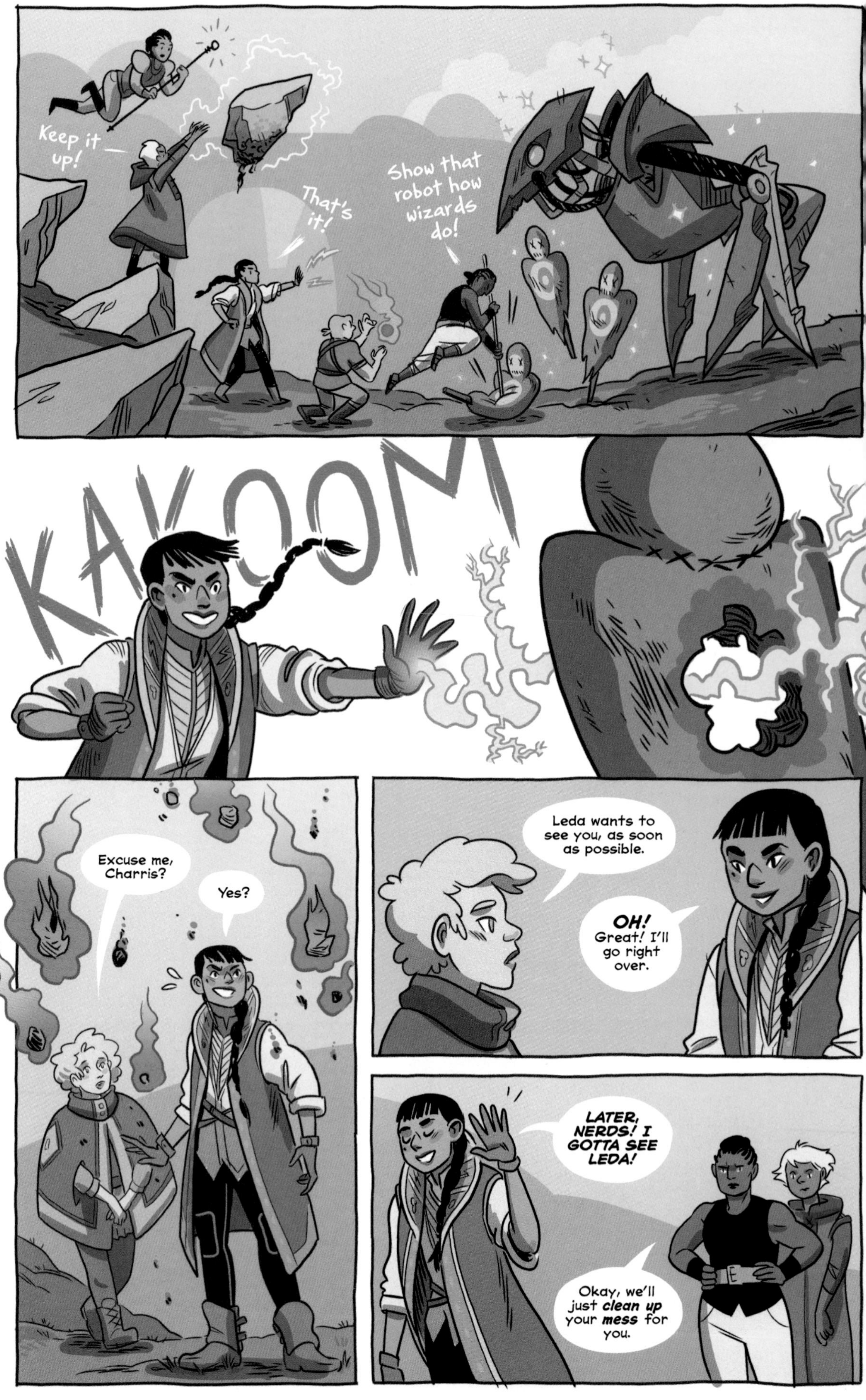

Keep it up!
That's it!
Show that robot how wizards do!
KAVOOM
Excuse me, Charris?
Yes?
Leda wants to see you, as soon as possible.
OH! Great! I'll go right over.
LATER, NERDS! I GOTTA SEE LEDA!
Okay, we'll just clean up your mess for you.

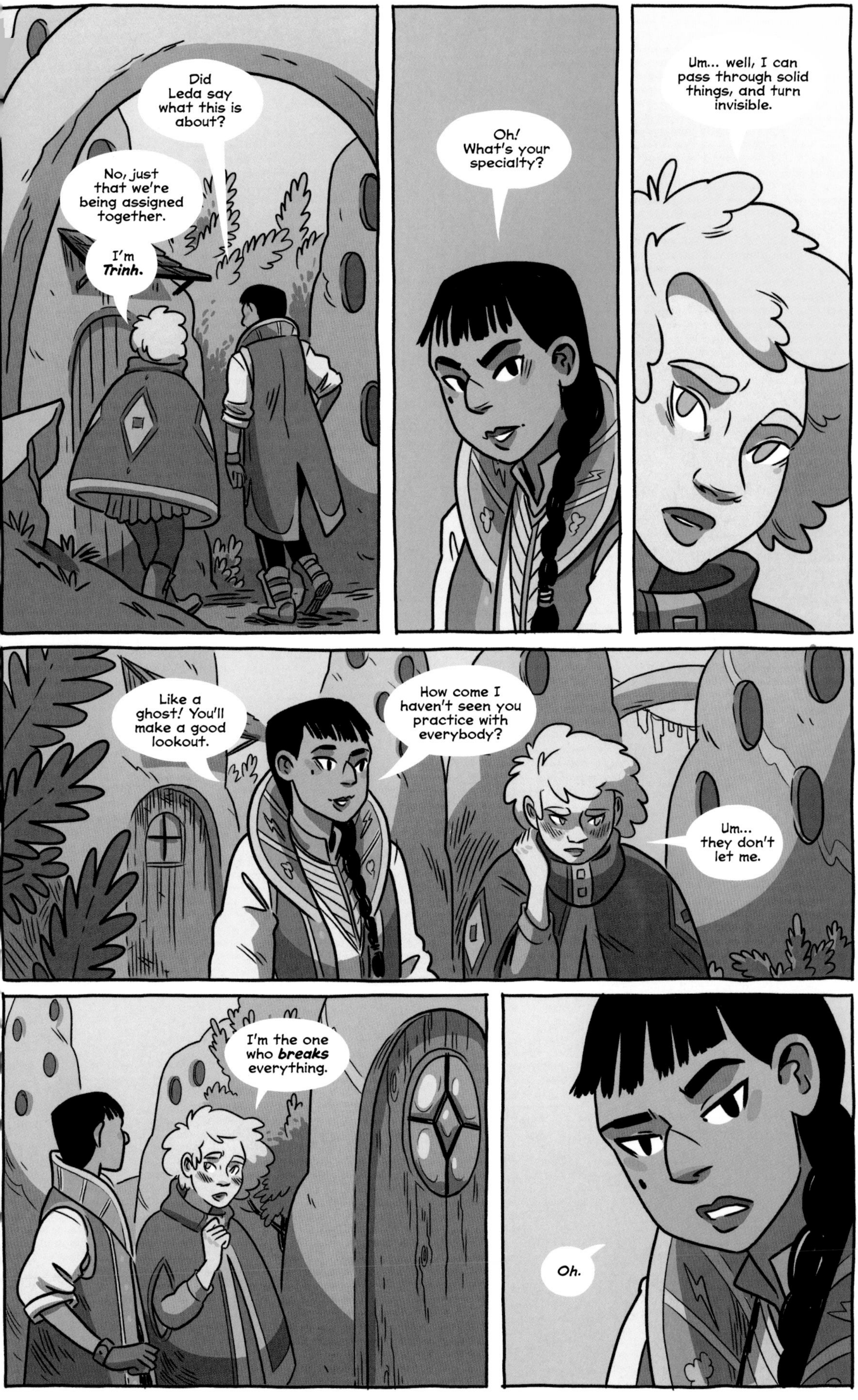
Did Leda say what this is about?
No, just that we're being assigned together.
I'm **Trinh.**
Oh! What's your specialty?
Um... well, I can pass through solid things, and turn invisible.
Like a ghost! You'll make a good lookout.
How come I haven't seen you practice with everybody?
Um... they don't let me.
I'm the one who **breaks** everything.
Oh.

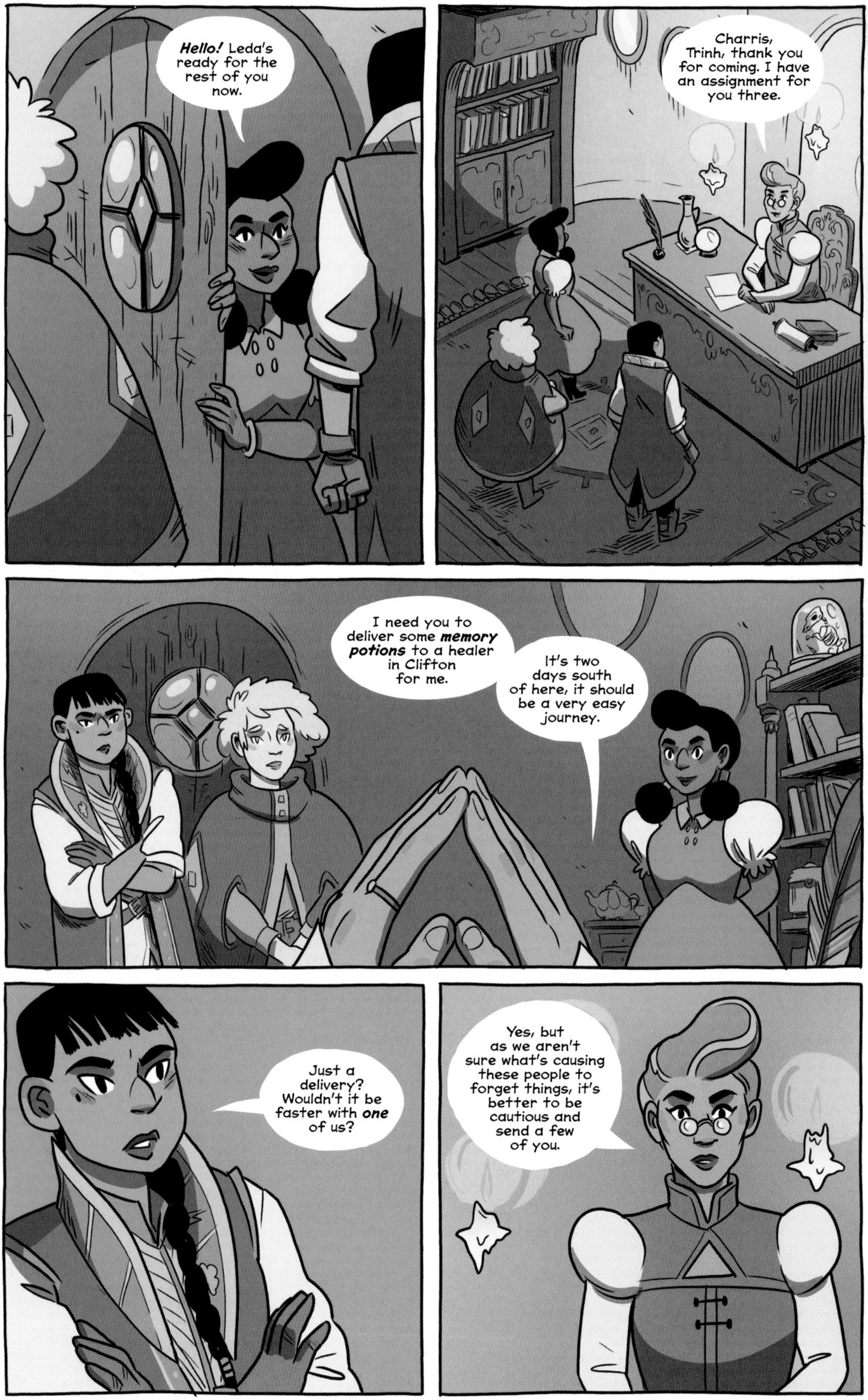
Hello! Leda's ready for the rest of you now.
Charris, Trinh, thank you for coming. I have an assignment for you three.
I need you to deliver some memory potions to a healer in Clifton for me.
It's two days south of here, it should be a very easy journey.
Just a delivery? Wouldn't it be faster with one of us?
Yes, but as we aren't sure what's causing these people to forget things, it's better to be cautious and send a few of you.

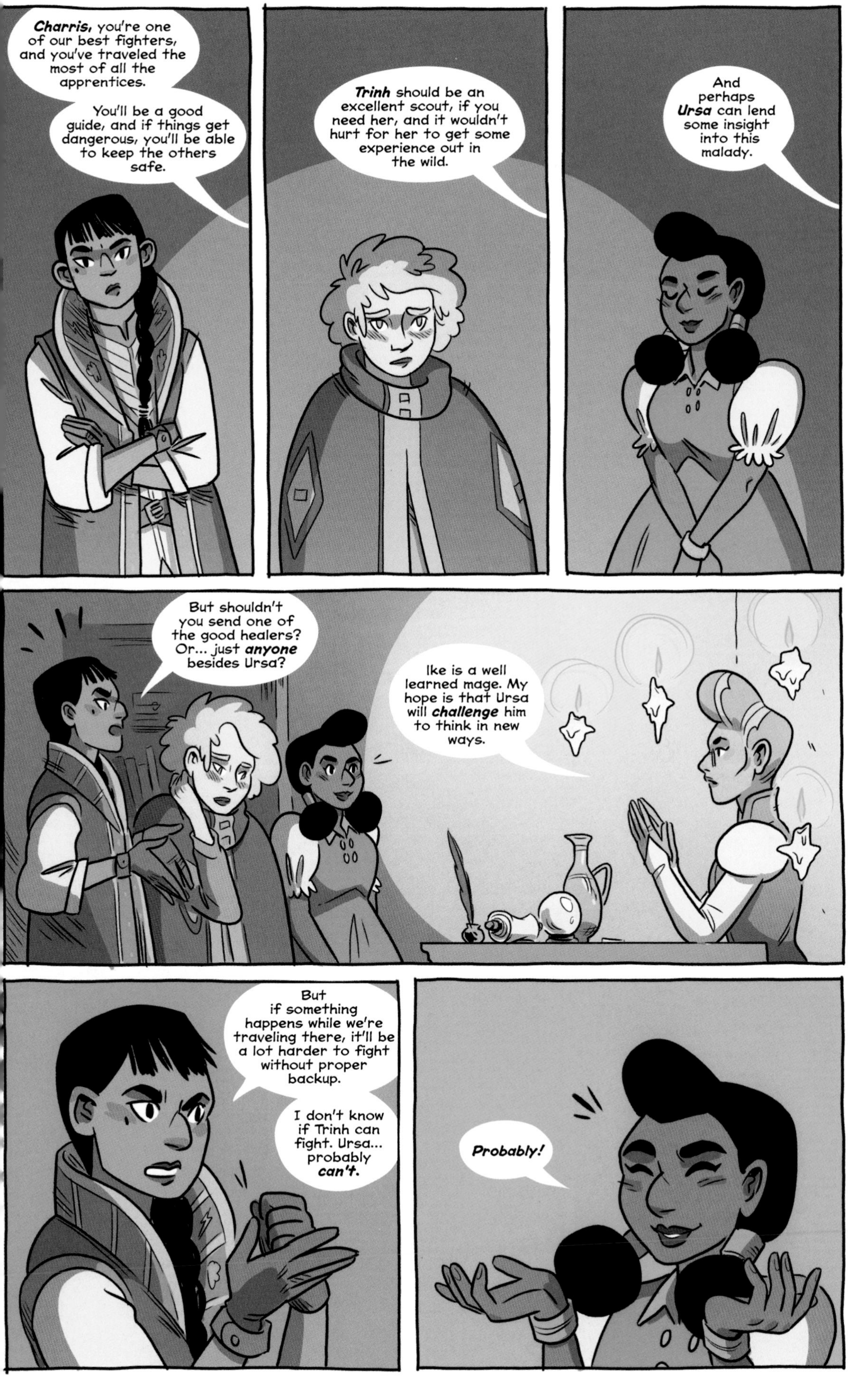
Charris, you're one of our best fighters, and you've traveled the most of all the apprentices.
You'll be a good guide, and if things get dangerous, you'll be able to keep the others safe.
Trinh should be an excellent scout, if you need her, and it wouldn't hurt for her to get some experience out in the wild.
And perhaps Ursa can lend some insight into this malady.
But shouldn't you send one of the good healers? Or... just anyone besides Ursa?
Ike is a well learned mage. My hope is that Ursa will challenge him to think in new ways.
But if something happens while we're traveling there, it'll be a lot harder to fight without proper backup.
I don't know if Trinh can fight. Ursa... probably can't.
Probably!

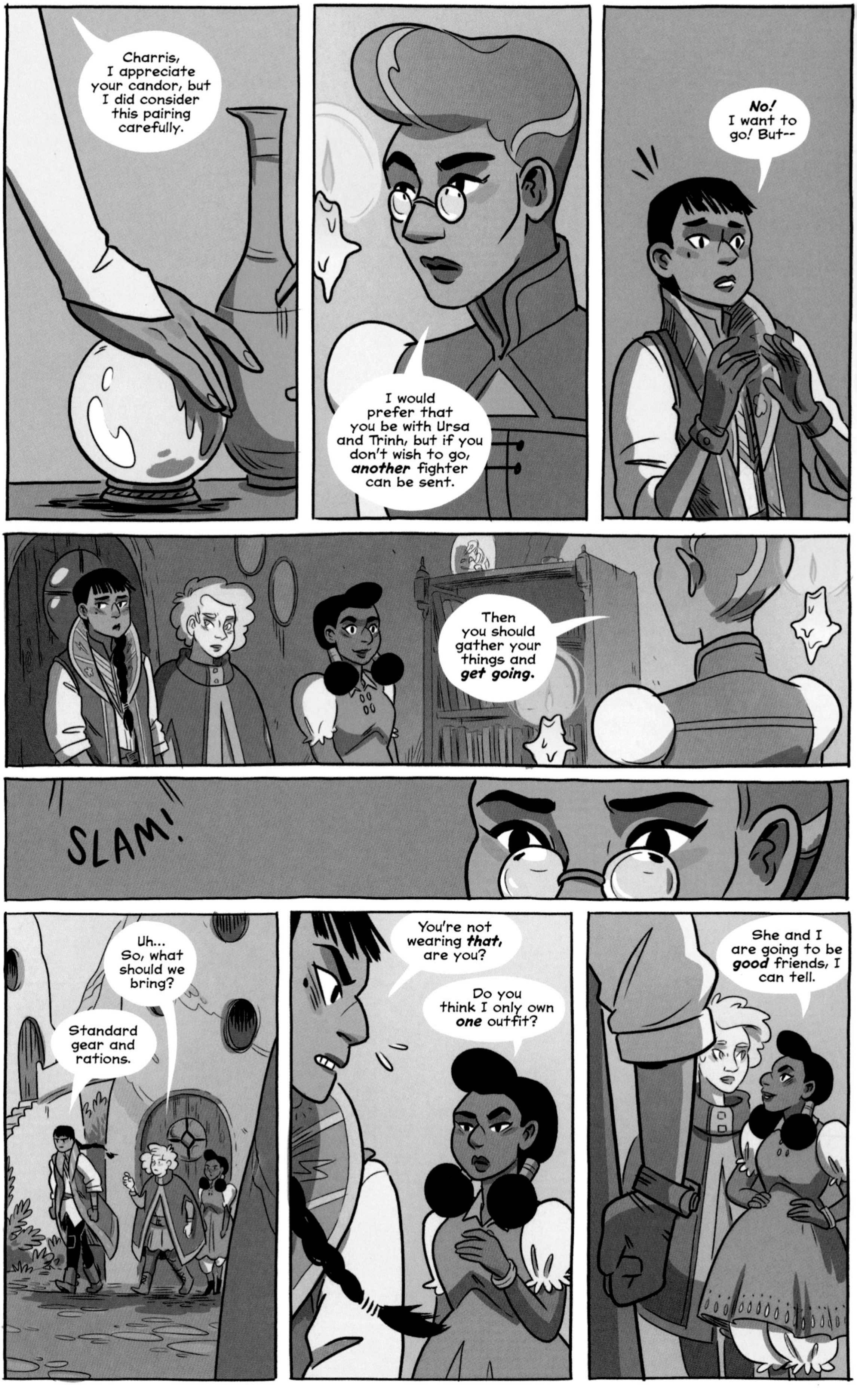
Charris, I appreciate your candor, but I did consider this pairing carefully.
I would prefer that you be with Ursa and Trinh, but if you don't wish to go, *another* fighter can be sent.
No! I want to go! But--
Then you should gather your things and *get going.*
SLAM!
Uh... So, what should we bring?
Standard gear and rations.
You're not wearing *that,* are you?
Do you think I only own *one* outfit?
She and I are going to be *good* friends, I can tell.

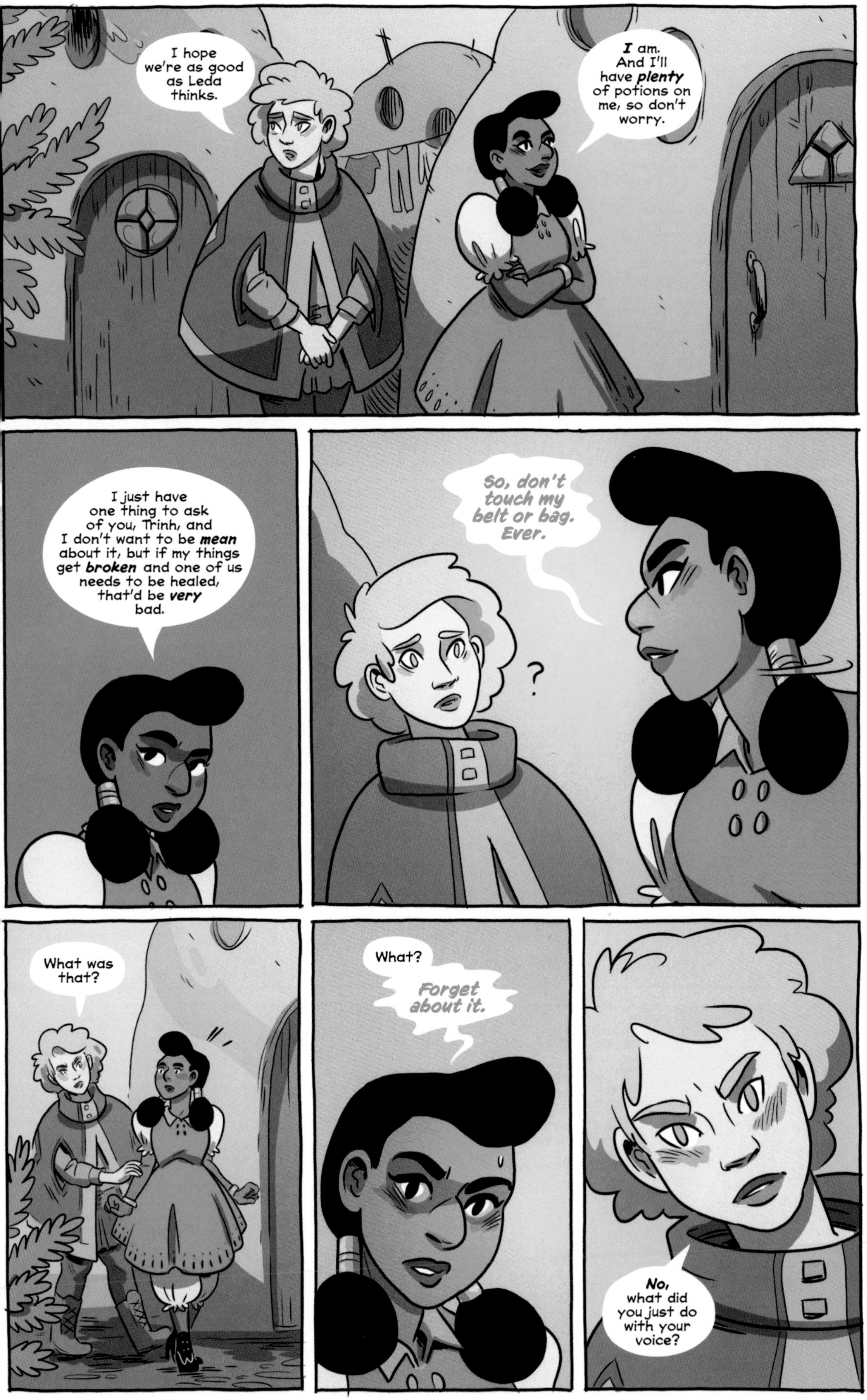
I hope we're as good as Leda thinks.
I am. And I'll have plenty of potions on me, so don't worry.
I just have one thing to ask of you, Trinh, and I don't want to be mean about it, but if my things get broken and one of us needs to be healed, that'd be very bad.
So, don't touch my belt or bag. Ever.
?
What was that?
What?
Forget about it.
No, what did you just do with your voice?

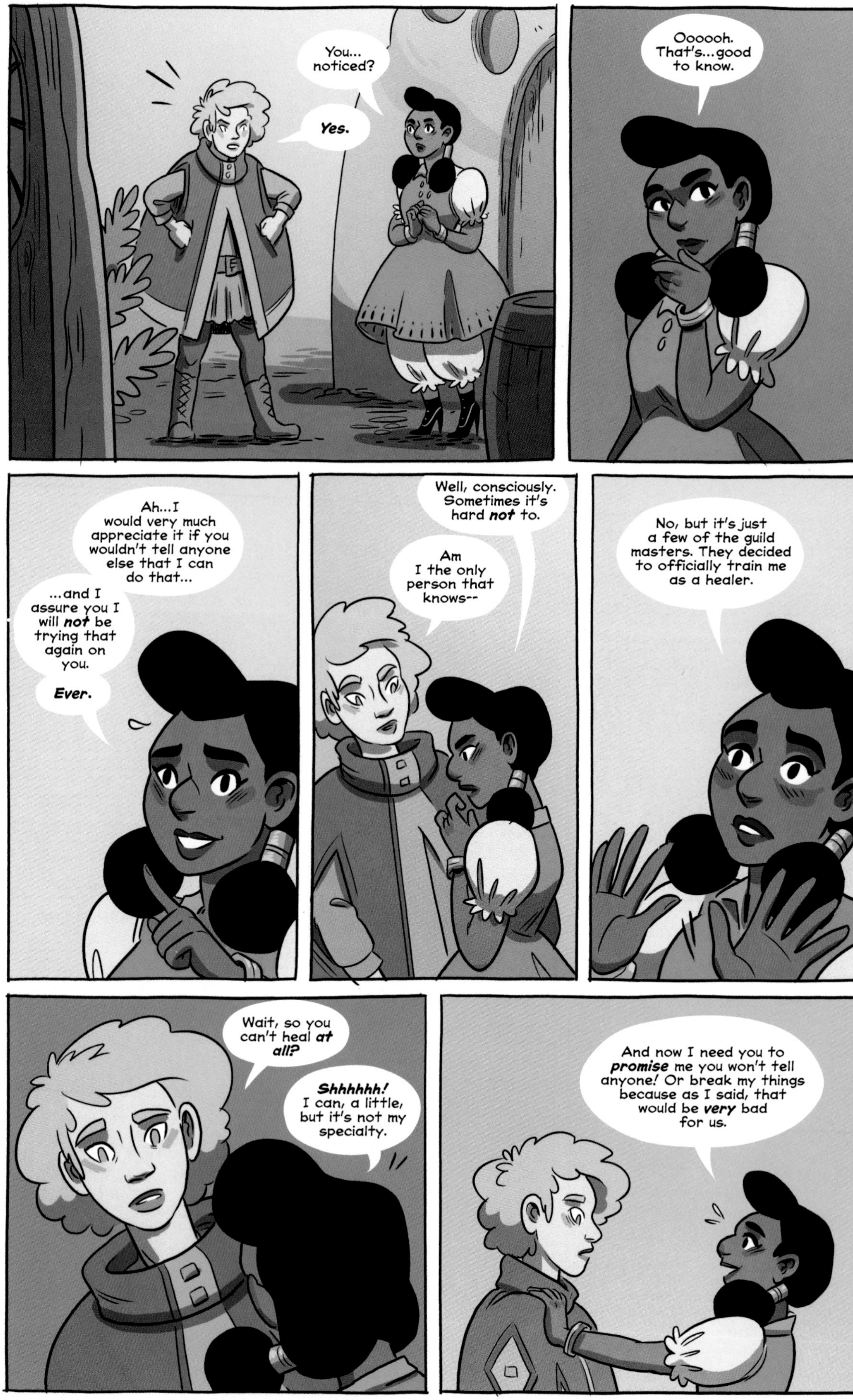

You... noticed?
Yes.
Oooooh. That's...good to know.
Ah...I would very much appreciate it if you wouldn't tell anyone else that I can do that...
...and I assure you I will not be trying that again on you.
Ever.
Well, consciously. Sometimes it's hard not to.
Am I the only person that knows--
No, but it's just a few of the guild masters. They decided to officially train me as a healer.
Wait, so you can't heal at all?
Shhhhhh! I can, a little, but it's not my specialty.
And now I need you to promise me you won't tell anyone! Or break my things because as I said, that would be very bad for us.

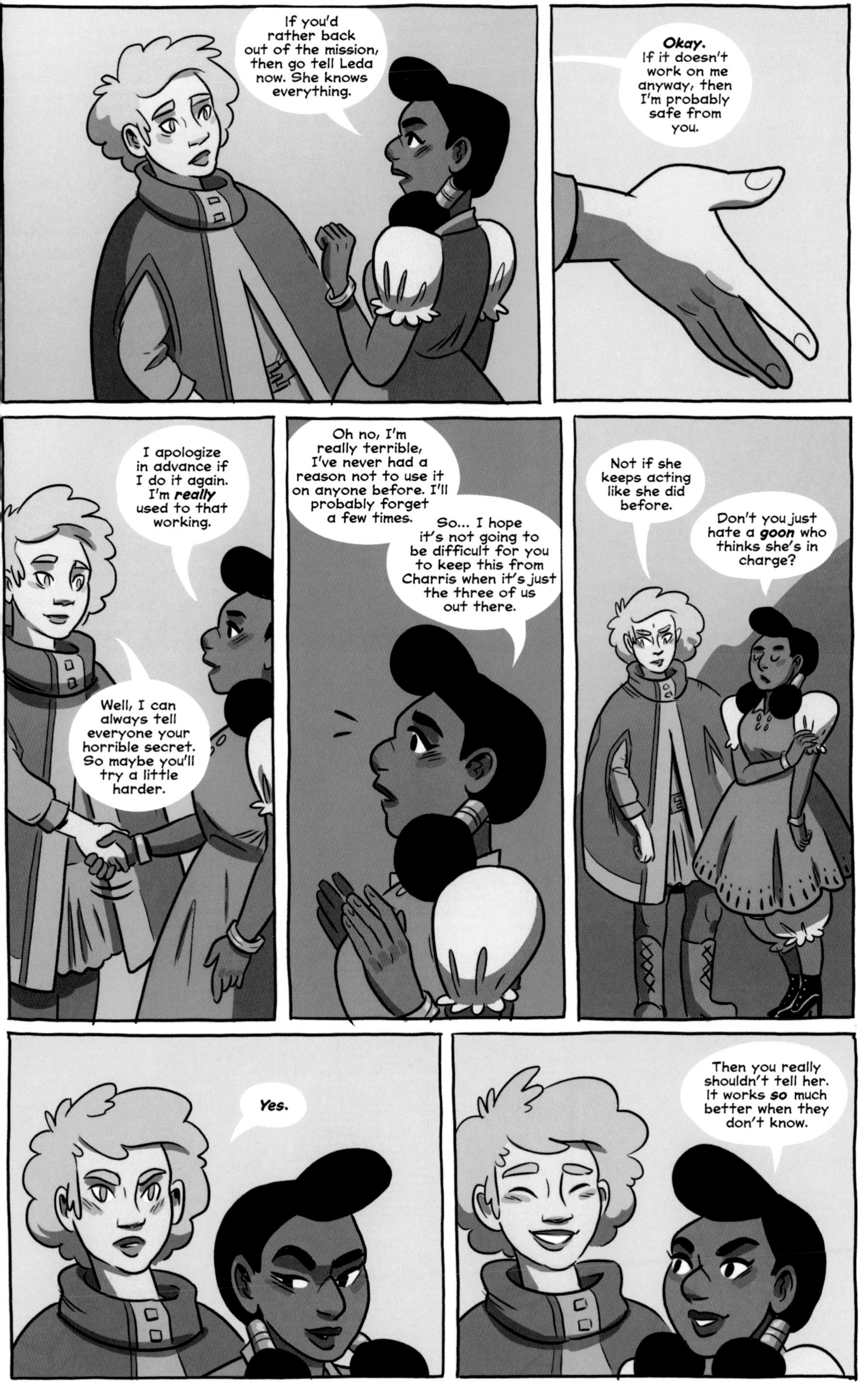

If you'd rather back out of the mission, then go tell Leda now. She knows everything.
Okay. If it doesn't work on me anyway, then I'm probably safe from you.
I apologize in advance if I do it again. I'm **really** used to that working.
Well, I can always tell everyone your horrible secret. So maybe you'll try a little harder.
Oh no, I'm really terrible, I've never had a reason not to use it on anyone before. I'll probably forget a few times.
So... I hope it's not going to be difficult for you to keep this from Charris when it's just the three of us out there.
Not if she keeps acting like she did before.
Don't you just hate a **goon** who thinks she's in charge?
Yes.
Then you really shouldn't tell her. It works **so** much better when they don't know.

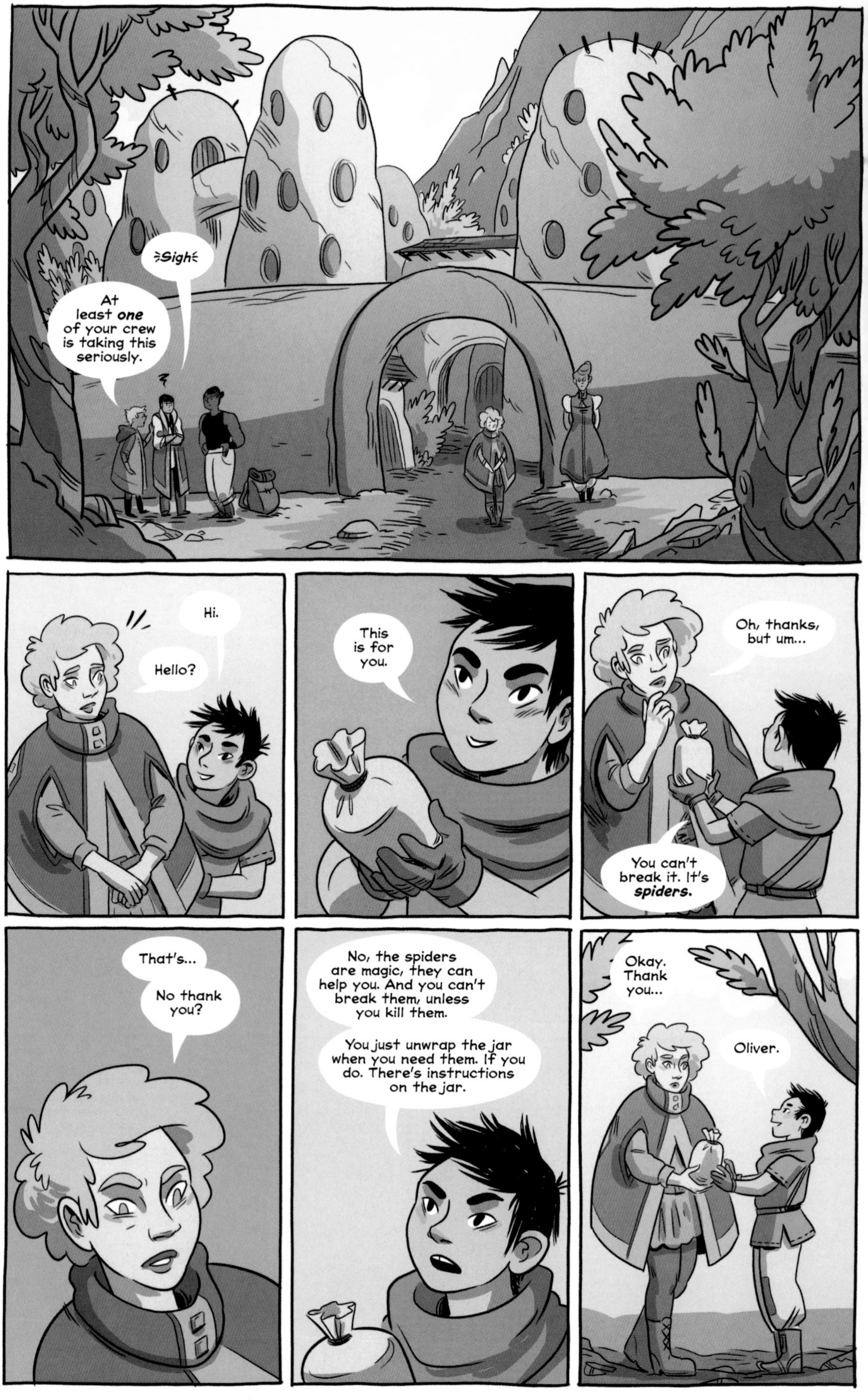

≈Sigh≈
At least **one** of your crew is taking this seriously.
Hi.
Hello?
This is for you.
Oh, thanks, but um...
You can't break it. It's **spiders.**
That's...
No thank you?
No, the spiders are magic, they can help you. And you can't break them, unless you kill them.
You just unwrap the jar when you need them. If you do. There's instructions on the jar.
Okay. Thank you...
Oliver.

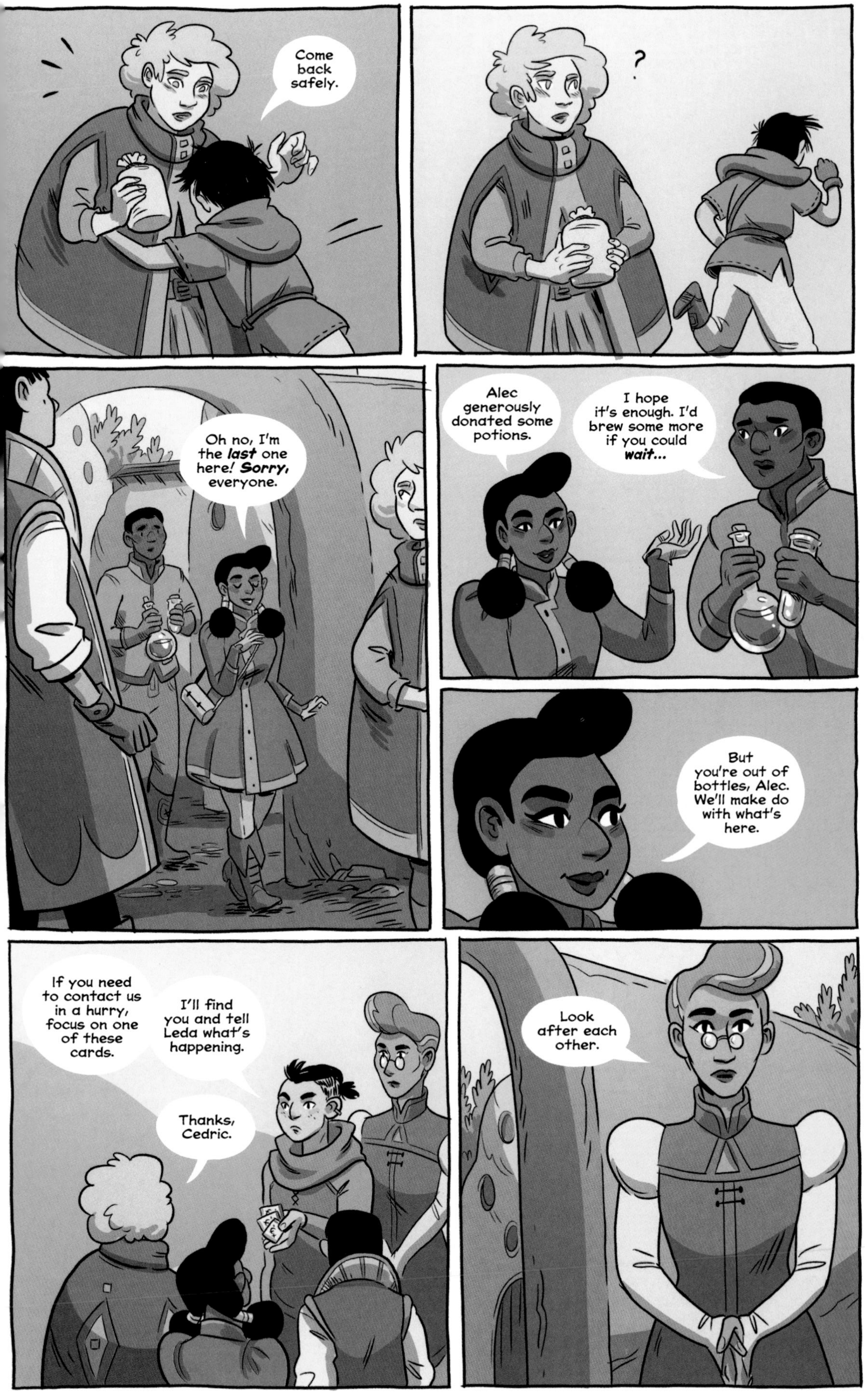
Come back safely.
?
Oh no, I'm the *last* one here! *Sorry,* everyone.
Alec generously donated some potions.
I hope it's enough. I'd brew some more if you could *wait...*
But you're out of bottles, Alec. We'll make do with what's here.
If you need to contact us in a hurry, focus on one of these cards.
I'll find you and tell Leda what's happening.
Thanks, Cedric.
Look after each other.

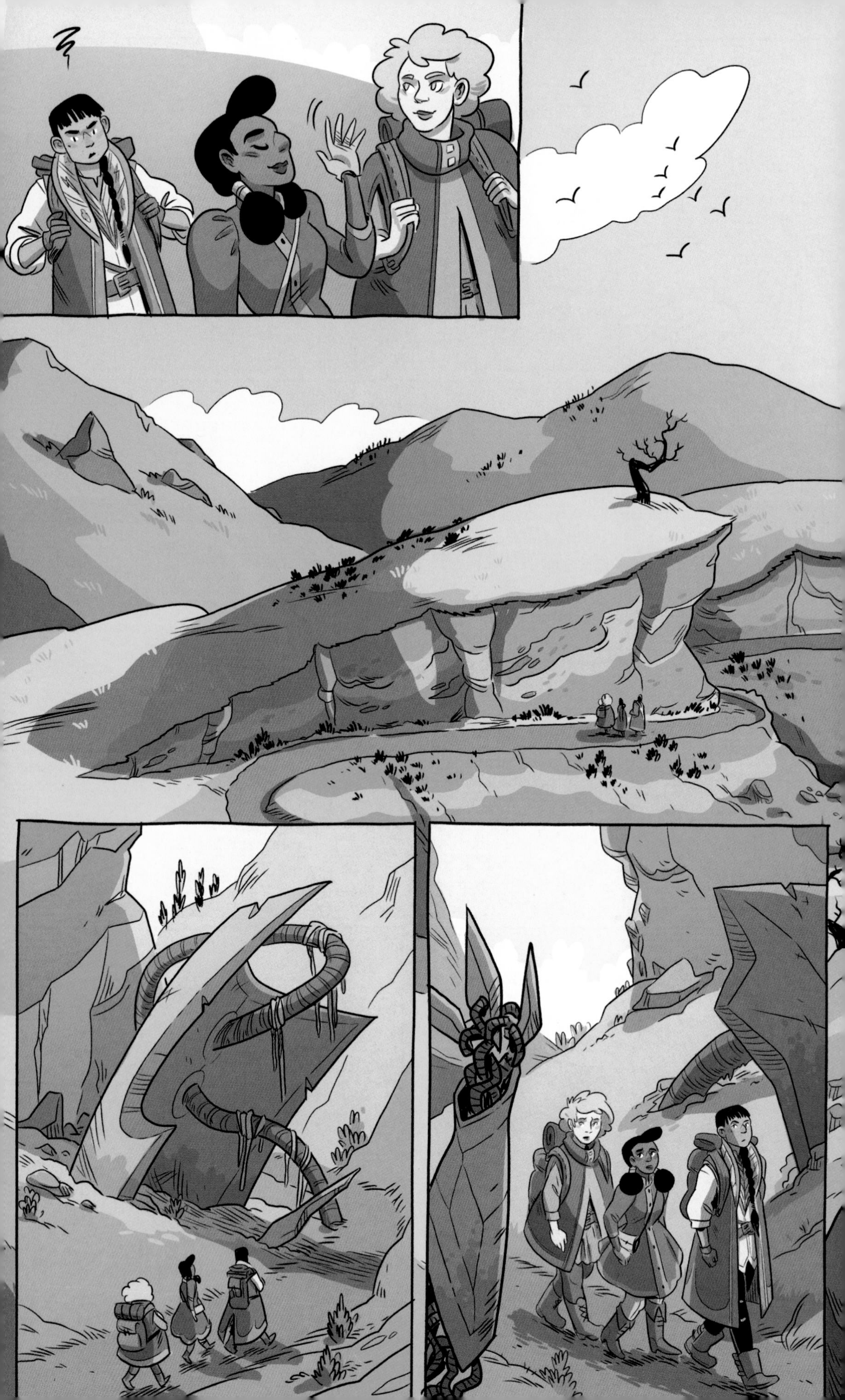

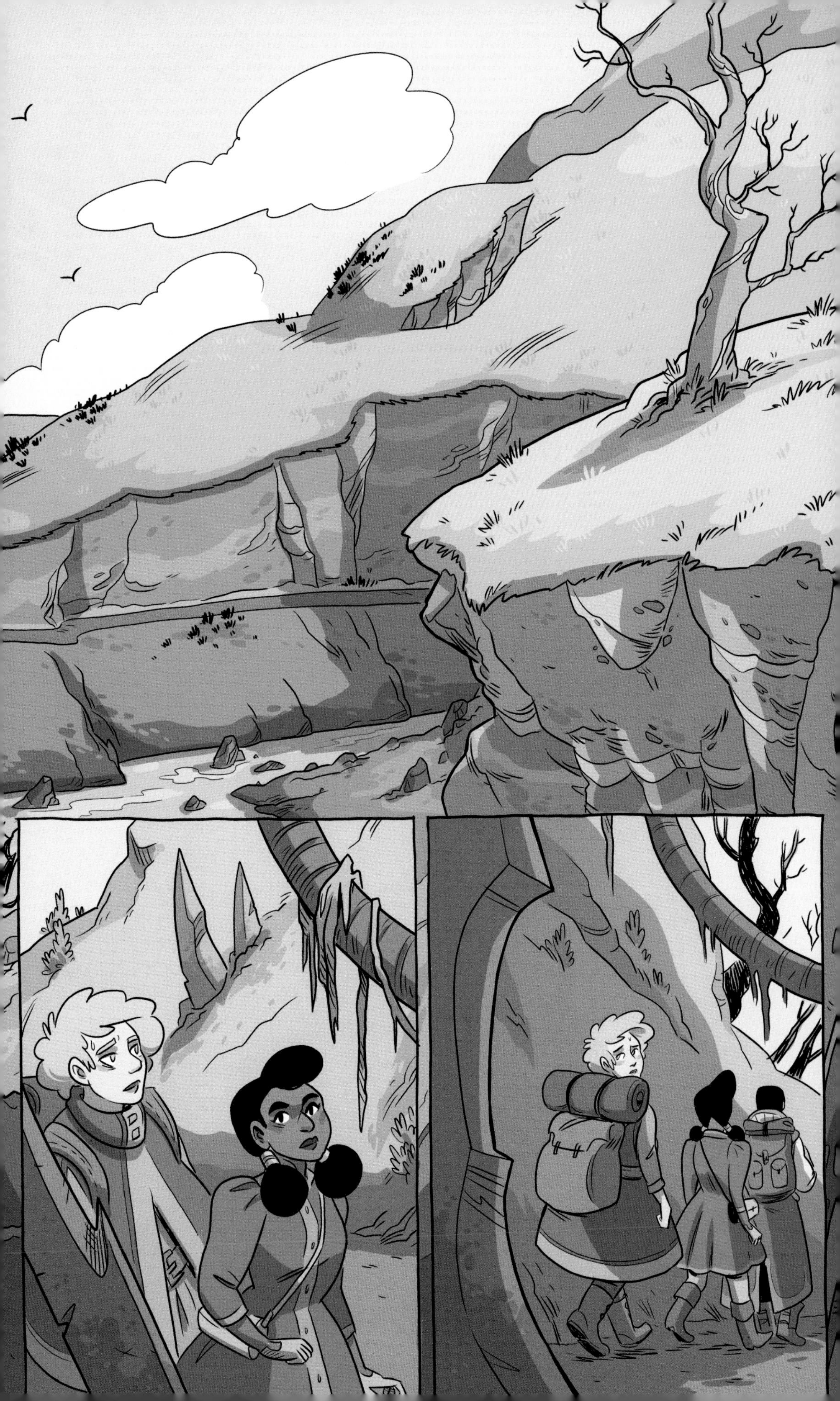

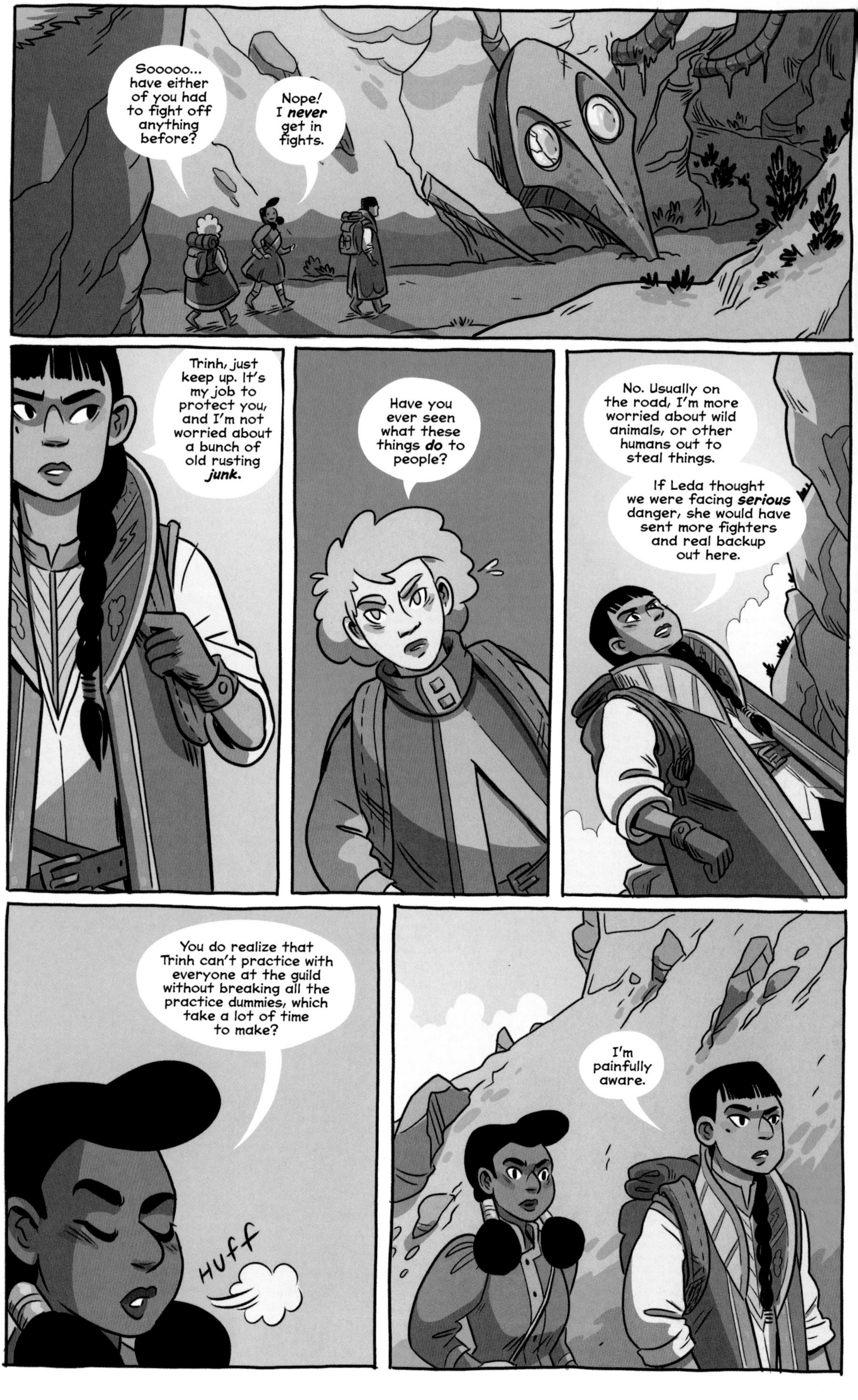
Sooooo... have either of you had to fight off anything before?
Nope! I ***never*** get in fights.
Trinh, just keep up. It's my job to protect you, and I'm not worried about a bunch of old rusting ***junk.***
Have you ever seen what these things ***do*** to people?
No. Usually on the road, I'm more worried about wild animals, or other humans out to steal things.
If Leda thought we were facing ***serious*** danger, she would have sent more fighters and real backup out here.
You do realize that Trinh can't practice with everyone at the guild without breaking all the practice dummies, which take a lot of time to make?
HUFF
I'm painfully aware.

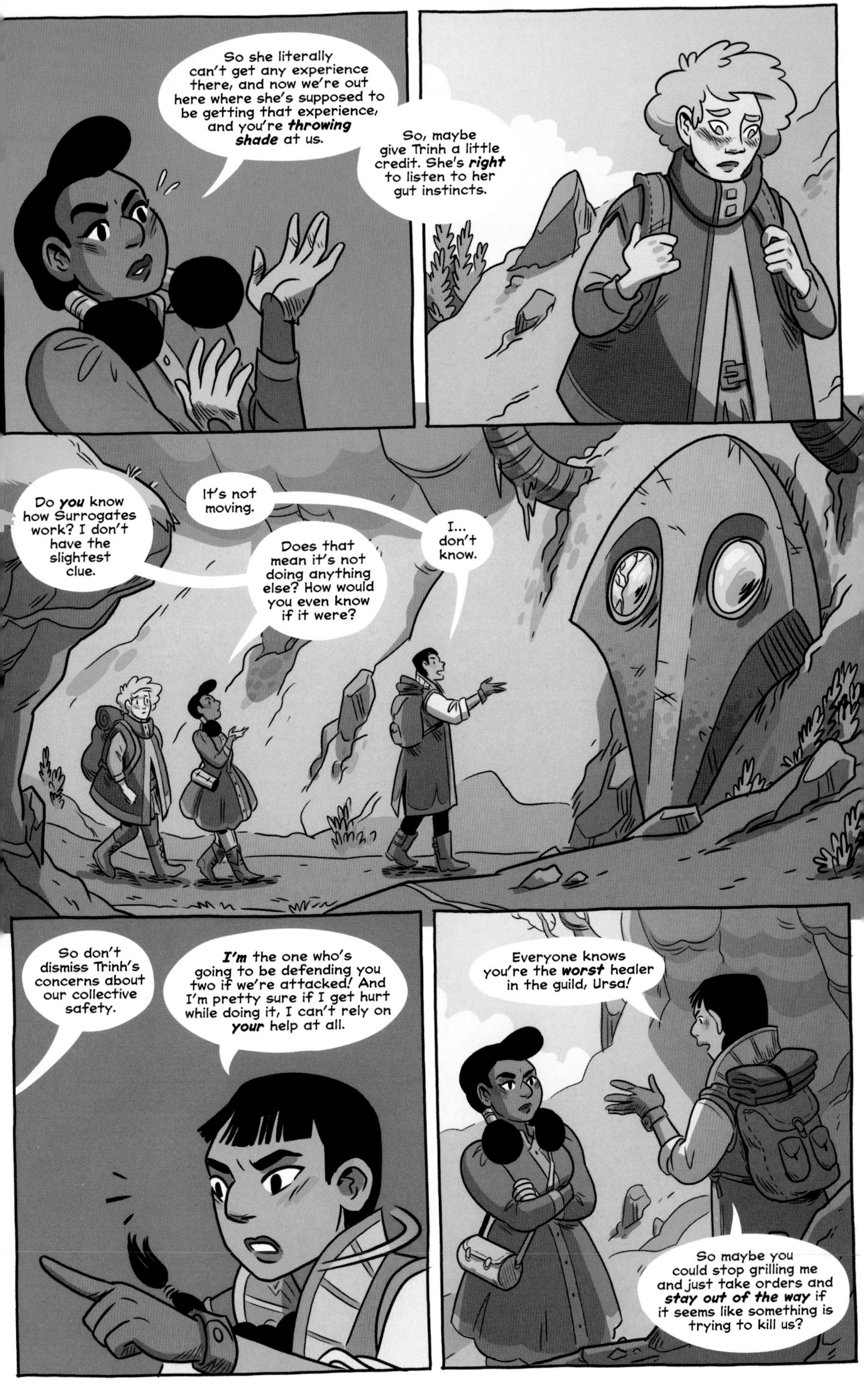
So she literally can't get any experience there, and now we're out here where she's supposed to be getting that experience, and you're ***throwing shade*** at us.
So, maybe give Trinh a little credit. She's ***right*** to listen to her gut instincts.
It's not moving.
Do ***you*** know how Surrogates work? I don't have the slightest clue.
Does that mean it's not doing anything else? How would you even know if it were?
I... don't know.
So don't dismiss Trinh's concerns about our collective safety.
I'm the one who's going to be defending you two if we're attacked! And I'm pretty sure if I get hurt while doing it, I can't rely on ***your*** help at all.
Everyone knows you're the ***worst*** healer in the guild, Ursa!
So maybe you could stop grilling me and just take orders and ***stay out of the way*** if it seems like something is trying to kill us?

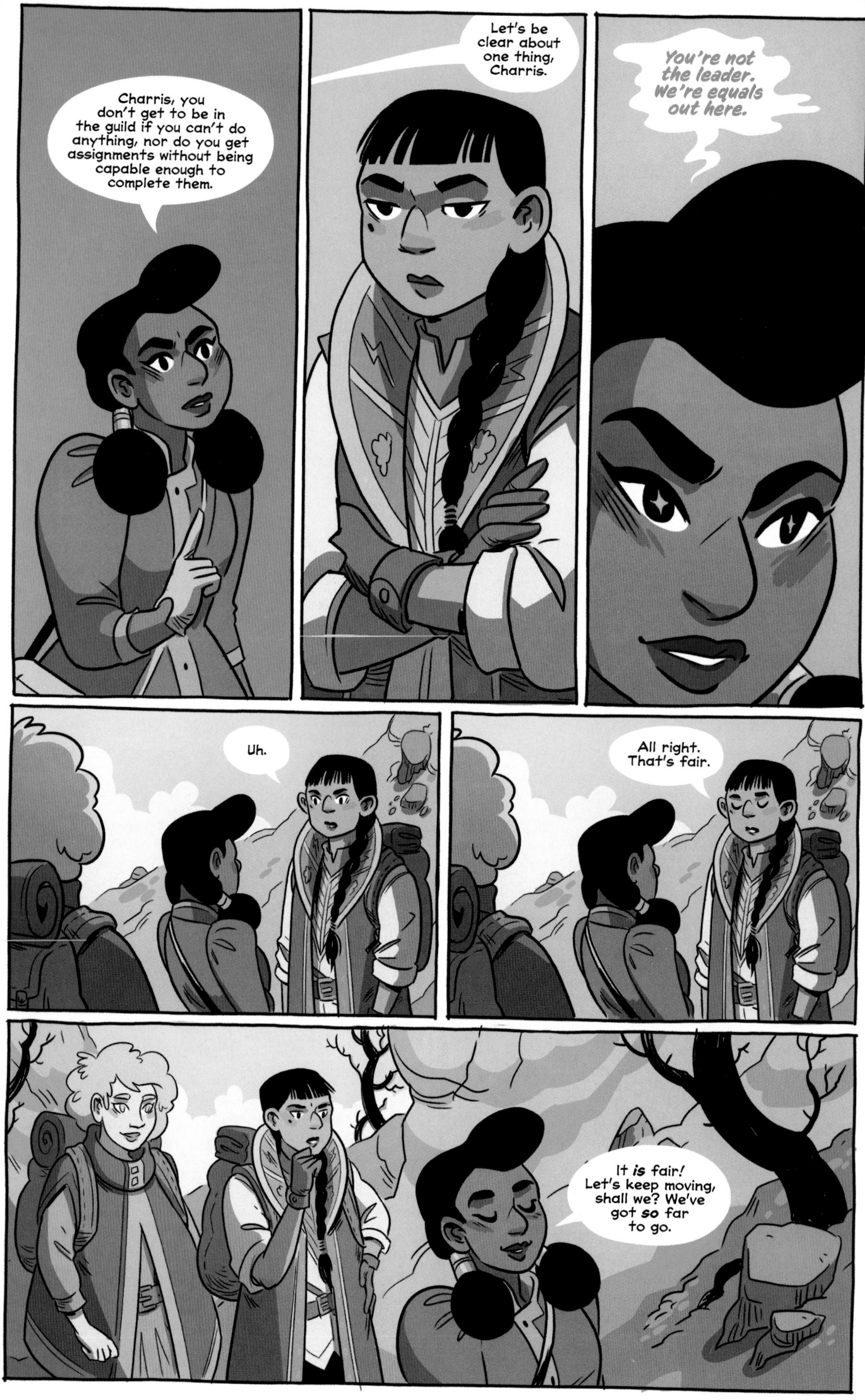

Charris, you don't get to be in the guild if you can't do anything, nor do you get assignments without being capable enough to complete them.
Let's be clear about one thing, Charris.
You're not the leader. We're equals out here.
Uh.
All right. That's fair.
It *is* fair! Let's keep moving, shall we? We've got *so* far to go.

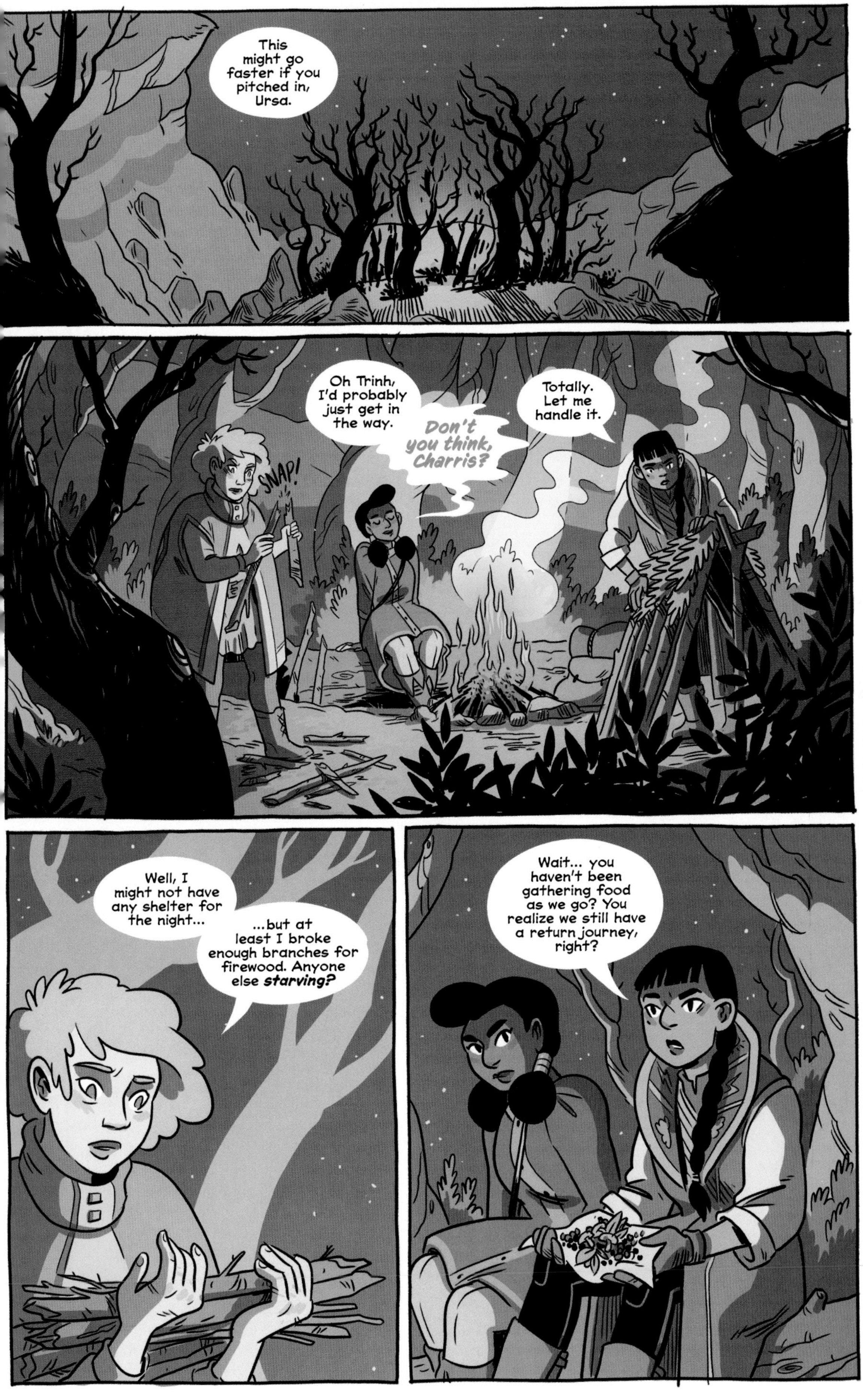
This might go faster if you pitched in, Ursa.
Oh Trinh, I'd probably just get in the way.
Don't you think, Charris?
Totally. Let me handle it.
SNAP!
Well, I might not have any shelter for the night...
...but at least I broke enough branches for firewood. Anyone else *starving?*
Wait... you haven't been gathering food as we go? You realize we still have a return journey, right?

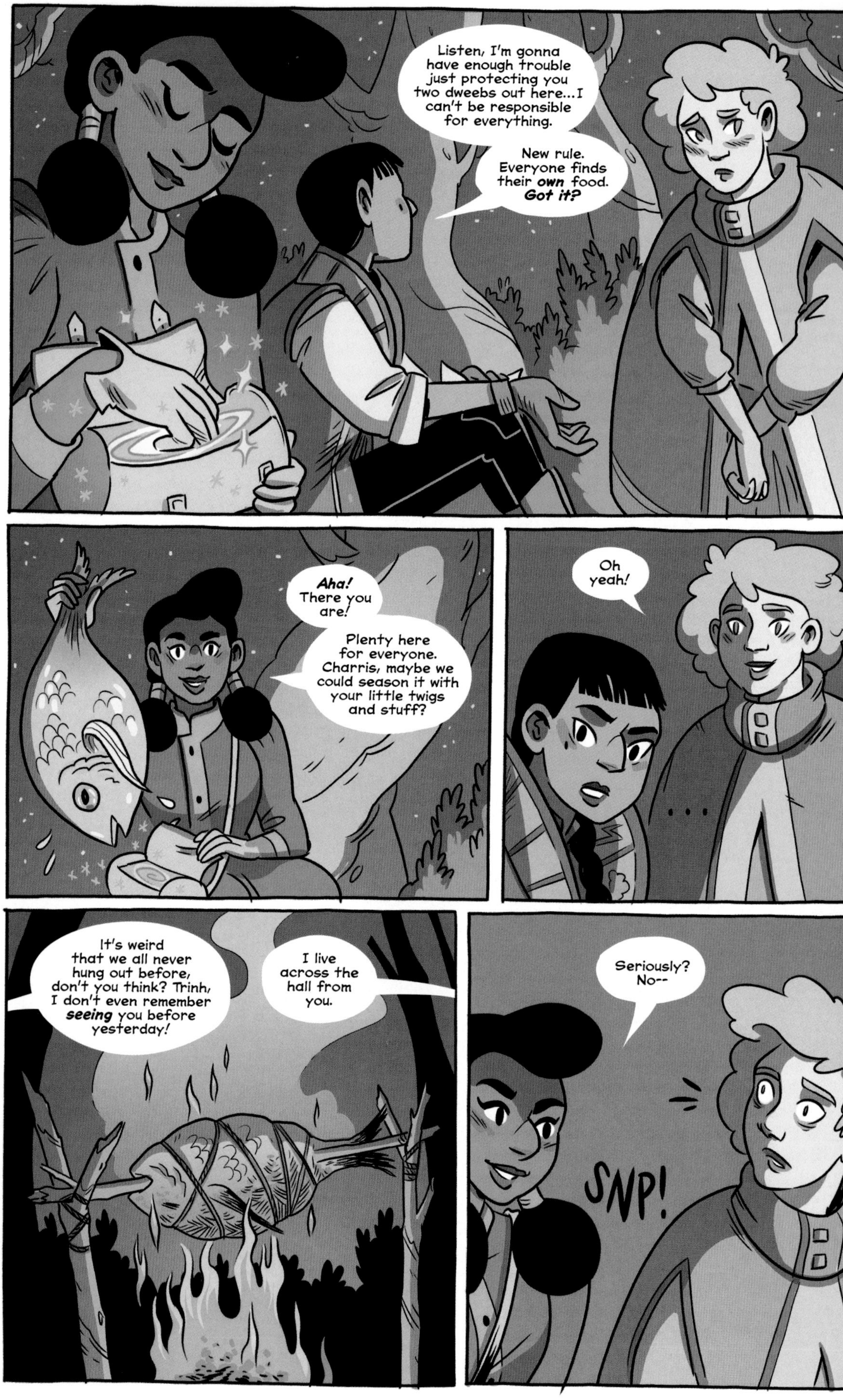

Listen, I'm gonna have enough trouble just protecting you two dweebs out here...I can't be responsible for everything.
New rule. Everyone finds their **own** food. ***Got it?***
Aha! There you are!
Plenty here for everyone. Charris, maybe we could season it with your little twigs and stuff?
Oh yeah!
...
It's weird that we all never hung out before, don't you think? Trinh, I don't even remember ***seeing*** you before yesterday!
I live across the hall from you.
Seriously? No--
SNP!

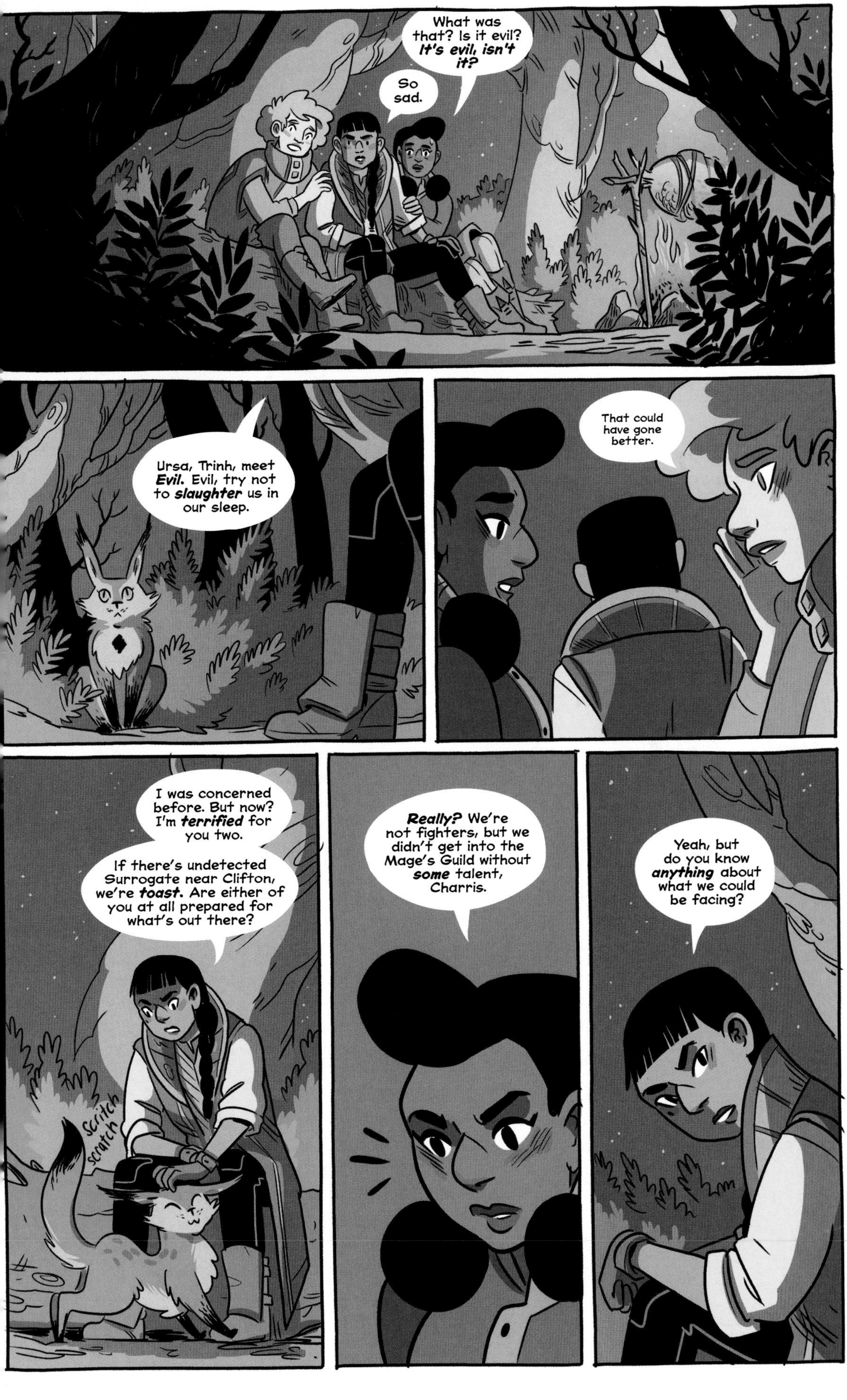
What was that? Is it evil? ***It's evil, isn't it?***
So sad.
Ursa, Trinh, meet ***Evil.*** Evil, try not to ***slaughter*** us in our sleep.
That could have gone better.
I was concerned before. But now? I'm ***terrified*** for you two.
If there's undetected Surrogate near Clifton, we're ***toast.*** Are either of you at all prepared for what's out there?
scritch scratch
Really? We're not fighters, but we didn't get into the Mage's Guild without ***some*** talent, Charris.
Yeah, but do you know ***anything*** about what we could be facing?

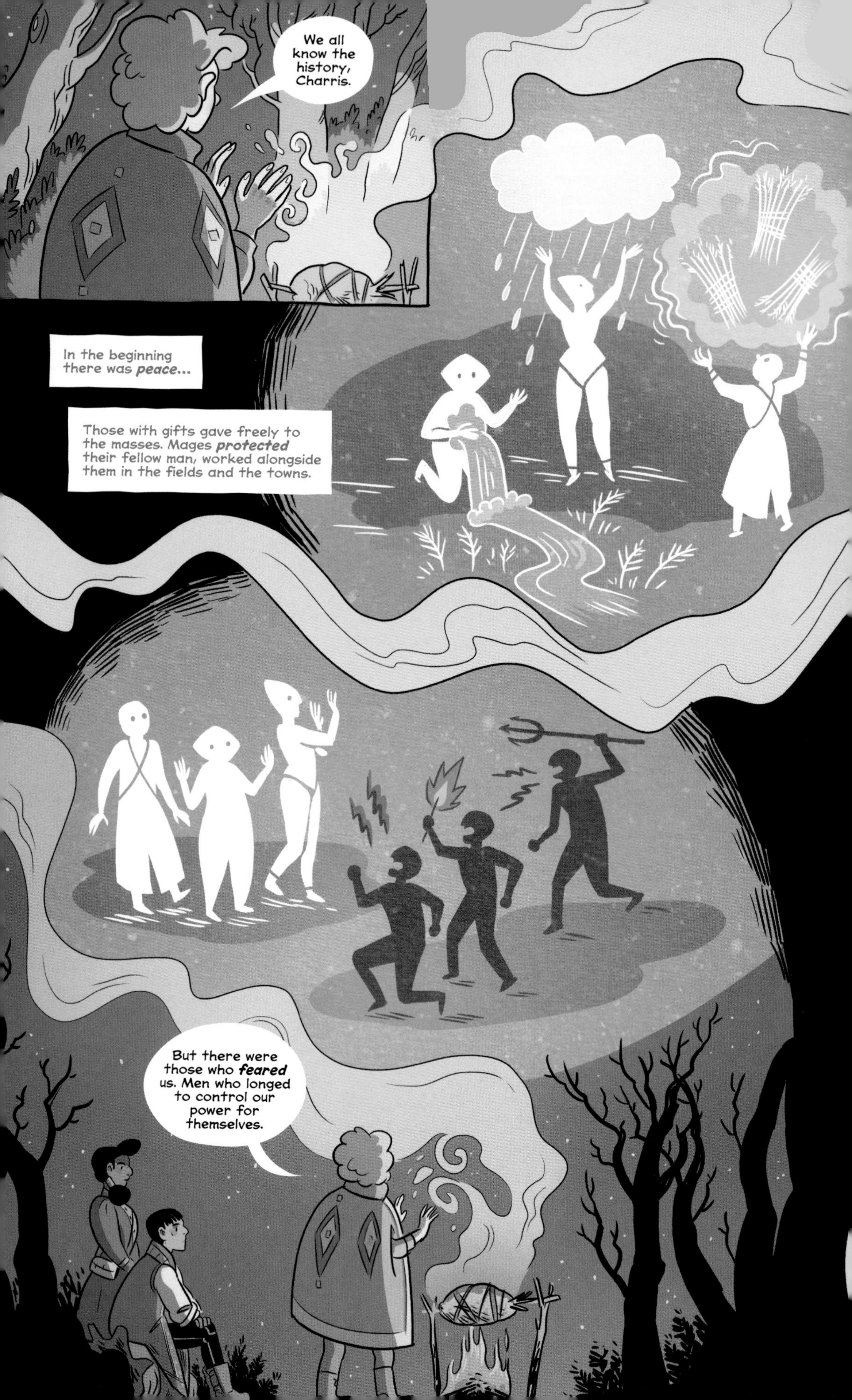
We all know the history, Charris.
In the beginning there was *peace*...
Those with gifts gave freely to the masses. Mages ***protected*** their fellow man, worked alongside them in the fields and the towns.
But there were those who ***feared*** us. Men who longed to control our power for themselves.

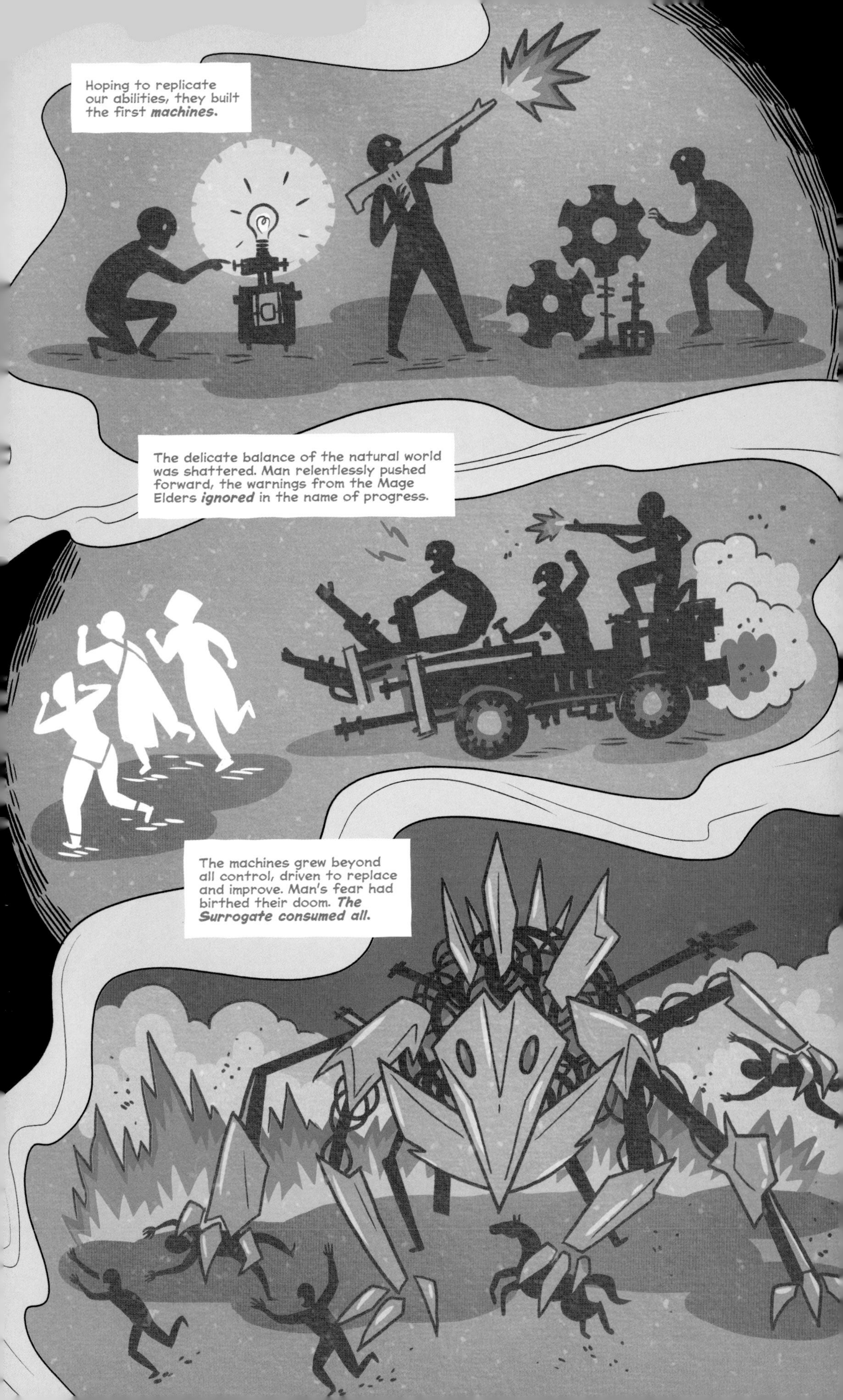
Hoping to replicate our abilities, they built the first ***machines.***
The delicate balance of the natural world was shattered. Man relentlessly pushed forward, the warnings from the Mage Elders ***ignored*** in the name of progress.
The machines grew beyond all control, driven to replace and improve. Man's fear had birthed their doom. ***The Surrogate consumed all.***

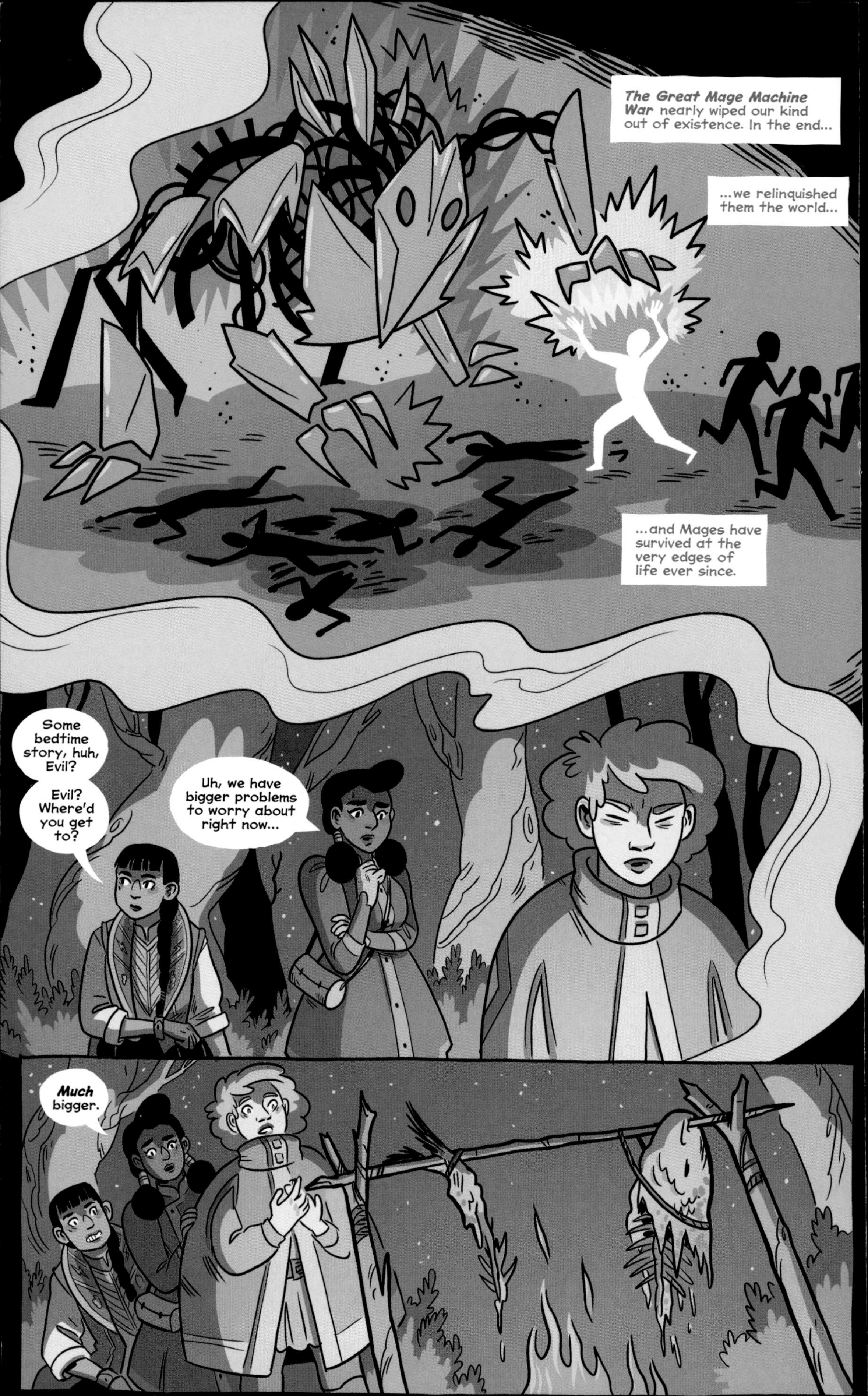
The Great Mage Machine War nearly wiped our kind out of existence. In the end...
...we relinquished them the world...
...and Mages have survived at the very edges of life ever since.
Some bedtime story, huh, Evil?
Evil? Where'd you get to?
Uh, we have bigger problems to worry about right now...
Much bigger.

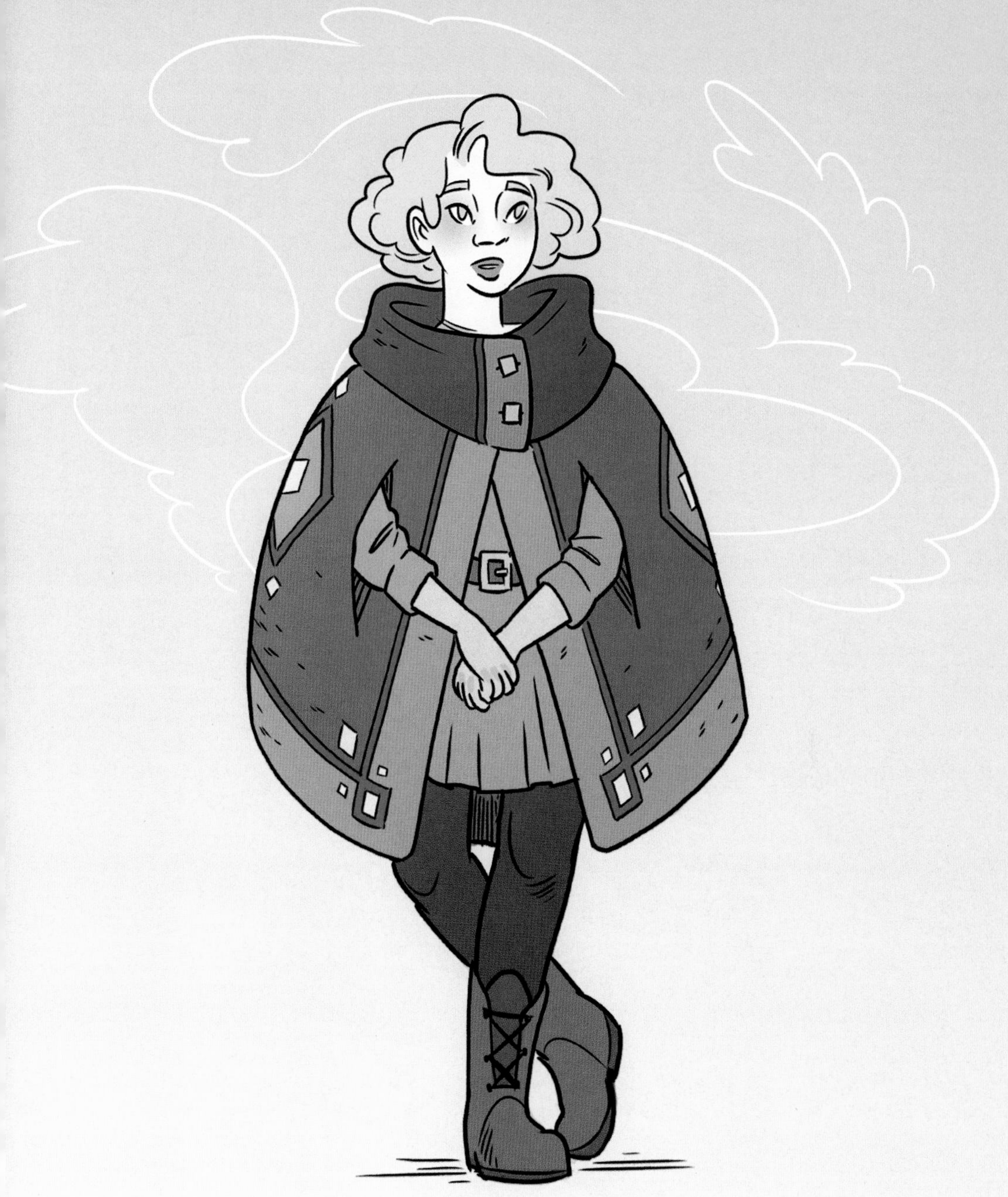

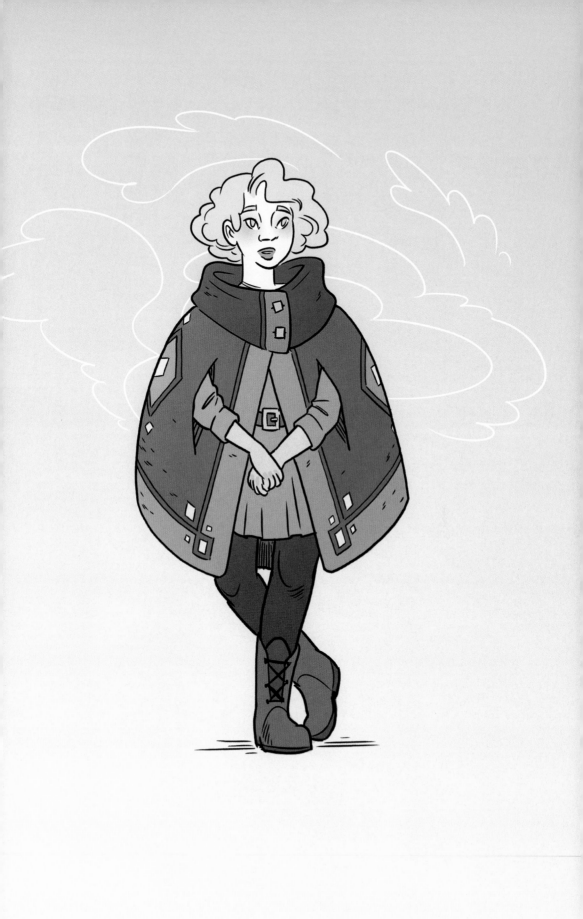

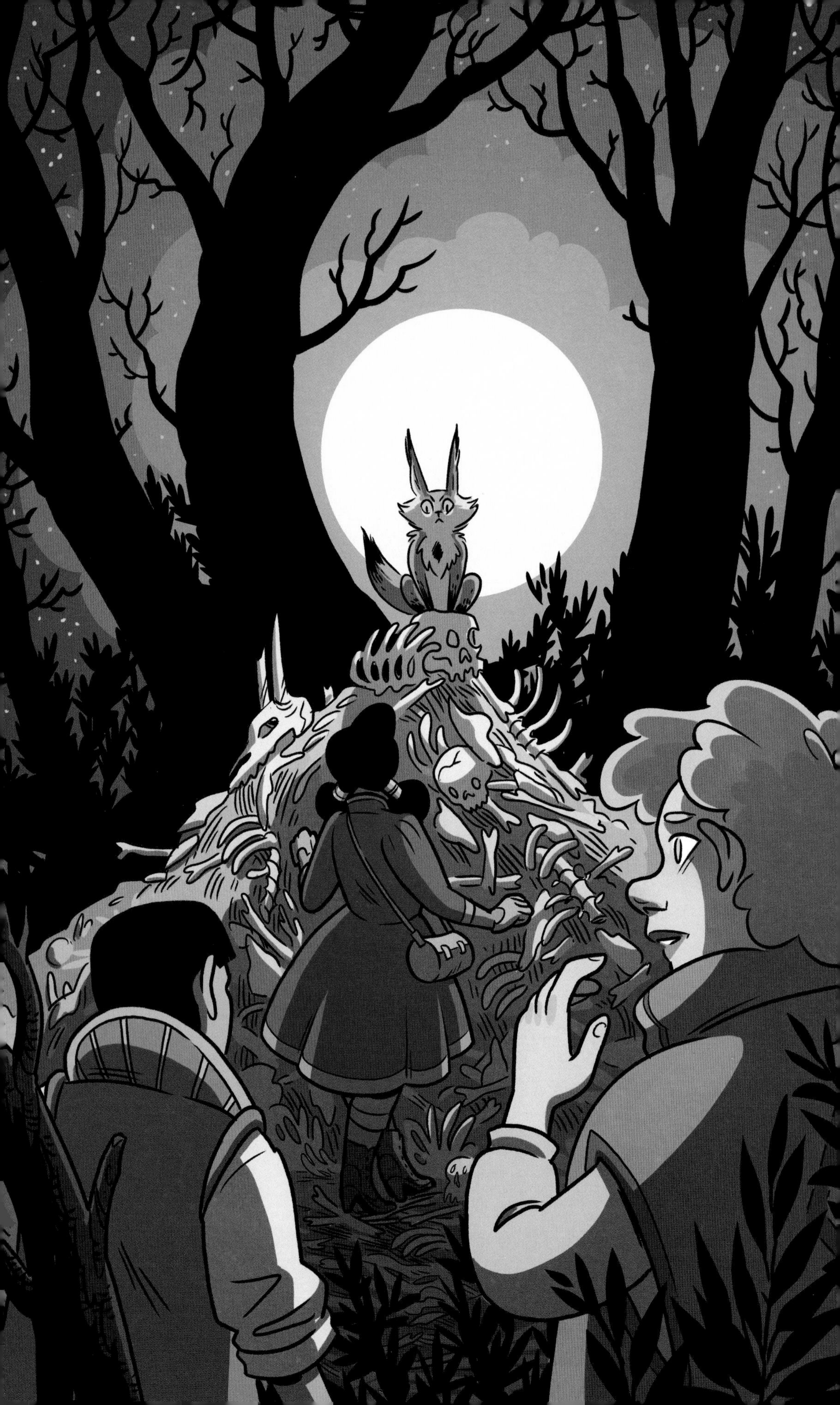

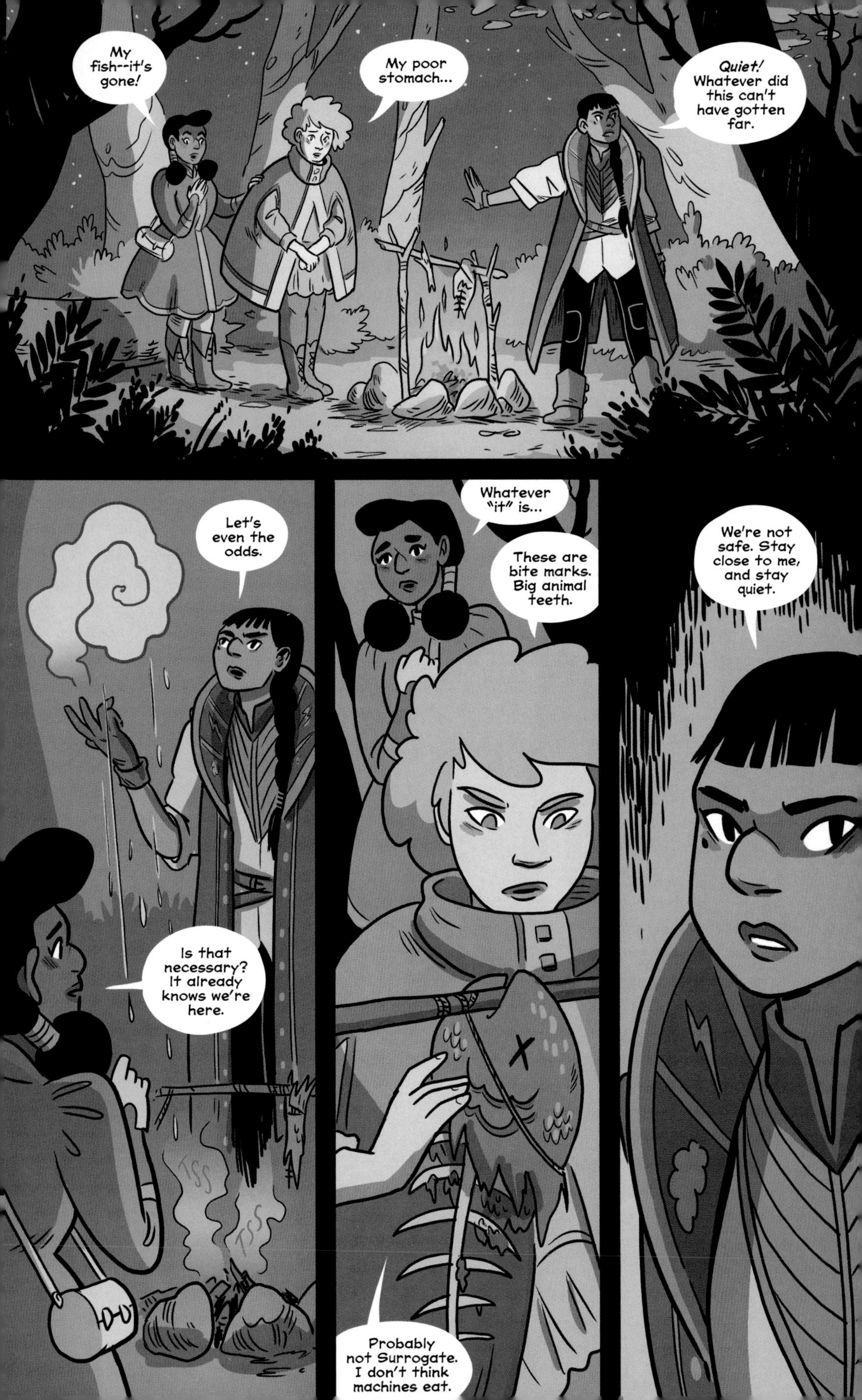
My fish--it's gone!
My poor stomach...
Quiet! Whatever did this can't have gotten far.
Let's even the odds.
Is that necessary? It already knows we're here.
Whatever "it" is...
These are bite marks. Big animal teeth.
Probably not Surrogate. I don't think machines eat.
TSS
TSS
We're not safe. Stay close to me, and stay quiet.

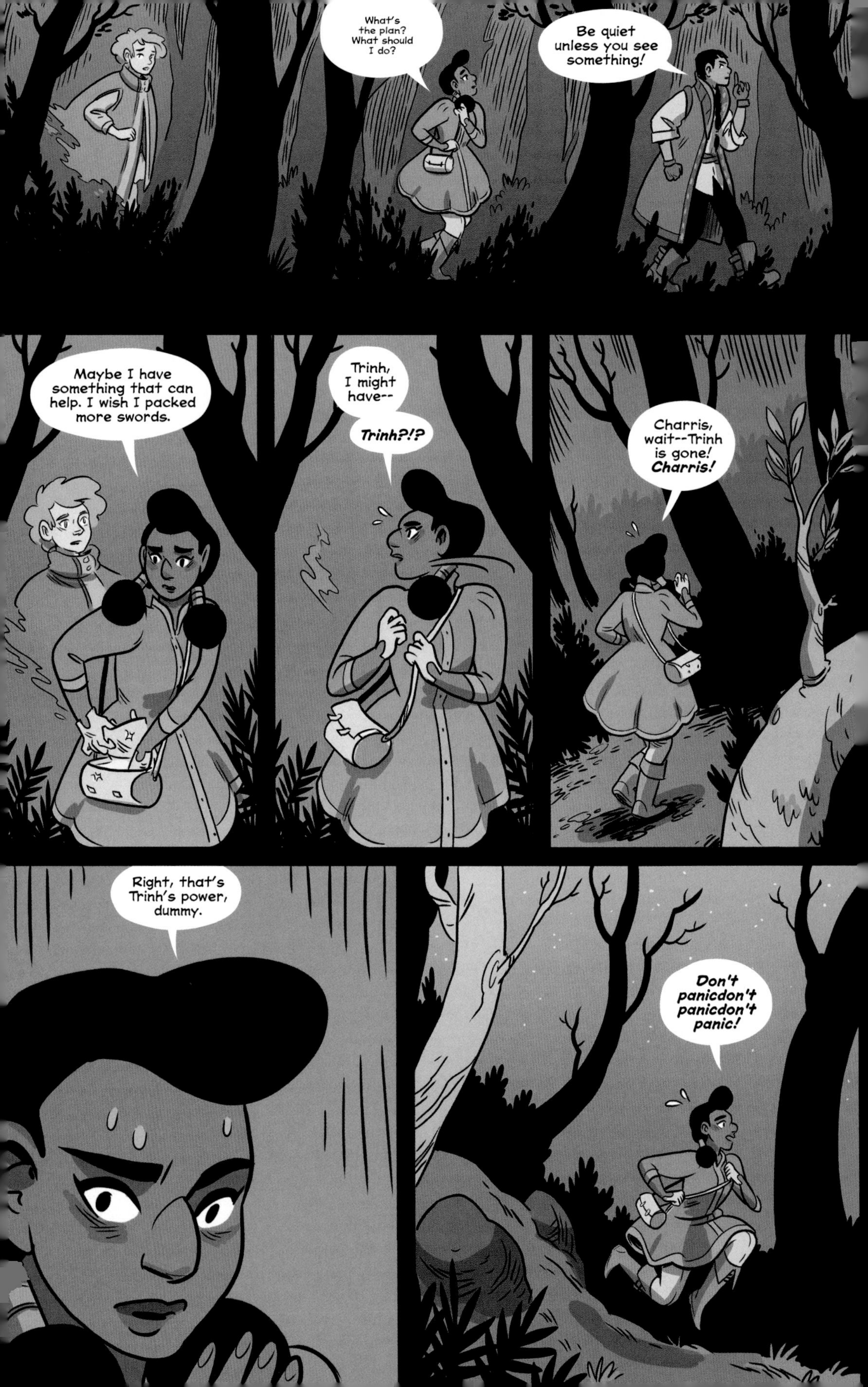
What's the plan? What should I do?
Be quiet unless you see something!
Maybe I have something that can help. I wish I packed more swords.
Trinh, I might have--
Trinh?!?
Charris, wait--Trinh is gone! Charris!
Right, that's Trinh's power, dummy.
Don't panicdon't panicdon't panic!

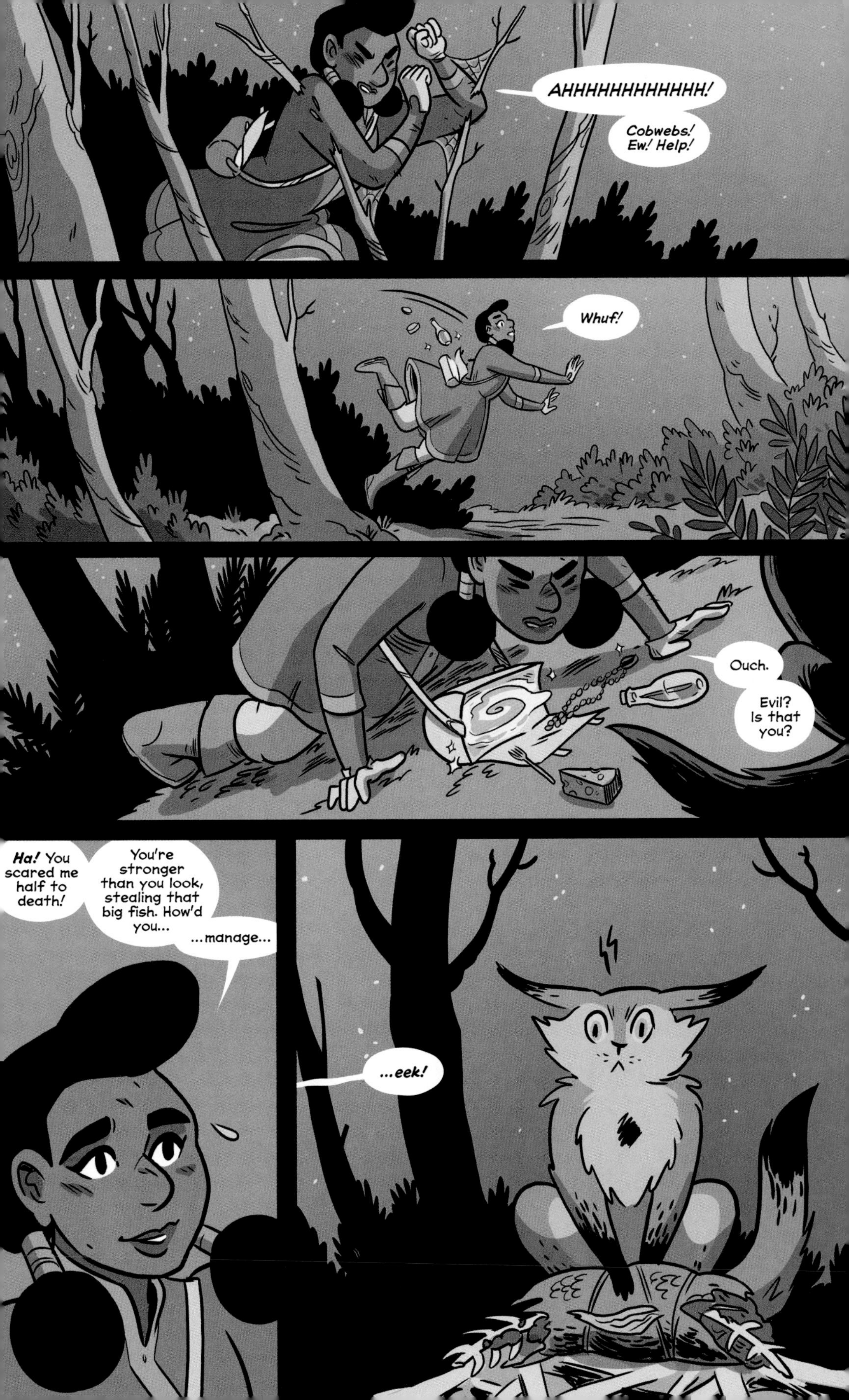
AHHHHHHHHHHHH!
Cobwebs! Ew! Help!
Whuf!
Ouch.
Evil? Is that you?
Ha! You scared me half to death!
You're stronger than you look, stealing that big fish. How'd you...
...manage...
...eek!

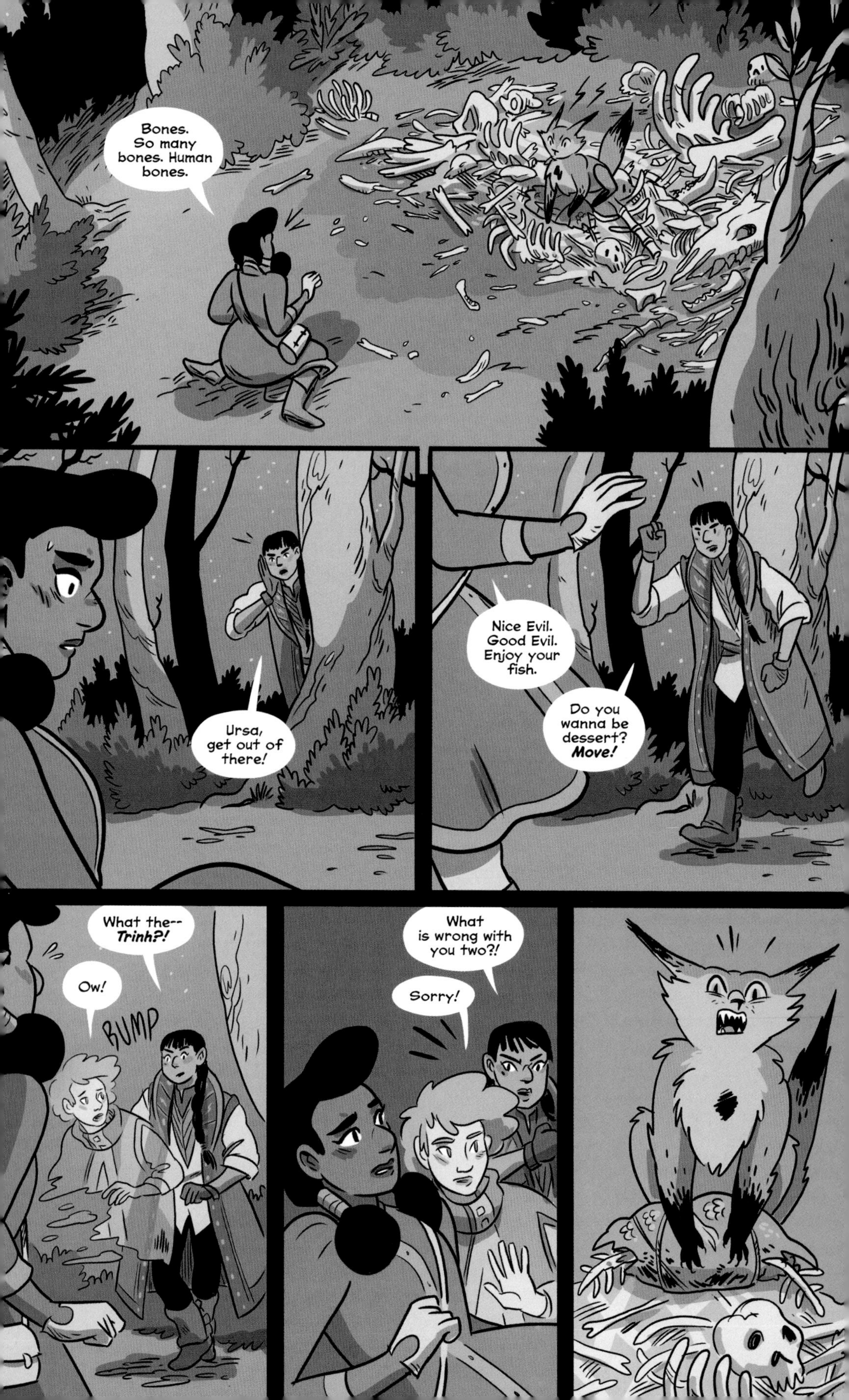
Bones.
So many
bones. Human
bones.
Ursa,
get out of
there!
Nice Evil.
Good Evil.
Enjoy your
fish.
Do you
wanna be
dessert?
Move!
What the--
Trinh?!
Ow!
BUMP
What
is wrong with
you two?!
Sorry!

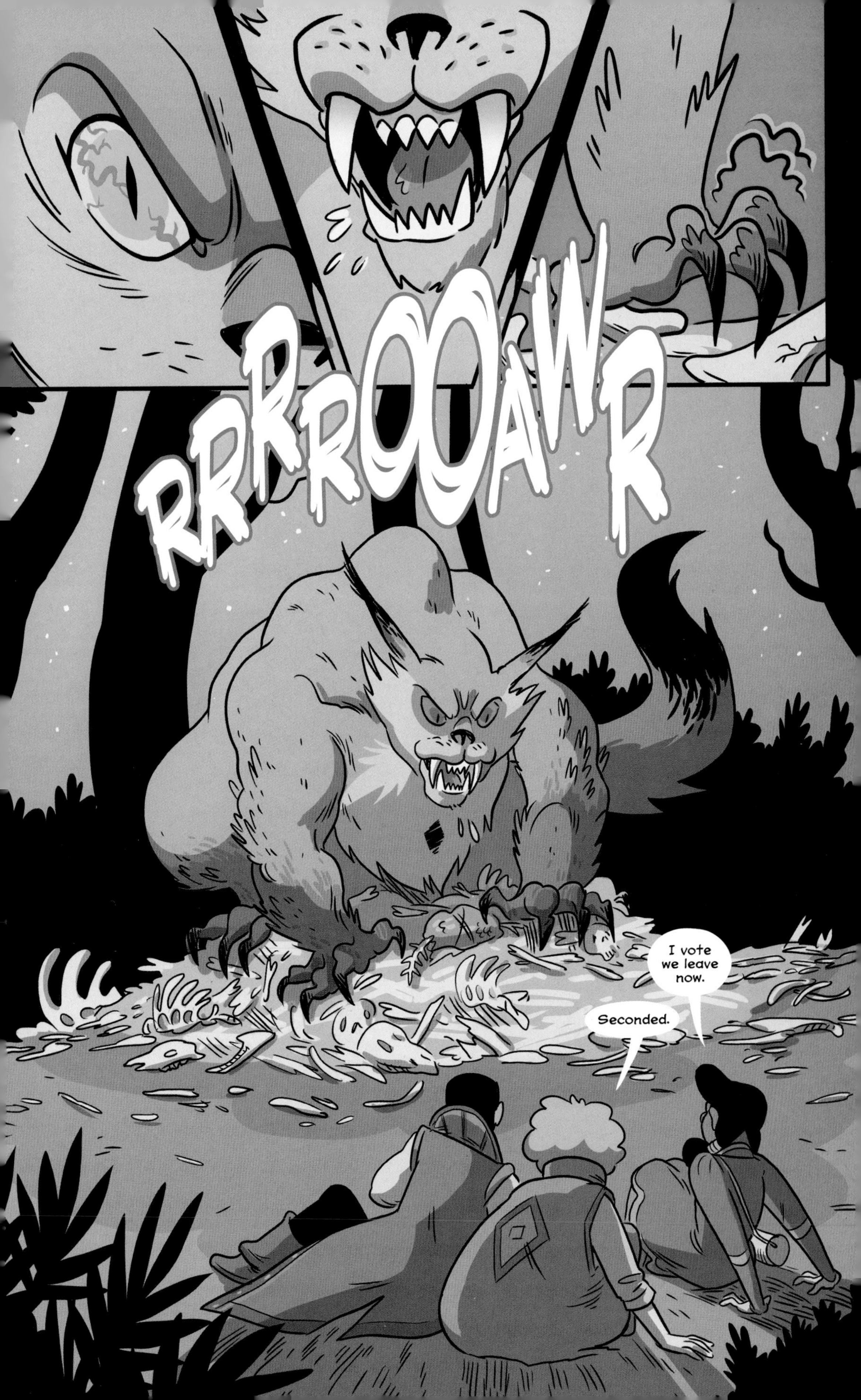
RRRROOOAWR
I vote we leave now.
Seconded.

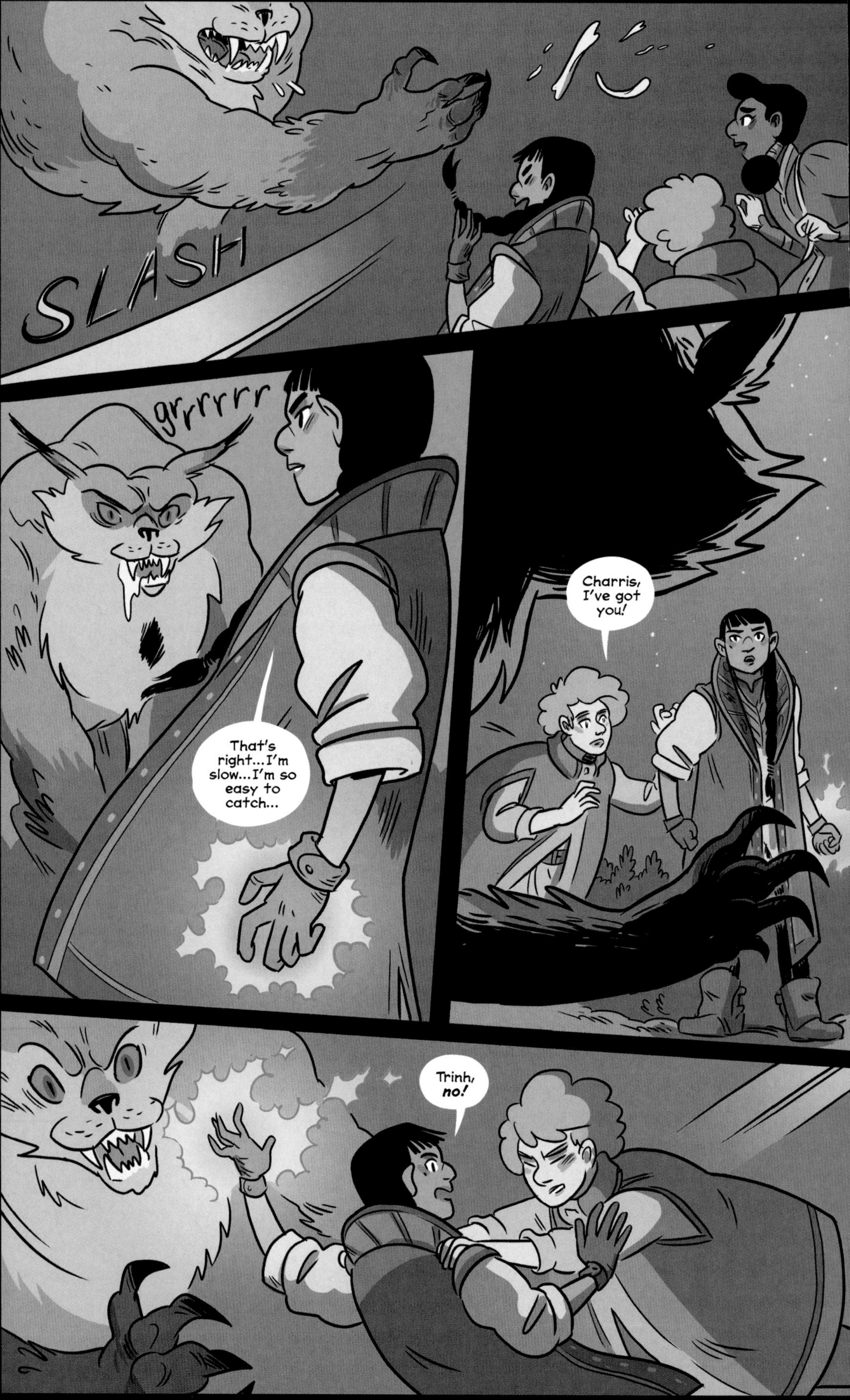
SLASH
grrrrr
That's right...I'm slow...I'm so easy to catch...
Charris, I've got you!
Trinh, *no!*

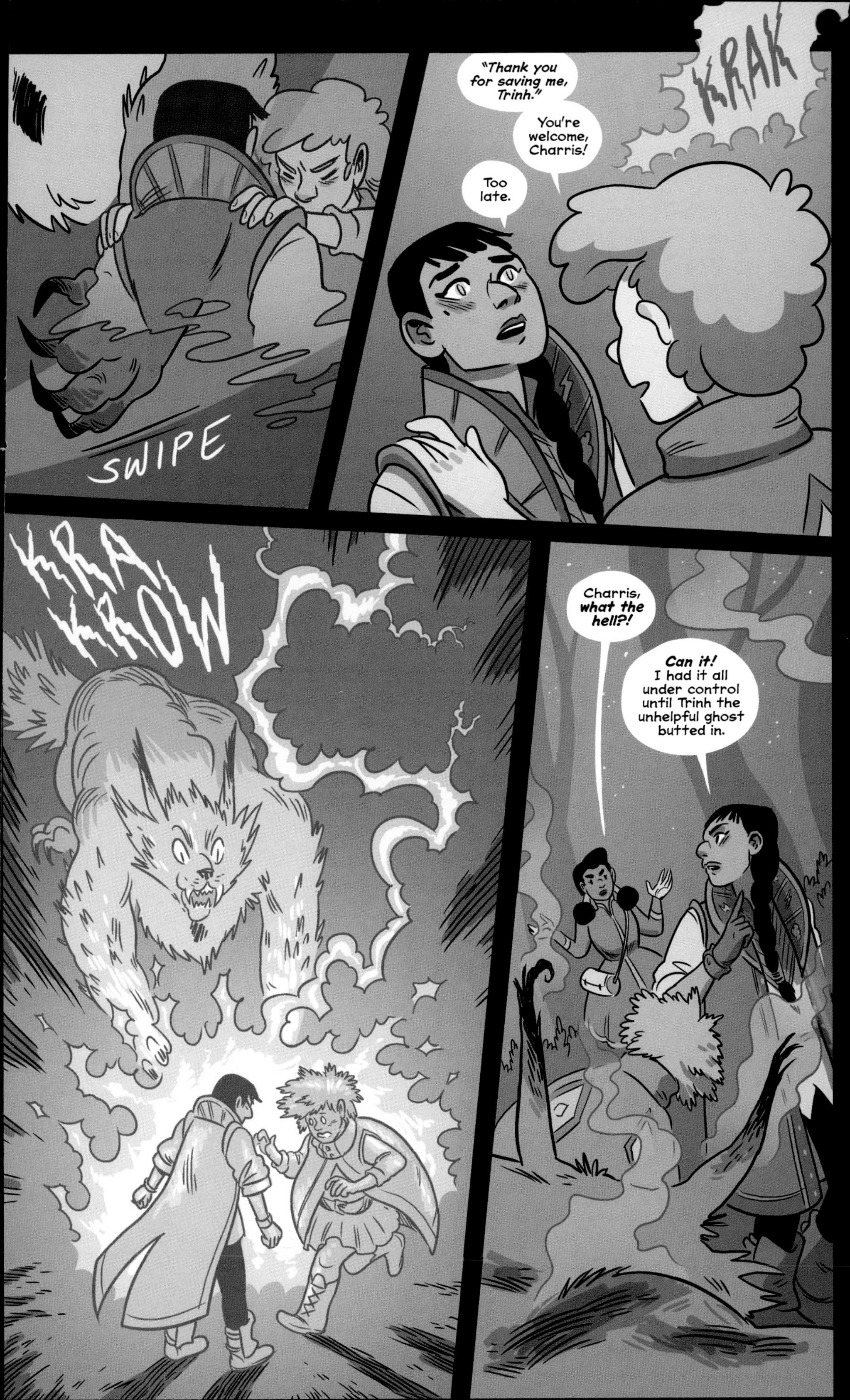
SWIPE
"Thank you for saving me, Trinh."
KRAK
You're welcome, Charris!
Too late.
KRA KROW
Charris, **what the hell?!**
Can it! I had it all under control until Trinh the unhelpful ghost butted in.

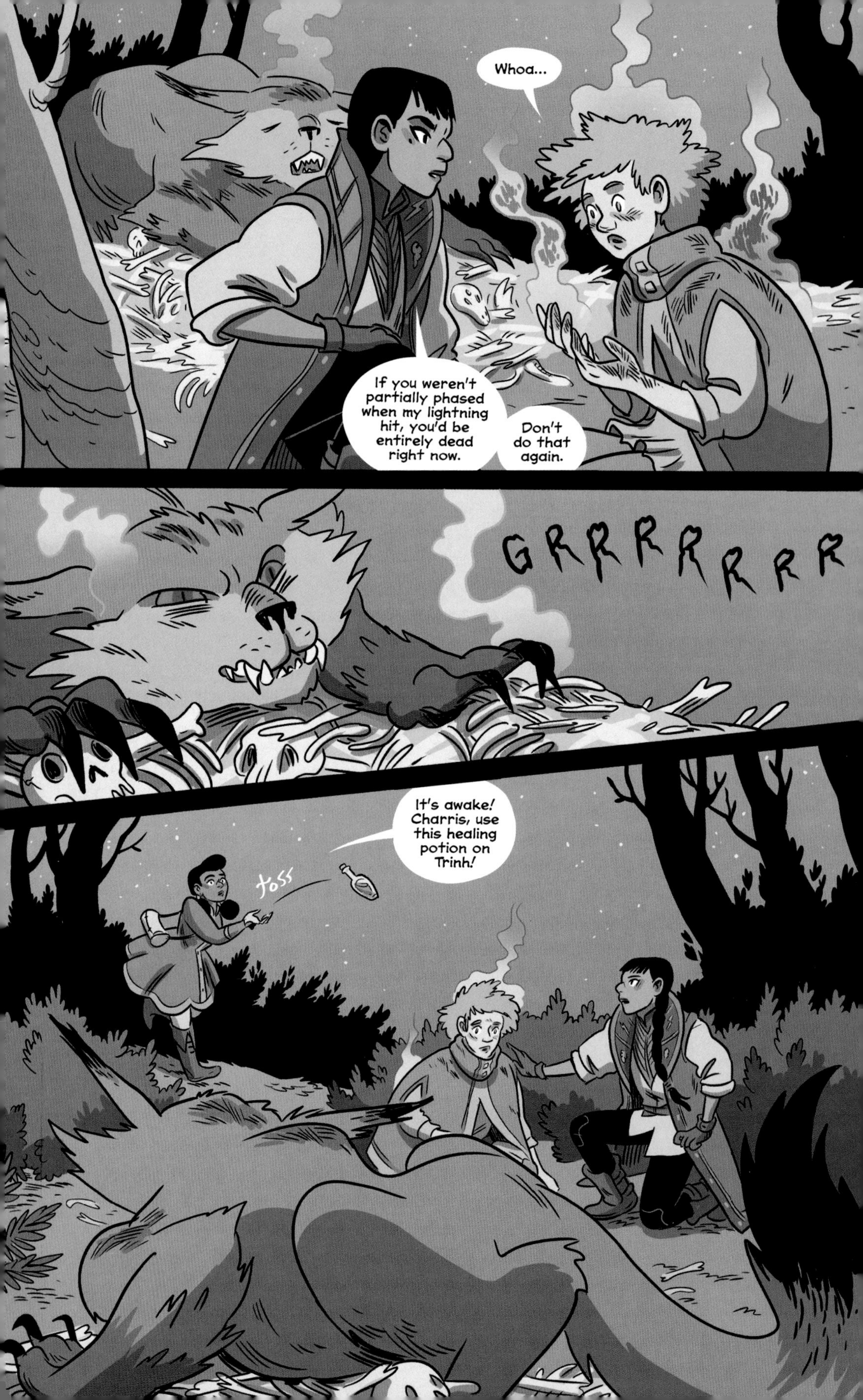
Whoa...
If you weren't partially phased when my lightning hit, you'd be entirely dead right now.
Don't do that again.
GRRRRRRR
It's awake! Charris, use this healing potion on Trinh!
toss

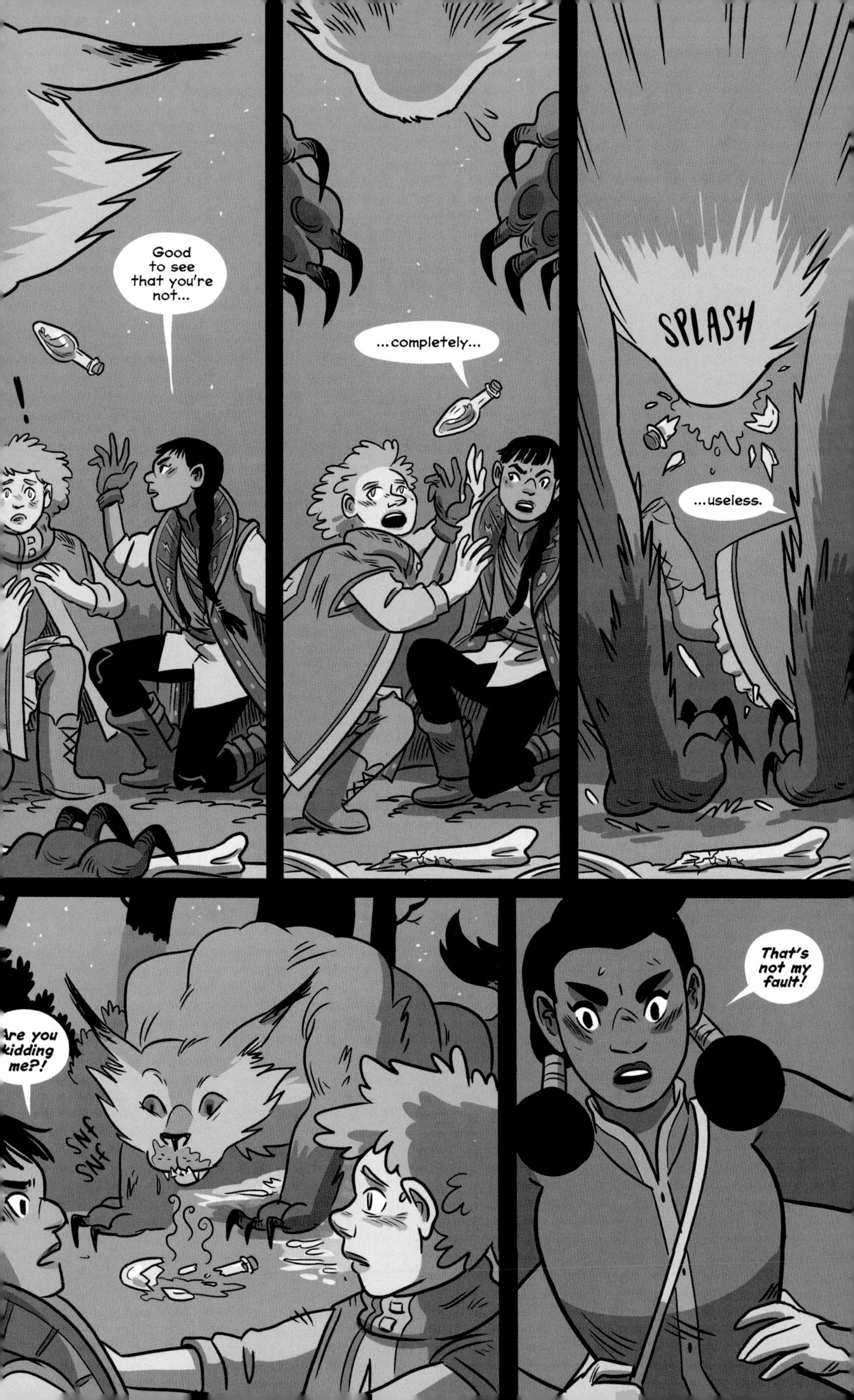
!
Good to see that you're not...
...completely...
SPLASH
...useless.
Are you kidding me?!
SNF SNF
That's not my fault!

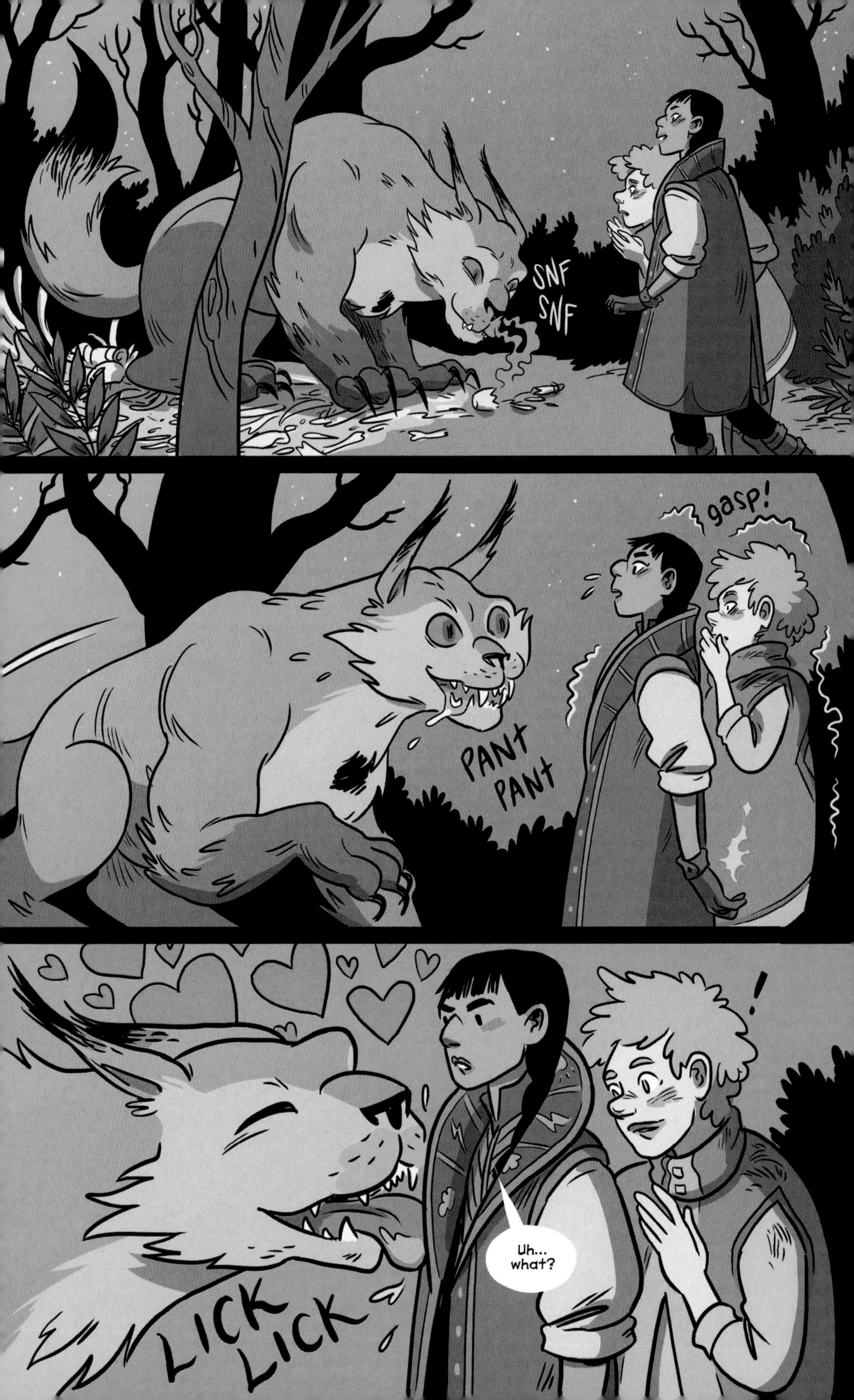
SNF
SNF
gasp!
PANT
PANT
!
Uh... what?
LICK
LICK

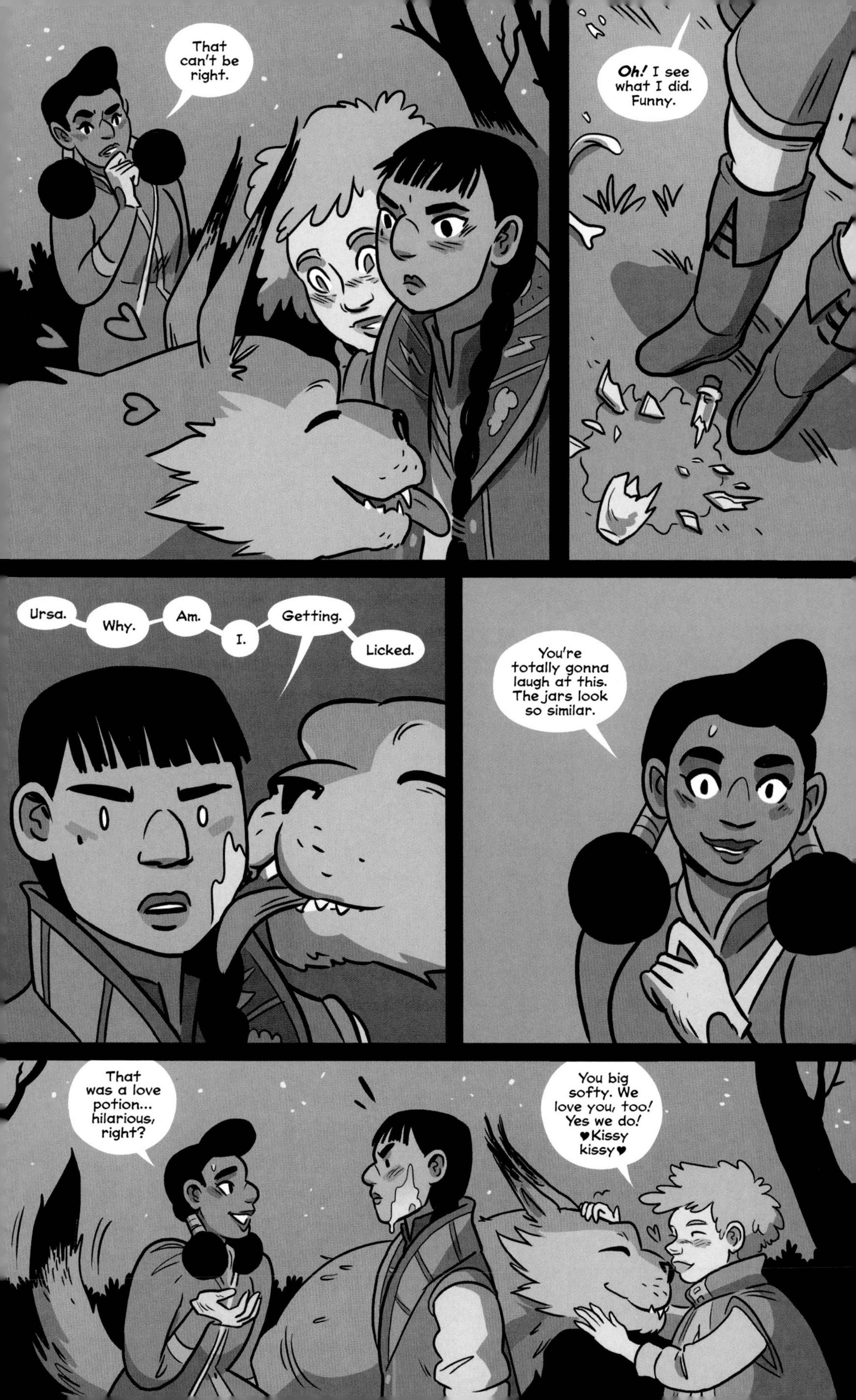
That can't be right.
Oh! I see what I did. Funny.
Ursa.
Why.
Am.
I.
Getting.
Licked.
You're totally gonna laugh at this. The jars look so similar.
That was a love potion... hilarious, right?
You big softy. We love you, too! Yes we do! ♥Kissy kissy♥

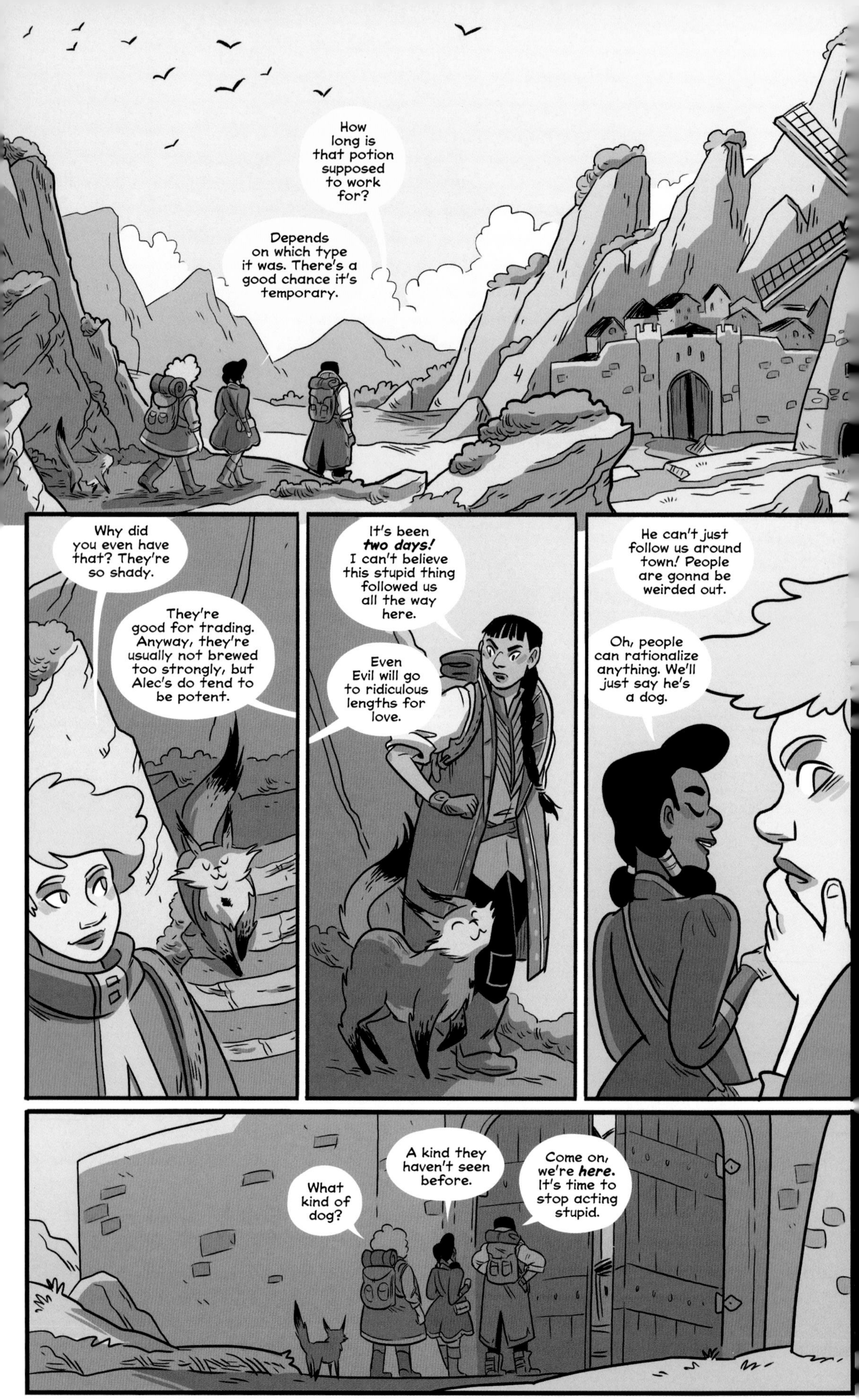
How long is that potion supposed to work for?
Depends on which type it was. There's a good chance it's temporary.
Why did you even have that? They're so shady.
They're good for trading. Anyway, they're usually not brewed too strongly, but Alec's do tend to be potent.
It's been **two days!** I can't believe this stupid thing followed us all the way here.
Even Evil will go to ridiculous lengths for love.
He can't just follow us around town! People are gonna be weirded out.
Oh, people can rationalize anything. We'll just say he's a dog.
What kind of dog?
A kind they haven't seen before.
Come on, we're **here.** It's time to stop acting stupid.

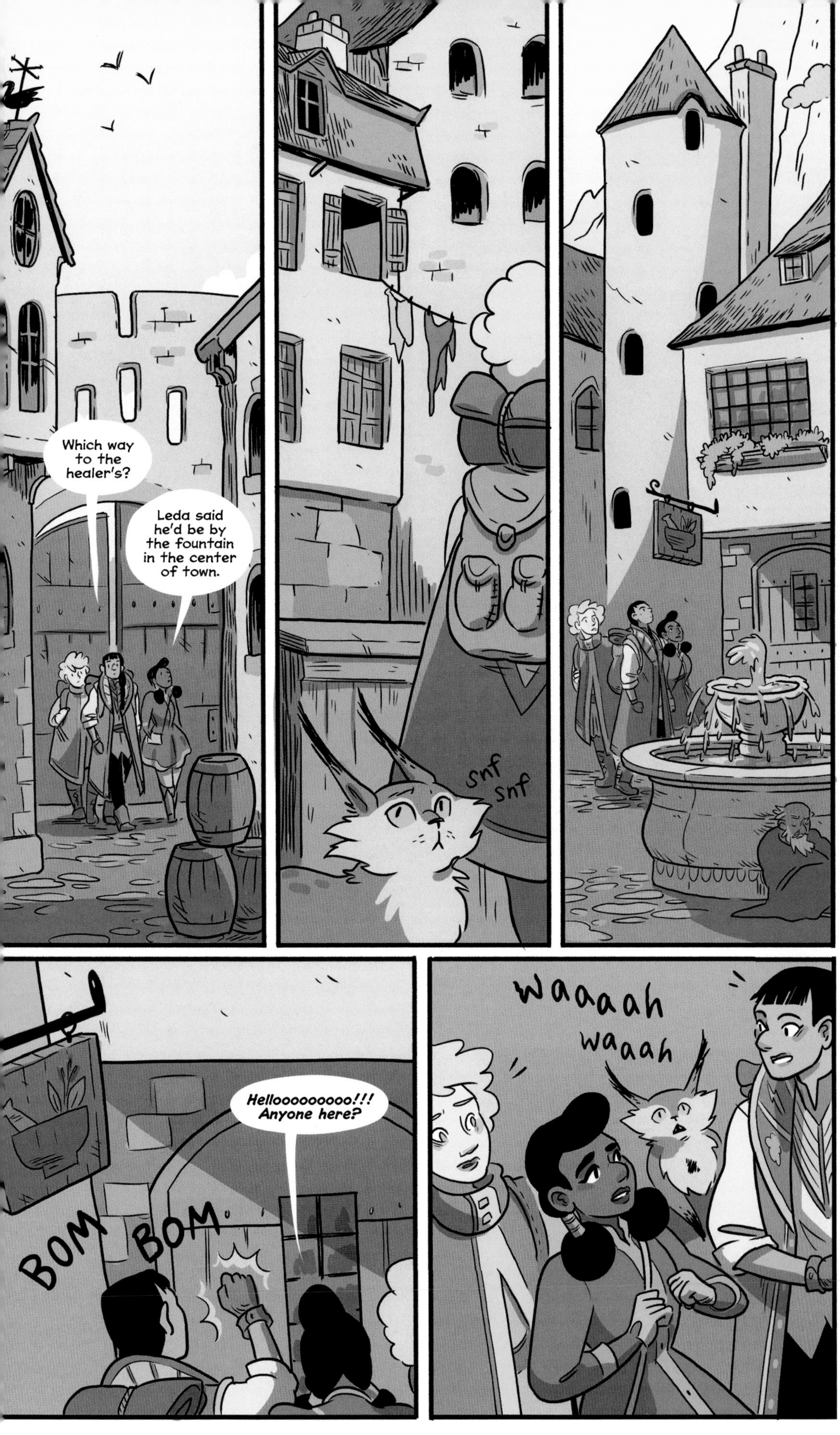

Which way to the healer's?
Leda said he'd be by the fountain in the center of town.
snf snf
Hellooooooooo!!! Anyone here?
BOM BOM
waaaah waaah

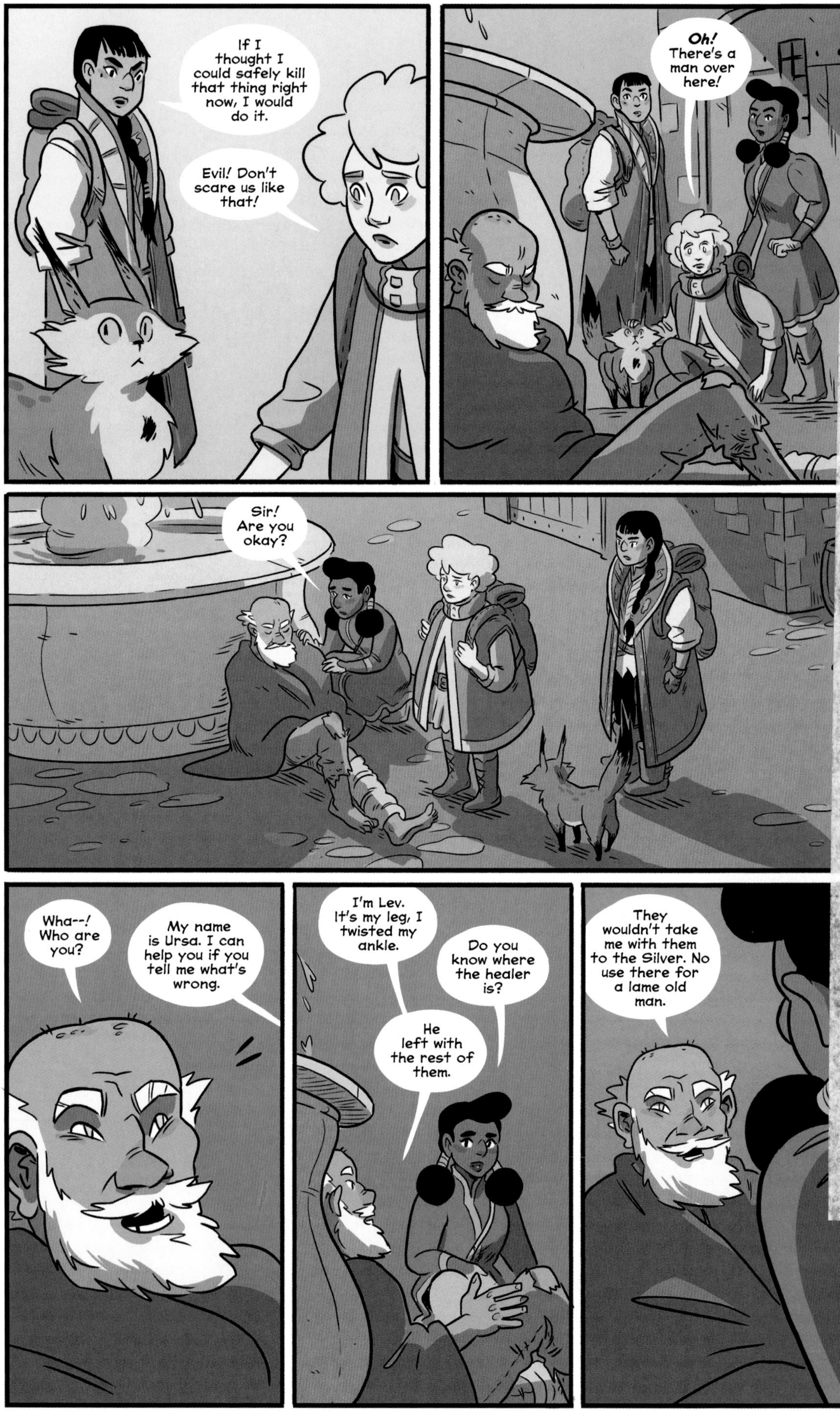
If I thought I could safely kill that thing right now, I would do it.
Evil! Don't scare us like that!
Oh! There's a man over here!
Sir! Are you okay?
Wha--! Who are you?
My name is Ursa. I can help you if you tell me what's wrong.
I'm Lev. It's my leg, I twisted my ankle.
Do you know where the healer is?
He left with the rest of them.
They wouldn't take me with them to the Silver. No use there for a lame old man.

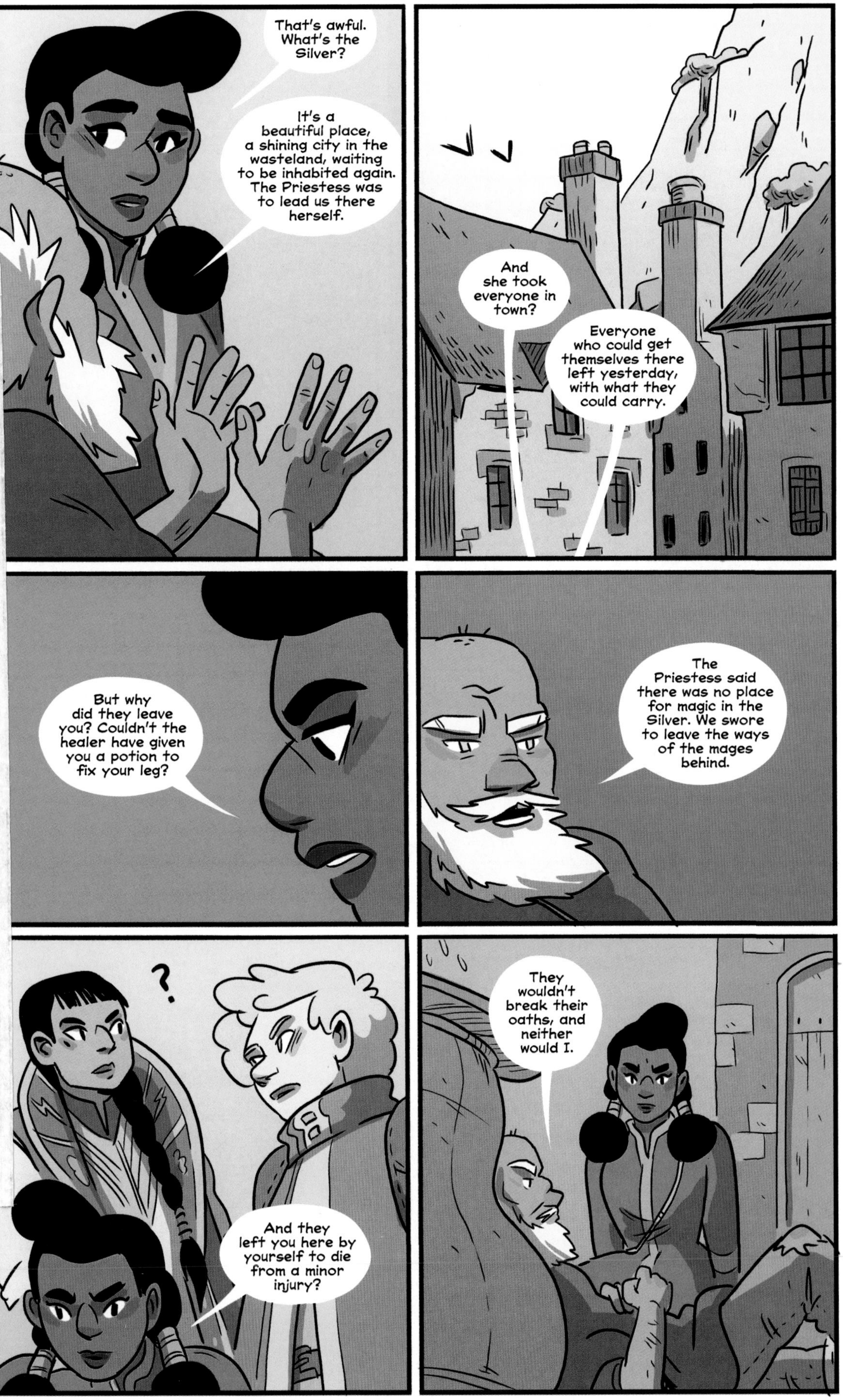
That's awful. What's the Silver?
It's a beautiful place, a shining city in the wasteland, waiting to be inhabited again. The Priestess was to lead us there herself.
And she took everyone in town?
Everyone who could get themselves there left yesterday, with what they could carry.
But why did they leave you? Couldn't the healer have given you a potion to fix your leg?
The Priestess said there was no place for magic in the Silver. We swore to leave the ways of the mages behind.
?
And they left you here by yourself to die from a minor injury?
They wouldn't break their oaths, and neither would I.

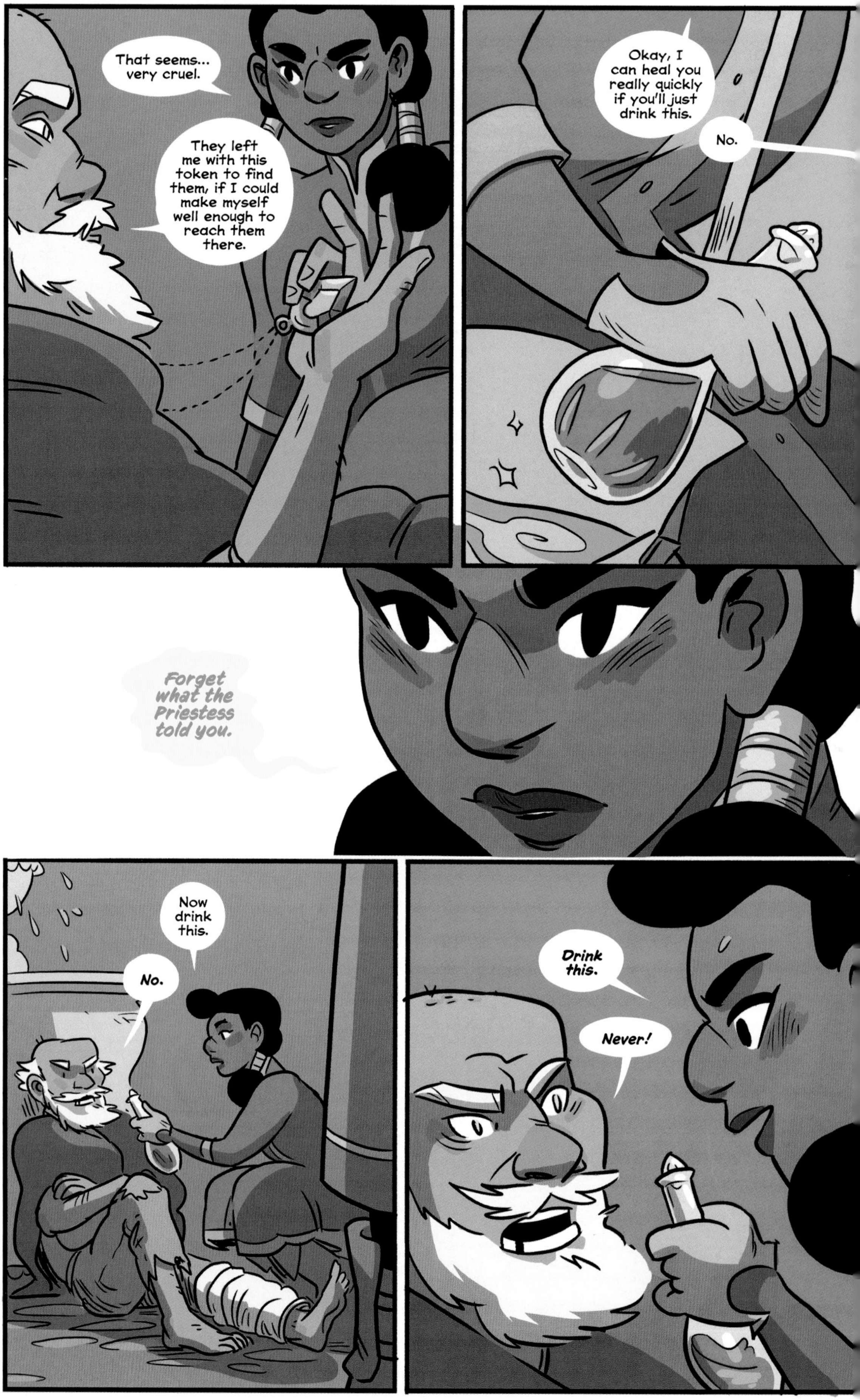
That seems... very cruel.
They left me with this token to find them, if I could make myself well enough to reach them there.
Okay, I can heal you really quickly if you'll just drink this.
No.
Forget what the Priestess told you.
Now drink this.
No.
Drink this.
Never!

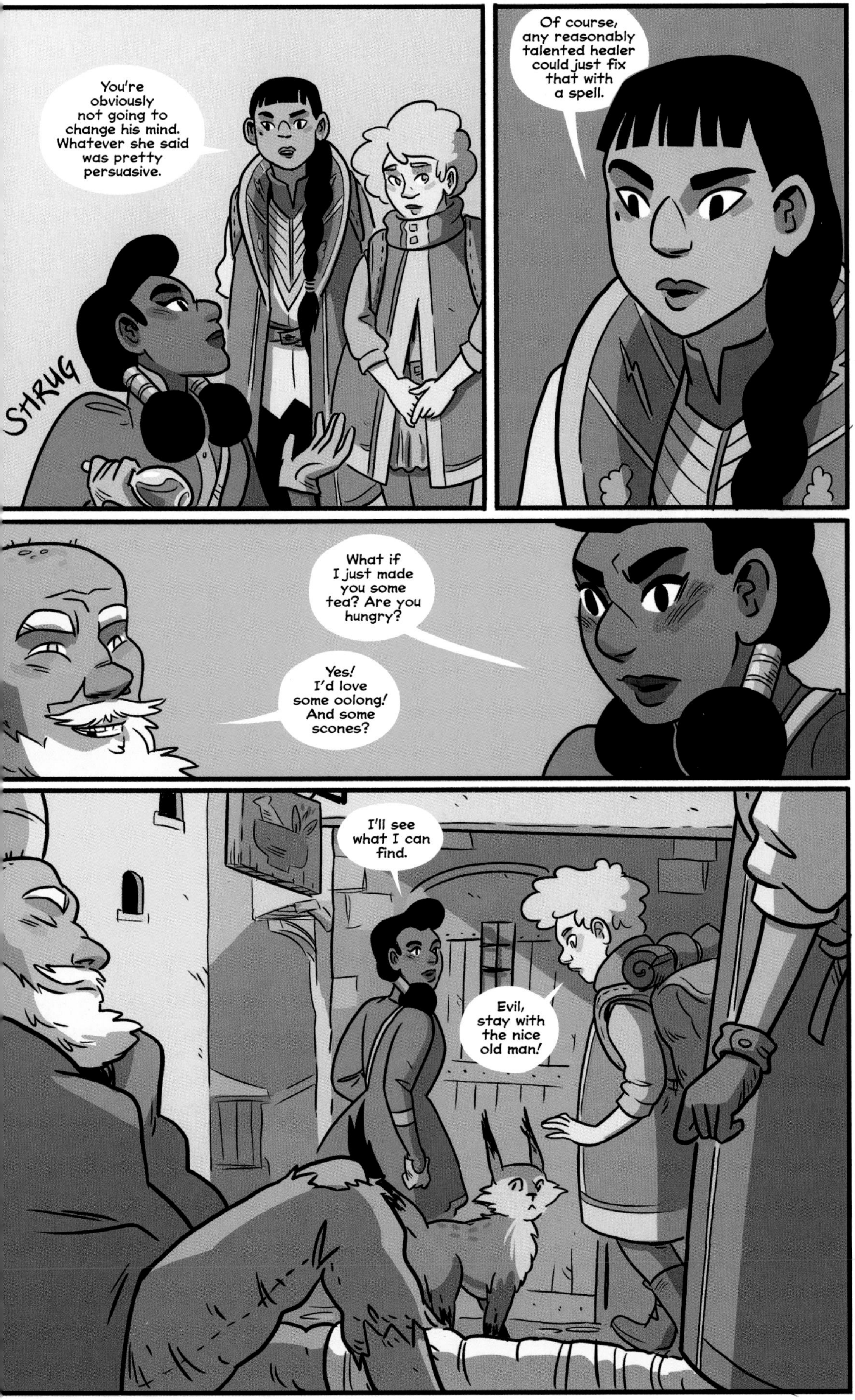
You're obviously not going to change his mind. Whatever she said was pretty persuasive.
SHRUG
Of course, any reasonably talented healer could just fix that with a spell.
What if I just made you some tea? Are you hungry?
Yes! I'd love some oolong! And some scones?
I'll see what I can find.
Evil, stay with the nice old man!

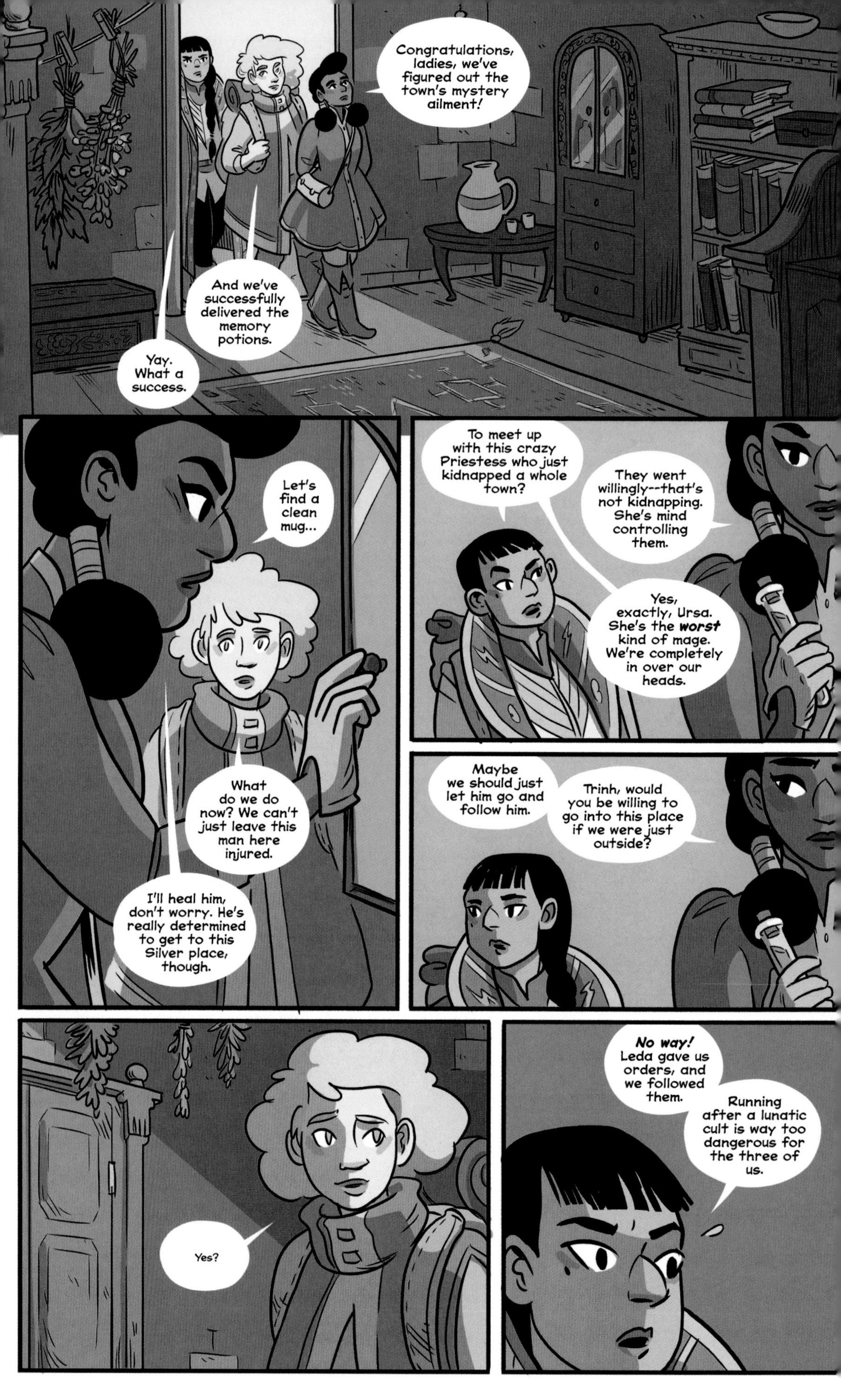
Congratulations, ladies, we've figured out the town's mystery ailment!
And we've successfully delivered the memory potions.
Yay. What a success.
Let's find a clean mug...
What do we do now? We can't just leave this man here injured.
I'll heal him, don't worry. He's really determined to get to this Silver place, though.
To meet up with this crazy Priestess who just kidnapped a whole town?
They went willingly--that's not kidnapping. She's mind controlling them.
Yes, exactly, Ursa. She's the *worst* kind of mage. We're completely in over our heads.
Maybe we should just let him go and follow him.
Trinh, would you be willing to go into this place if we were just outside?
Yes?
No way! Leda gave us orders, and we followed them.
Running after a lunatic cult is way too dangerous for the three of us.

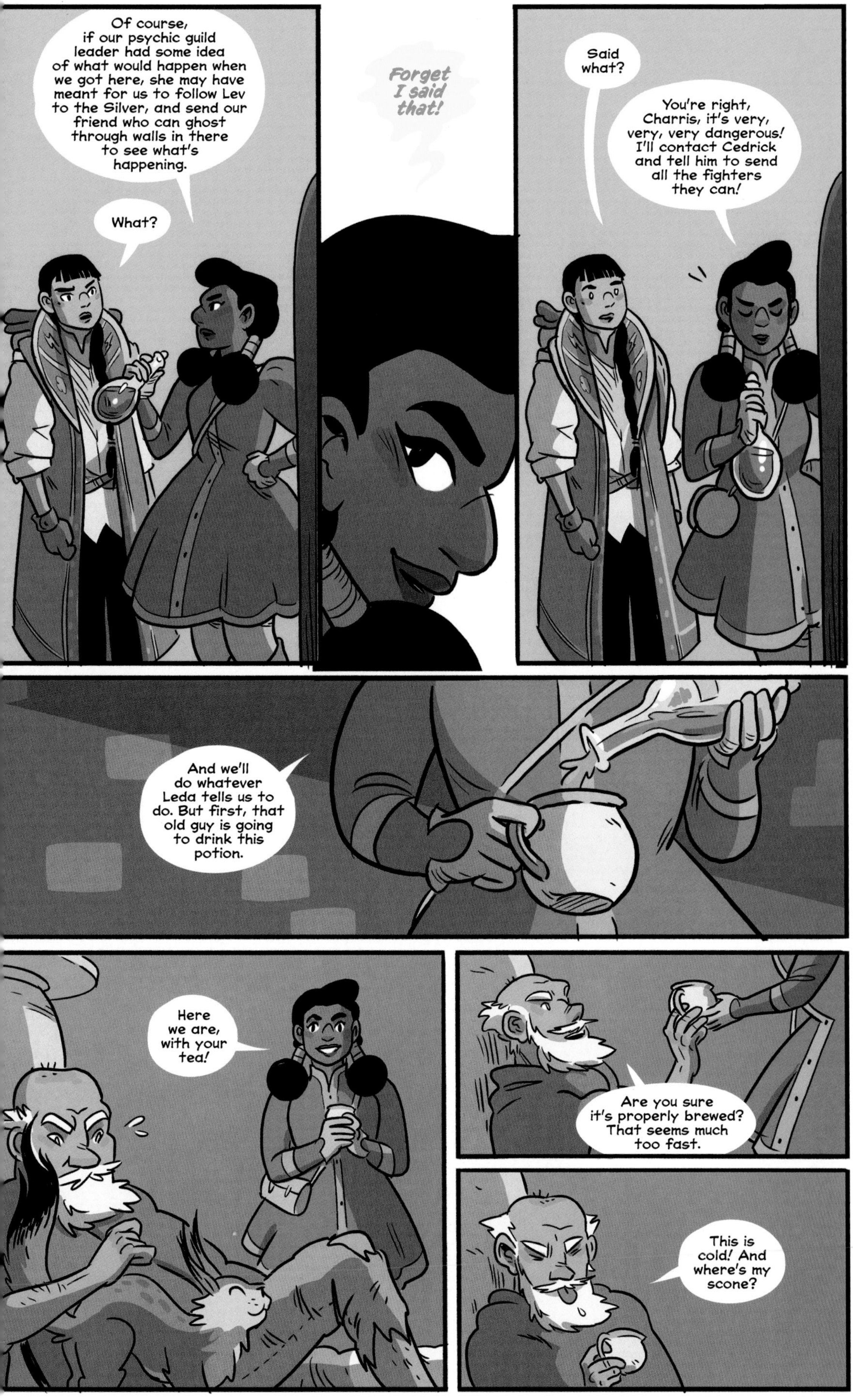
Of course, if our psychic guild leader had some idea of what would happen when we got here, she may have meant for us to follow Lev to the Silver, and send our friend who can ghost through walls in there to see what's happening.
What?
Forget I said that!
Said what?
You're right, Charris, it's very, very, very dangerous! I'll contact Cedrick and tell him to send all the fighters they can!
And we'll do whatever Leda tells us to do. But first, that old guy is going to drink this potion.
Here we are, with your tea!
Are you sure it's properly brewed? That seems much too fast.
This is cold! And where's my scone?

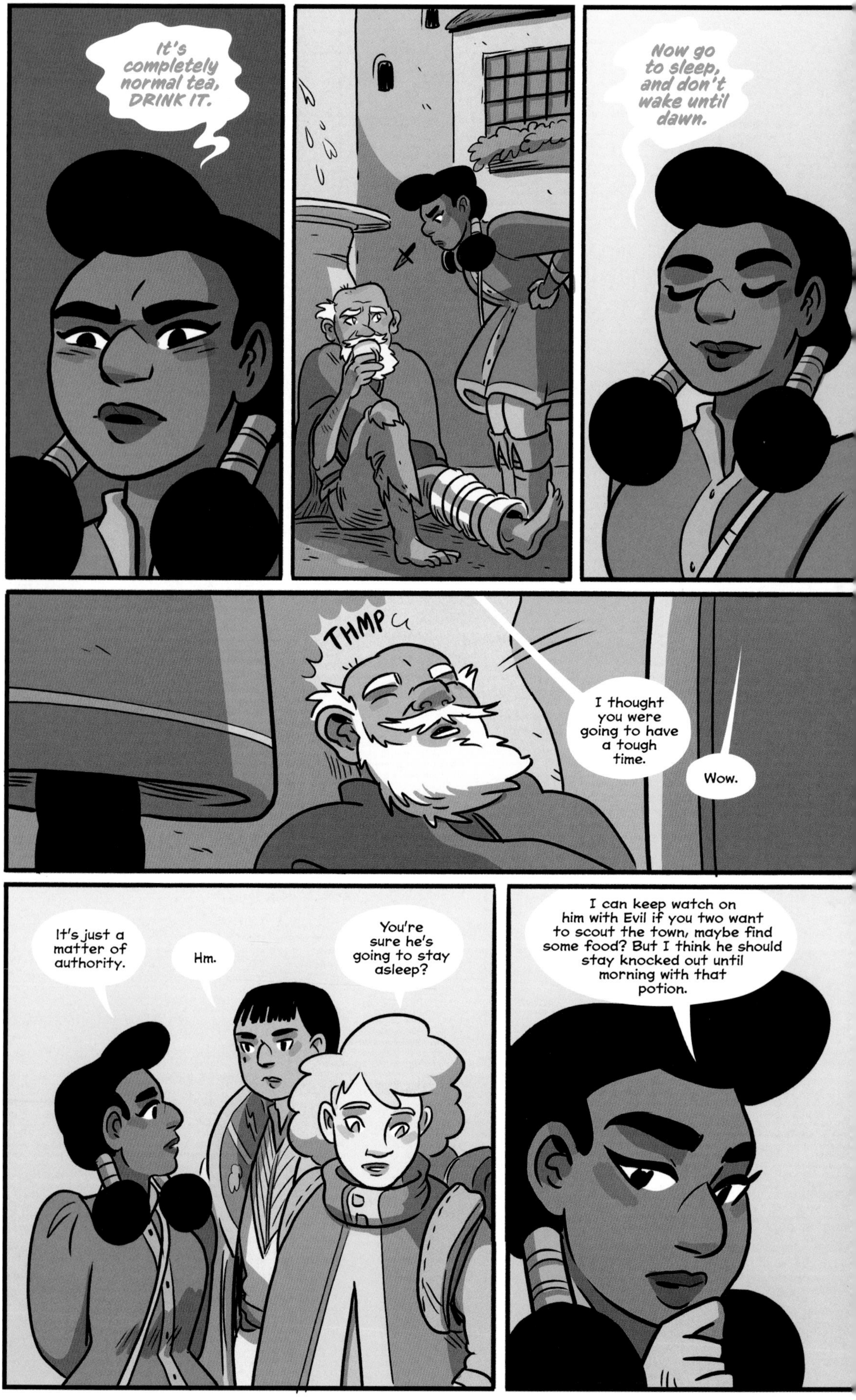

It's completely normal tea, DRINK IT.
Now go to sleep, and don't wake until dawn.
THMP
I thought you were going to have a tough time.
Wow.
It's just a matter of authority.
Hm.
You're sure he's going to stay asleep?
I can keep watch on him with Evil if you two want to scout the town, maybe find some food? But I think he should stay knocked out until morning with that potion.

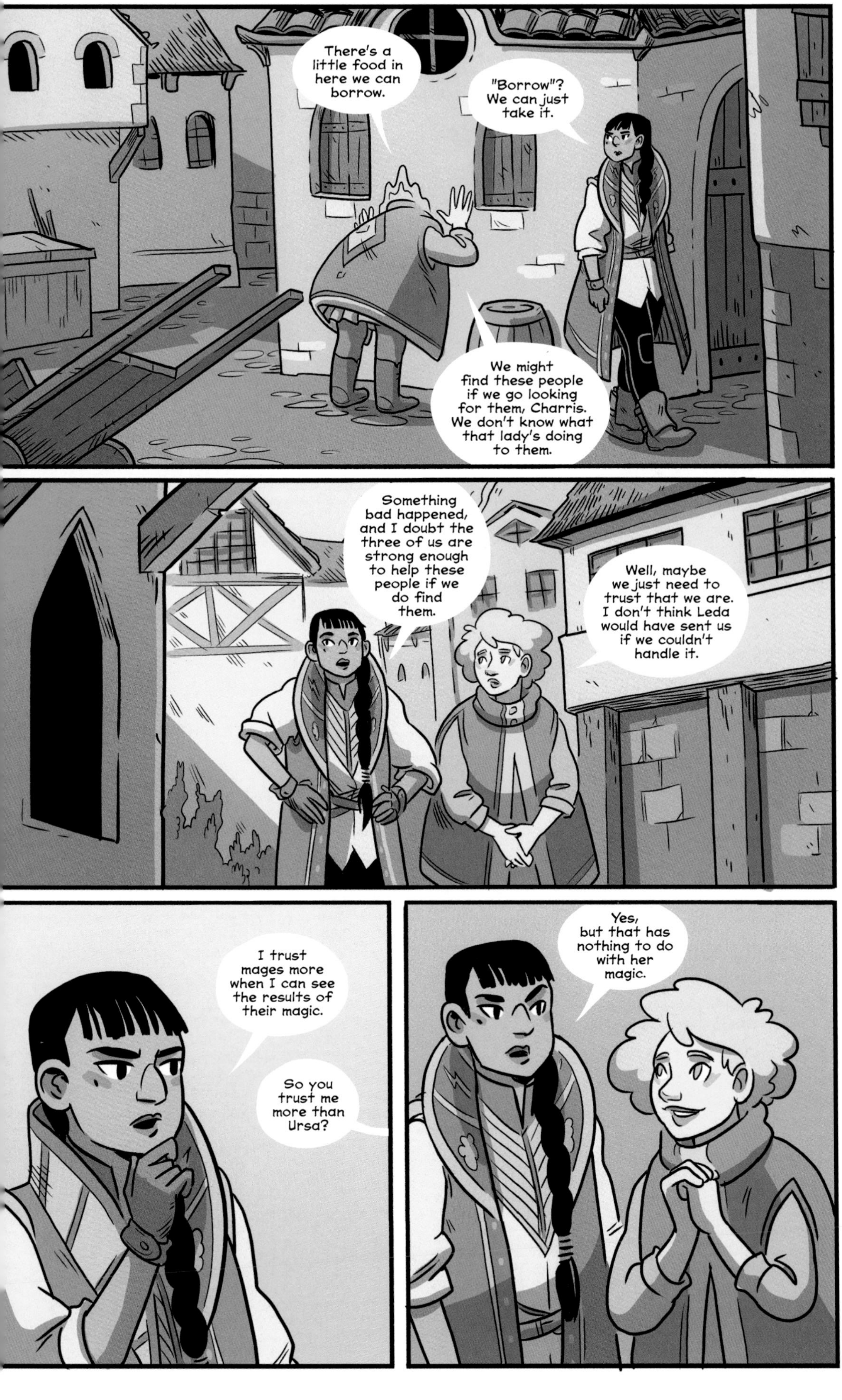
There's a little food in here we can borrow.
"Borrow"? We can just take it.
We might find these people if we go looking for them, Charris. We don't know what that lady's doing to them.
Something bad happened, and I doubt the three of us are strong enough to help these people if we do find them.
Well, maybe we just need to trust that we are. I don't think Leda would have sent us if we couldn't handle it.
I trust mages more when I can see the results of their magic.
So you trust me more than Ursa?
Yes, but that has nothing to do with her magic.

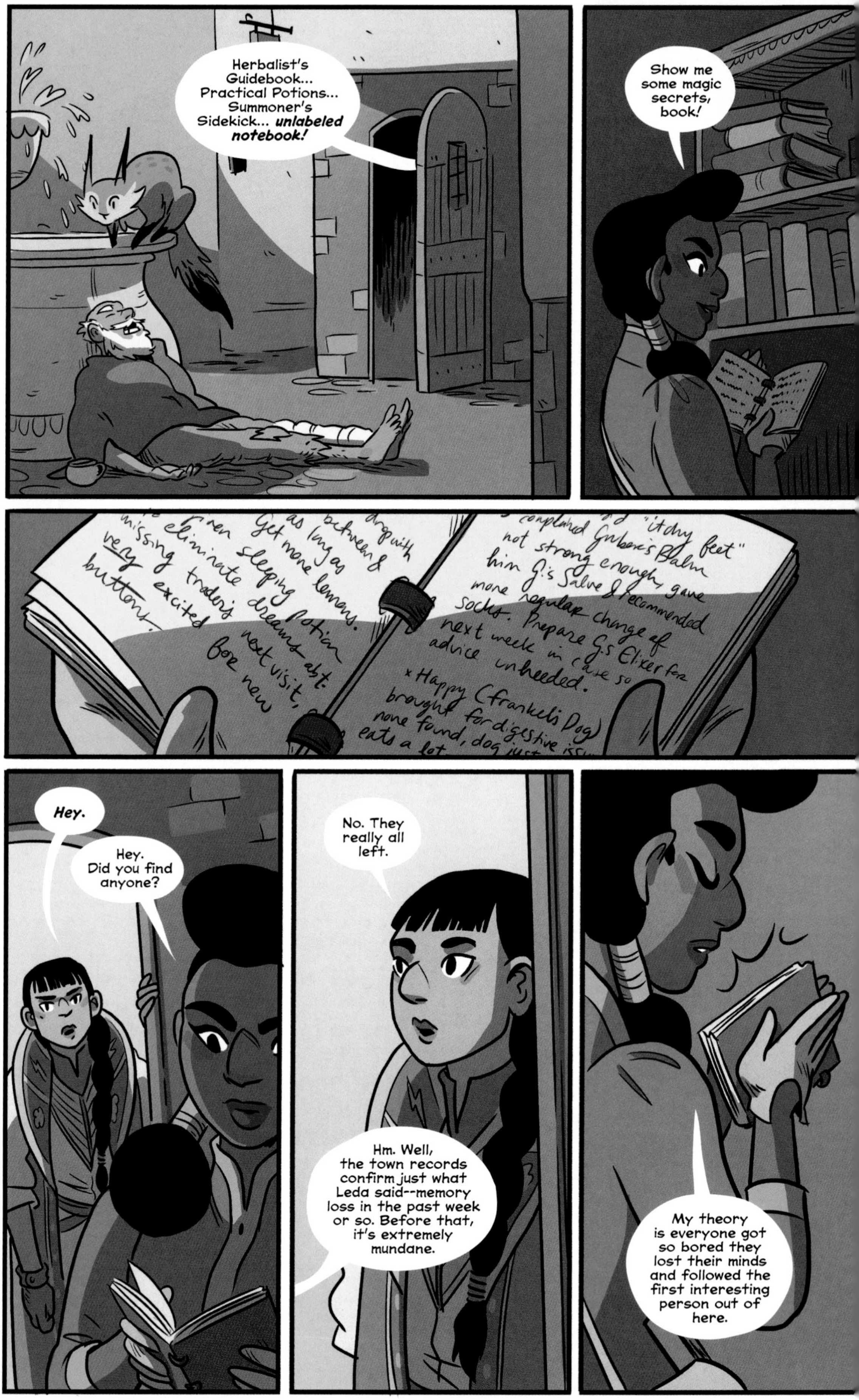

Herbalist's Guidebook... Practical Potions... Summoner's Sidekick... ***unlabeled notebook!***
Show me some magic secrets, book!
Get more lemons.
eliminate sleeping potion
very excited
not strong enough, gave
him G.'s Salve & recommended
more regular change of
socks. Prepare G.'s Elixer for
next week in case so
advice unheeded.
Hey.
Hey. Did you find anyone?
No. They really all left.
Hm. Well, the town records confirm just what Leda said--memory loss in the past week or so. Before that, it's extremely mundane.
My theory is everyone got so bored they lost their minds and followed the first interesting person out of here.

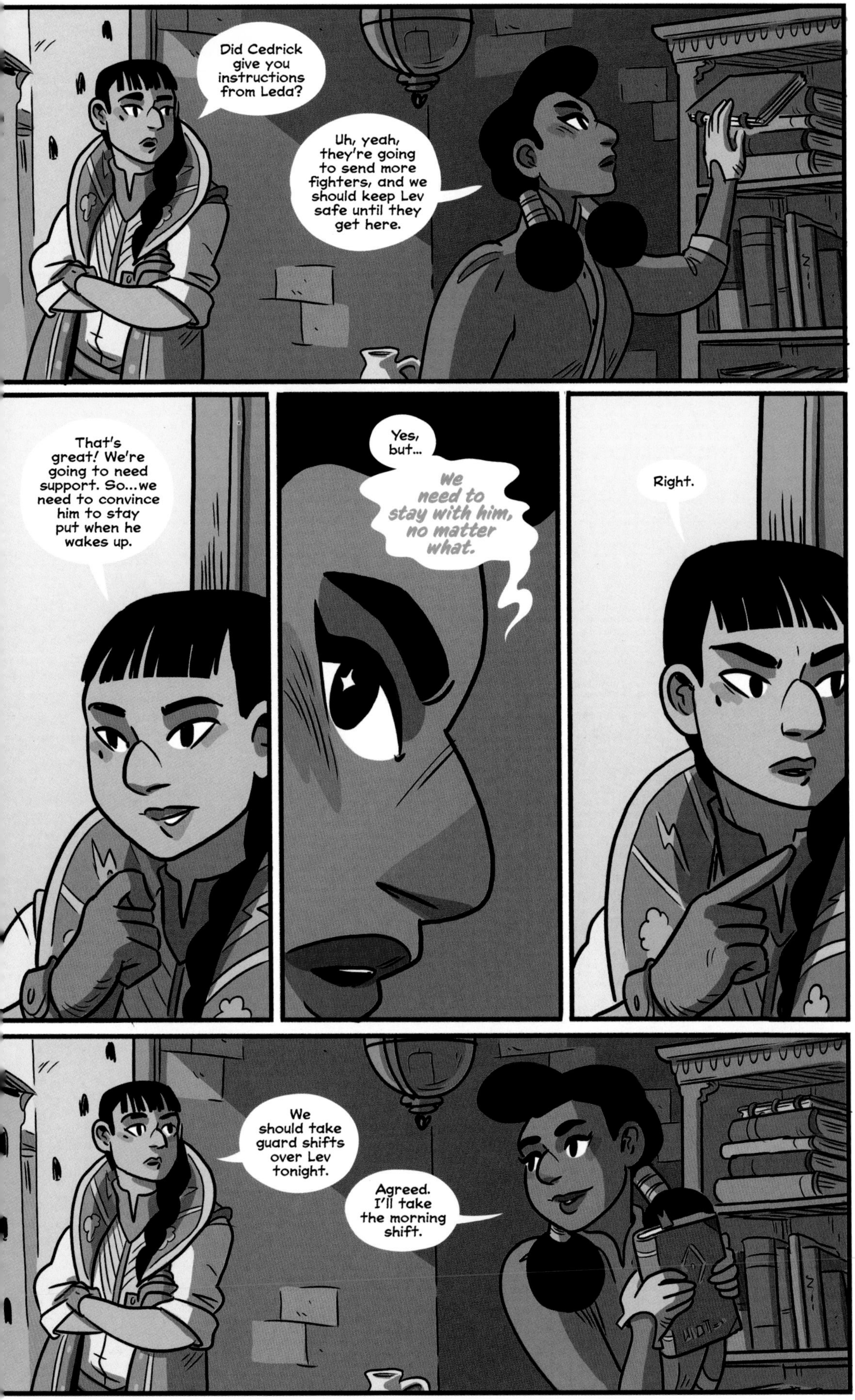
Did Cedrick give you instructions from Leda?
Uh, yeah, they're going to send more fighters, and we should keep Lev safe until they get here.
That's great! We're going to need support. So...we need to convince him to stay put when he wakes up.
Yes, but...
We need to stay with him, no matter what.
Right.
We should take guard shifts over Lev tonight.
Agreed. I'll take the morning shift.

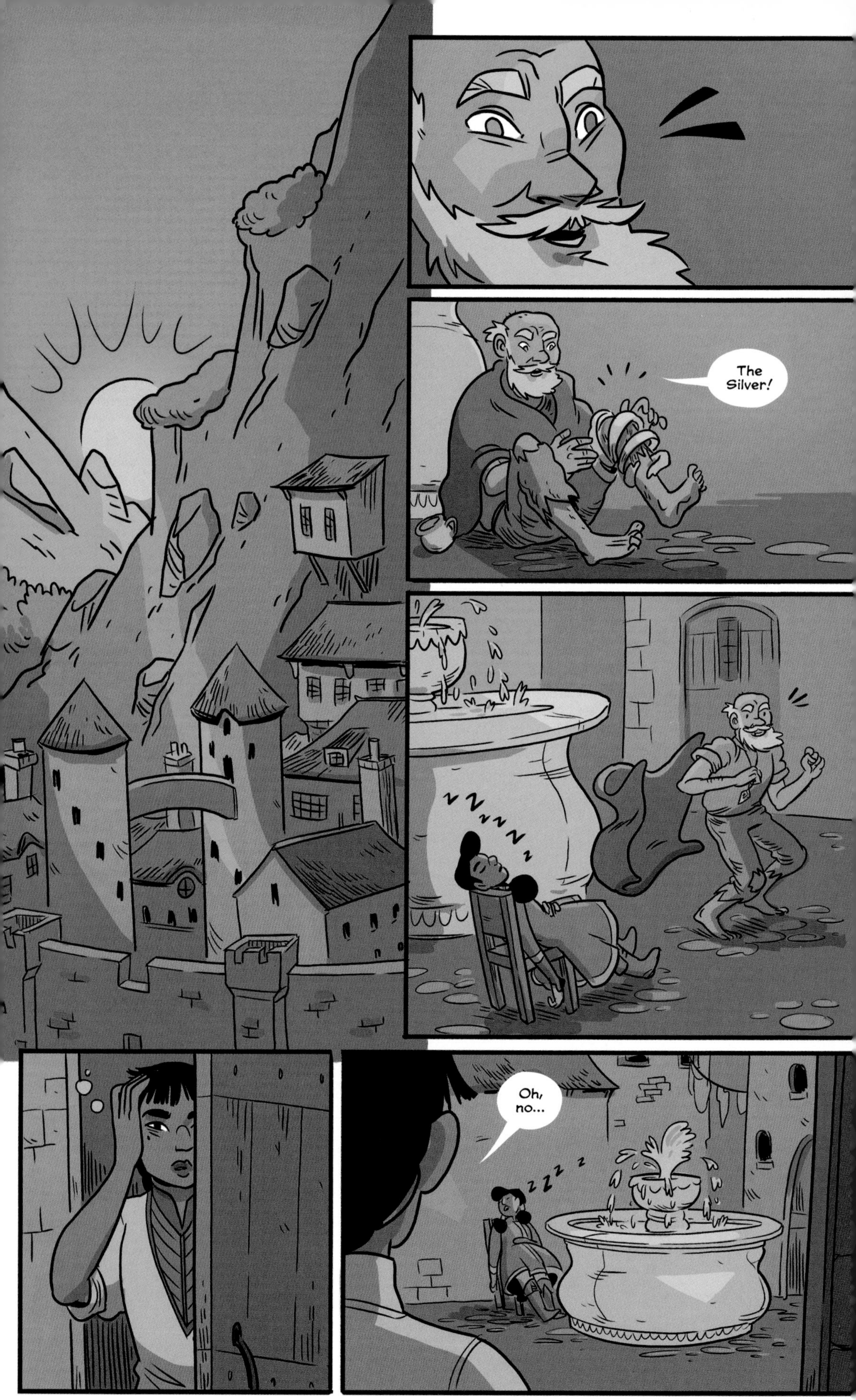
The Silver!
ZZZZZZ
Oh, no...
ZZZZ

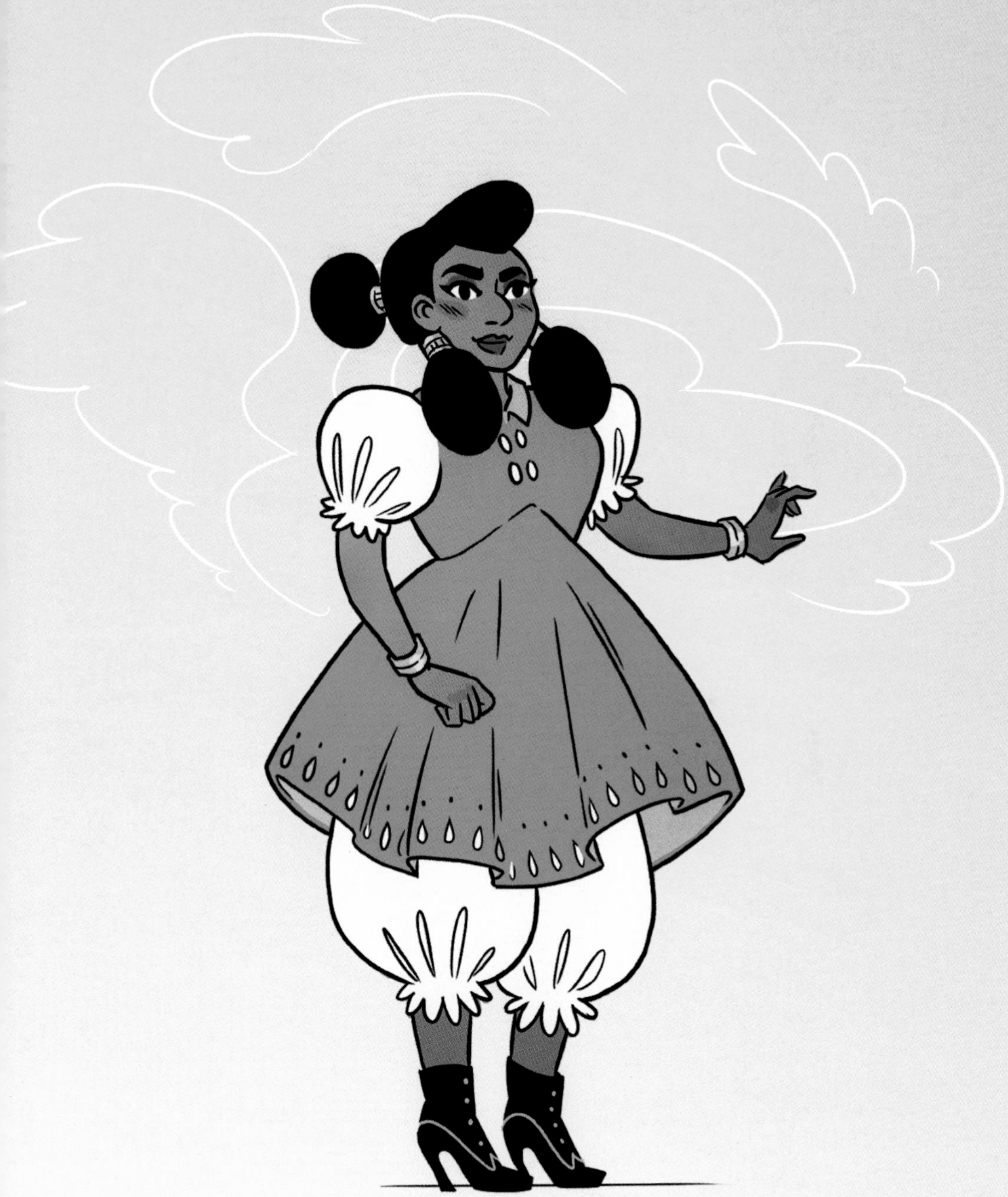

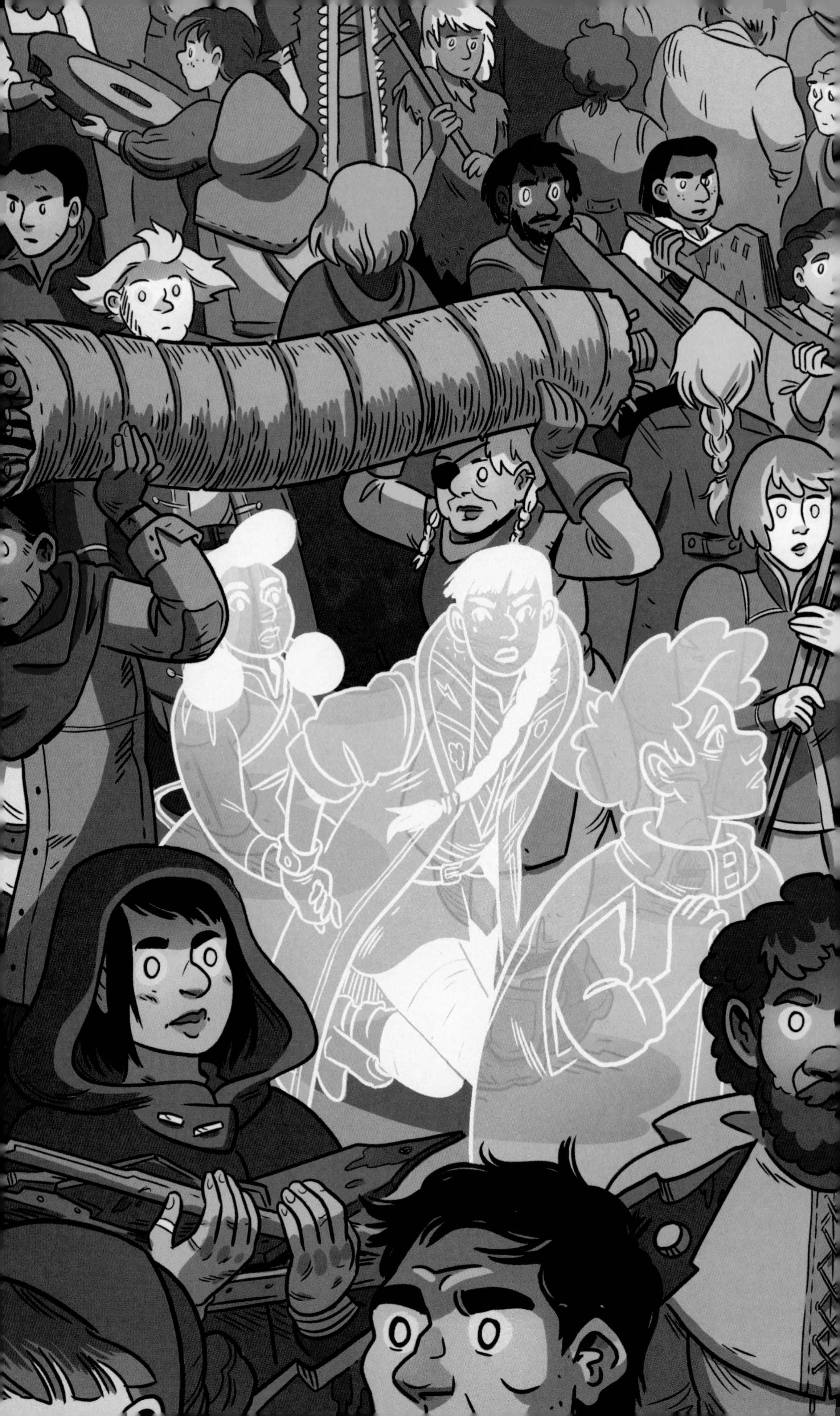

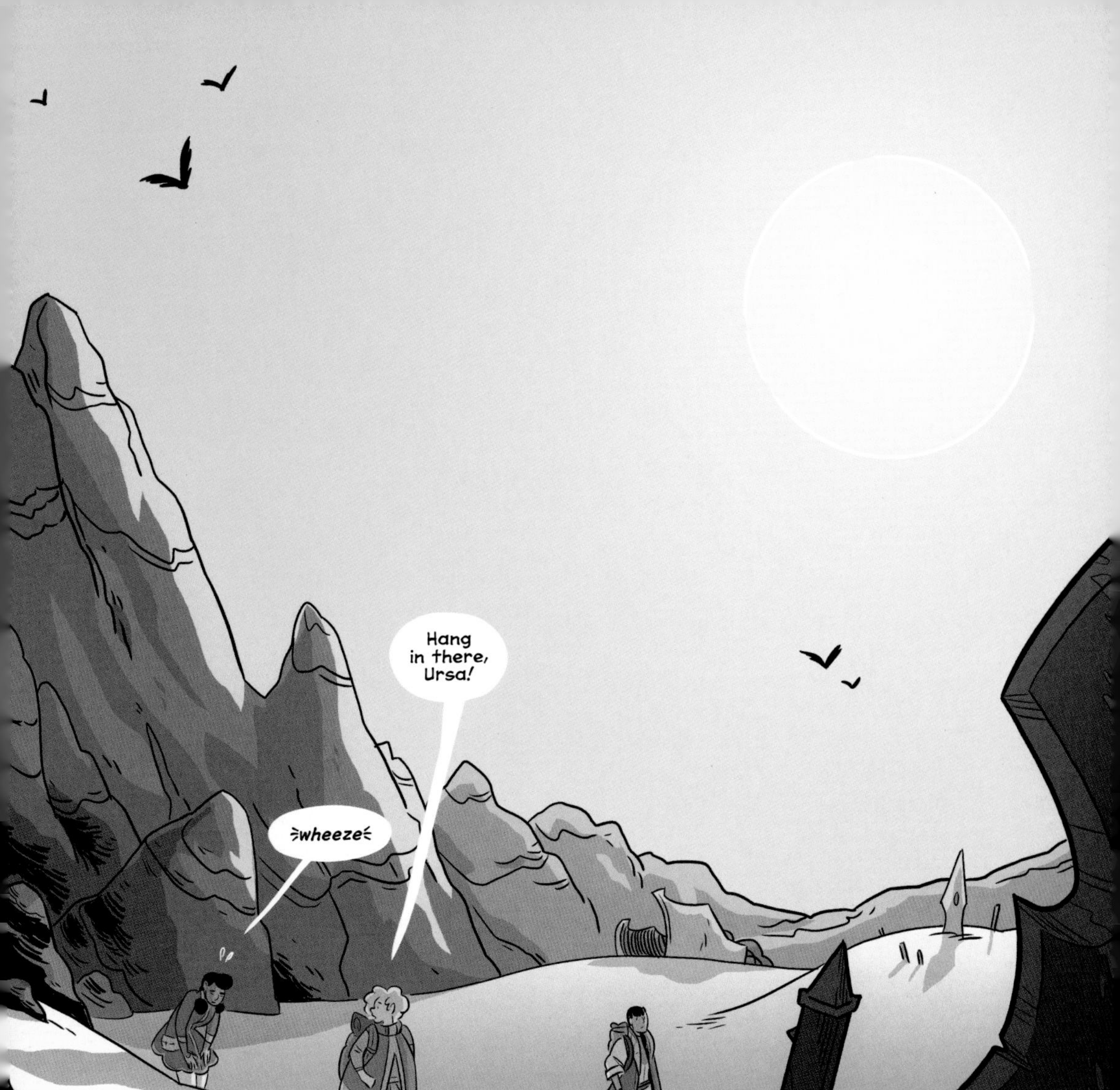
Hang in there, Ursa!
wheeze

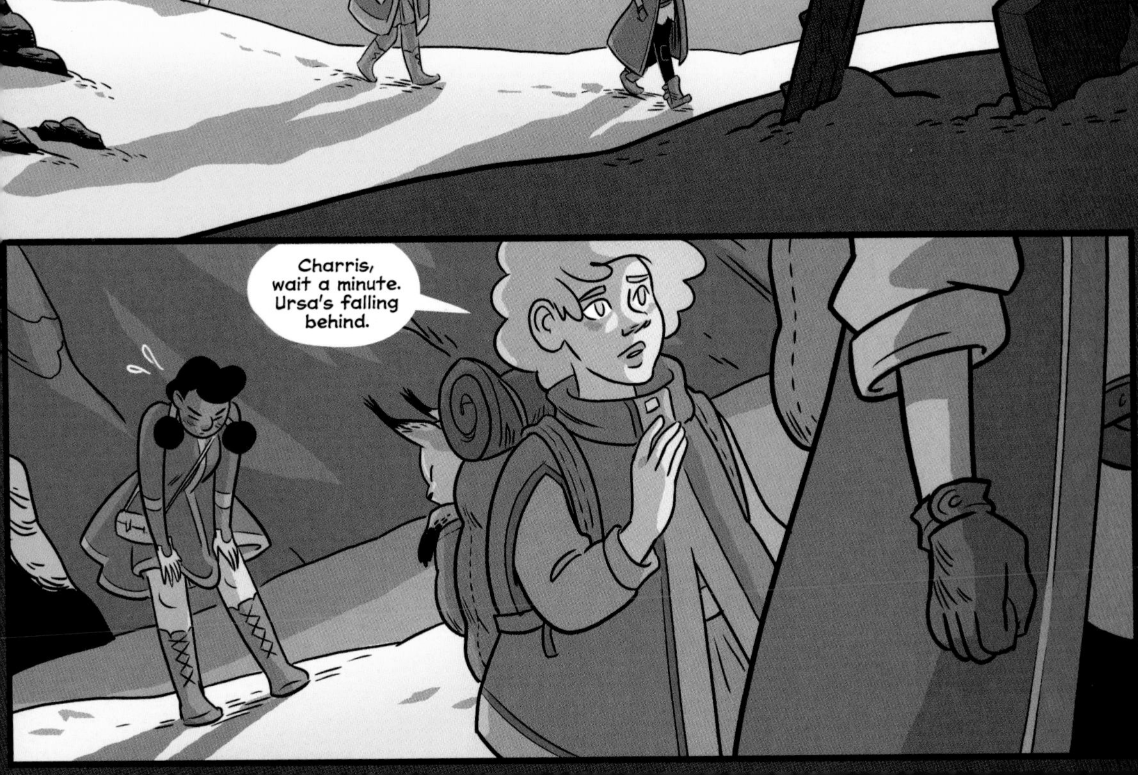
Charris, wait a minute. Ursa's falling behind.

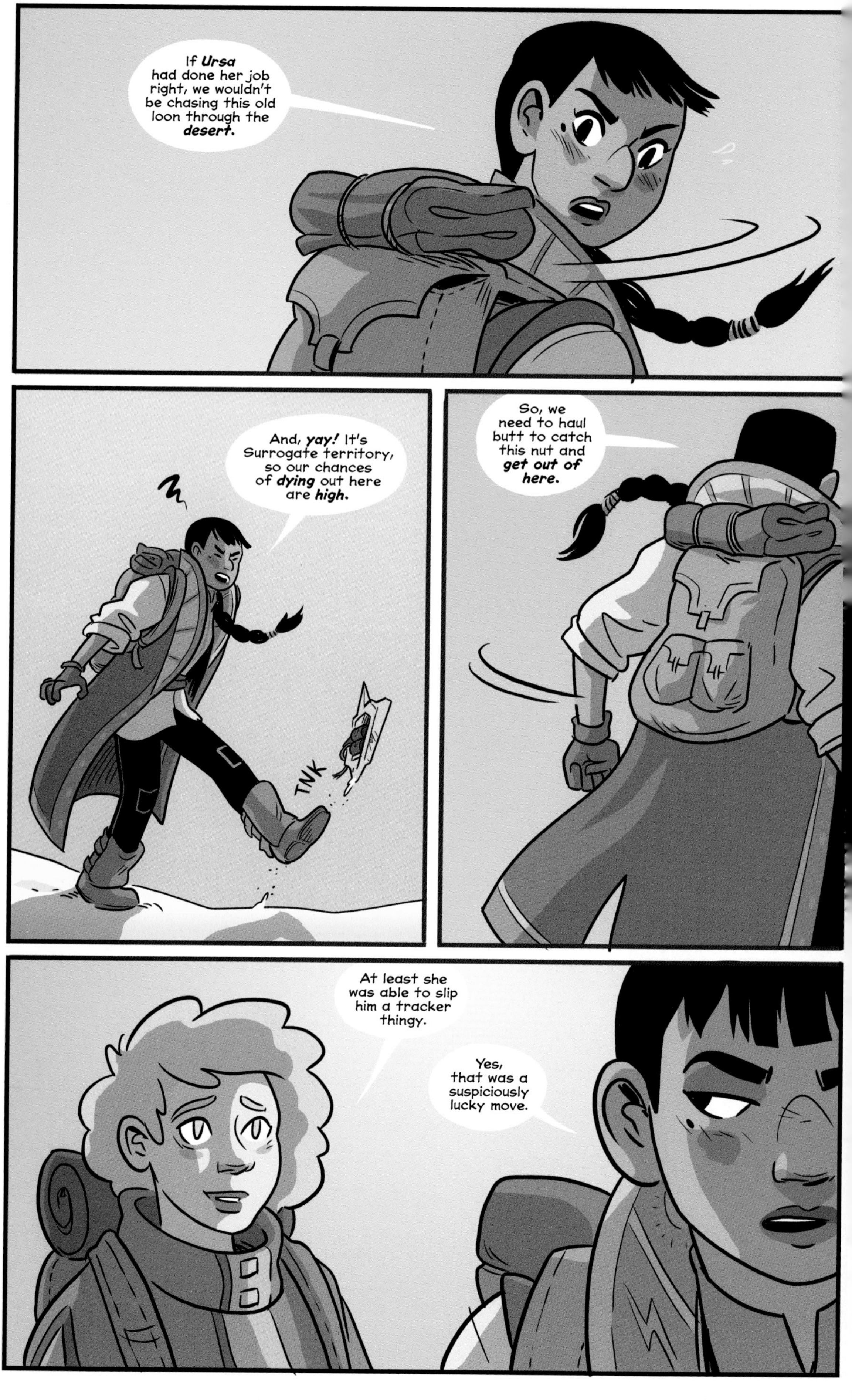
If ***Ursa*** had done her job right, we wouldn't be chasing this old loon through the ***desert.***
And, ***yay!*** It's Surrogate territory, so our chances of ***dying*** out here are ***high.***
TNK
So, we need to haul butt to catch this nut and ***get out of here.***
At least she was able to slip him a tracker thingy.
Yes, that was a suspiciously lucky move.

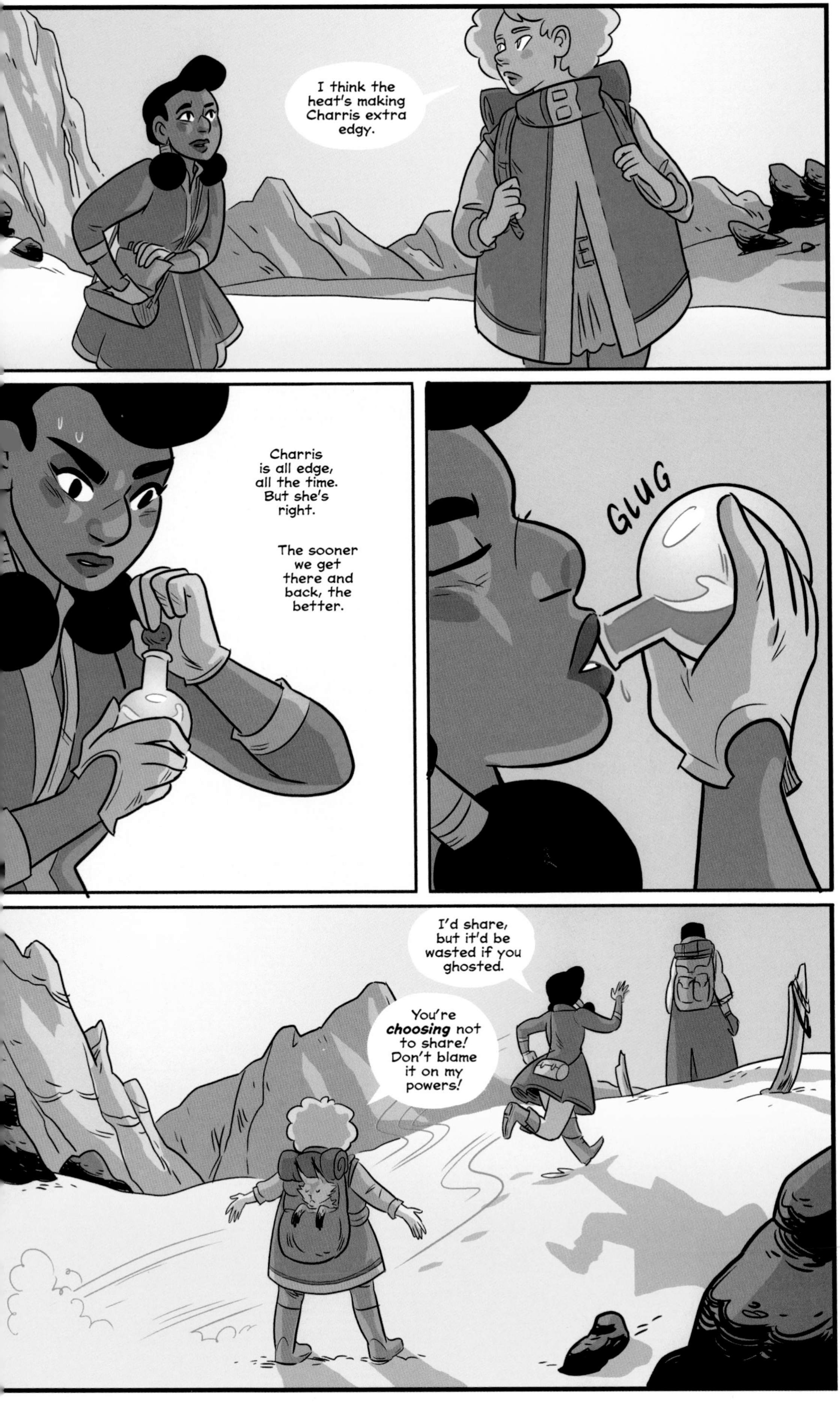
I think the heat's making Charris extra edgy.
Charris is all edge, all the time. But she's right.
The sooner we get there and back, the better.
GLUG
I'd share, but it'd be wasted if you ghosted.
You're *choosing* not to share! Don't blame it on my powers!

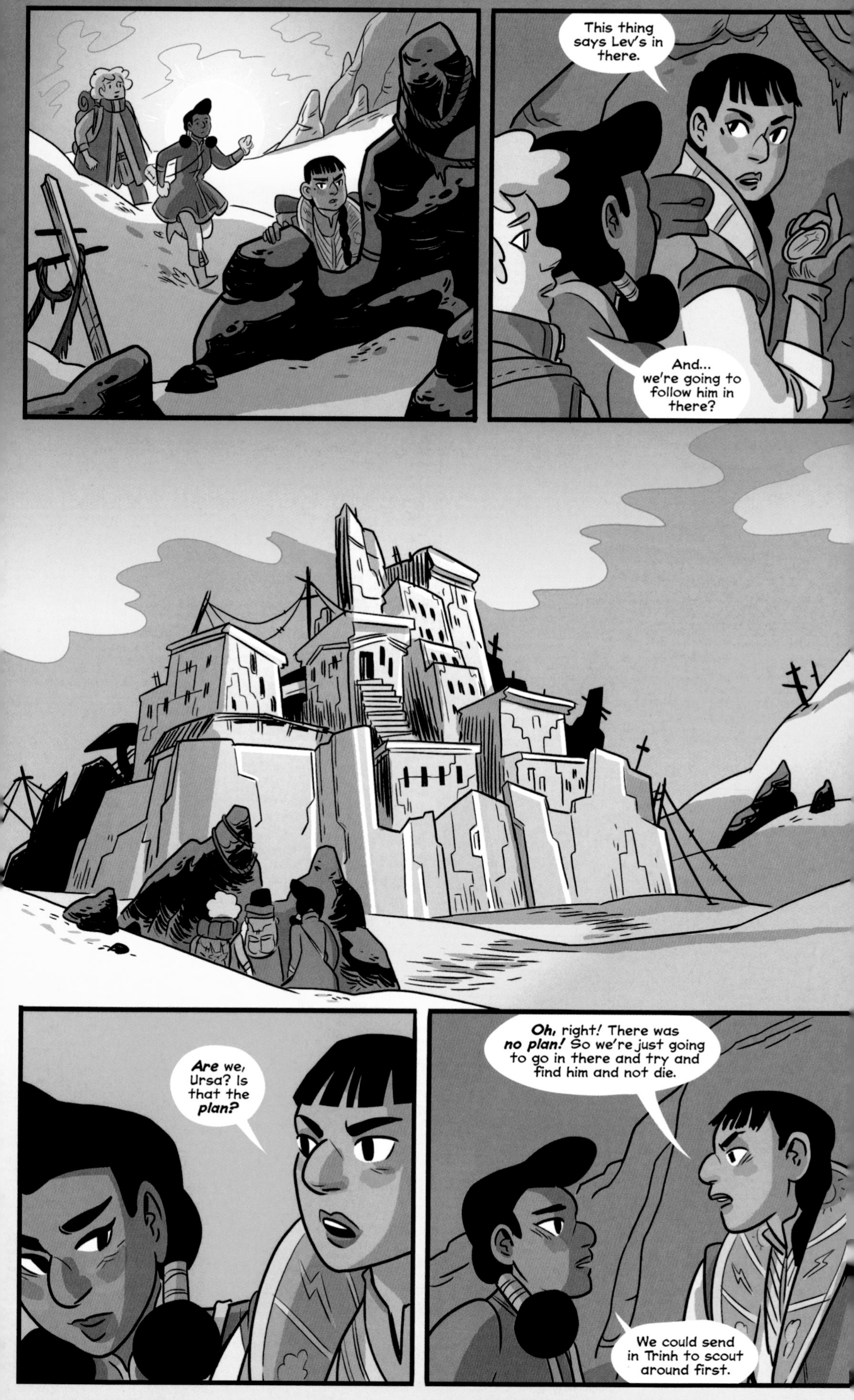
This thing says Lev's in there.
And... we're going to follow him in there?
Are we, Ursa? Is that the *plan?*
Oh, right! There was *no plan!* So we're just going to go in there and try and find him and not die.
We could send in Trinh to scout around first.

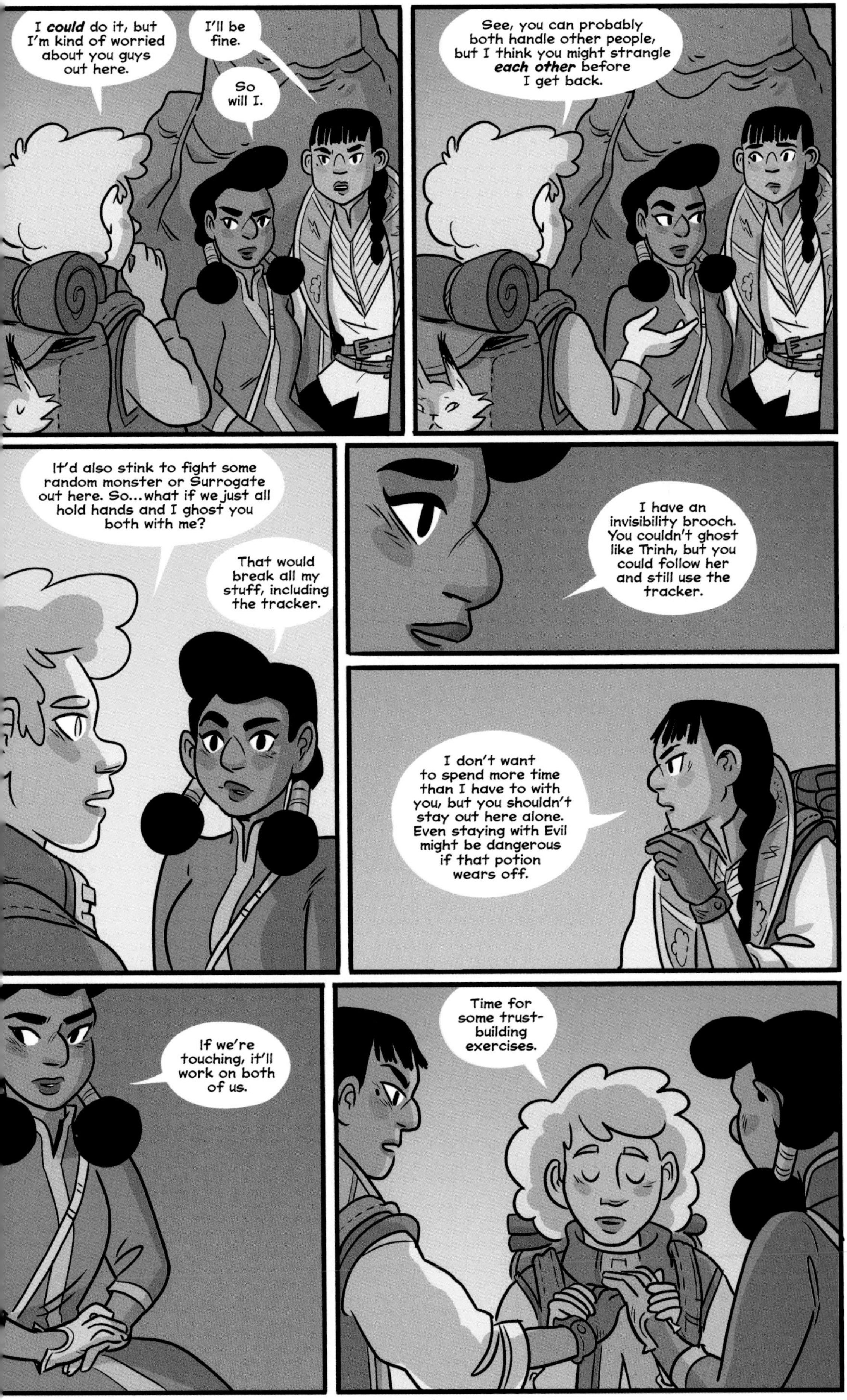
I *could* do it, but I'm kind of worried about you guys out here.
I'll be fine.
So will I.
See, you can probably both handle other people, but I think you might strangle *each other* before I get back.
It'd also stink to fight some random monster or Surrogate out here. So...what if we just all hold hands and I ghost you both with me?
That would break all my stuff, including the tracker.
I have an invisibility brooch. You couldn't ghost like Trinh, but you could follow her and still use the tracker.
I don't want to spend more time than I have to with you, but you shouldn't stay out here alone. Even staying with Evil might be dangerous if that potion wears off.
If we're touching, it'll work on both of us.
Time for some trust-building exercises.

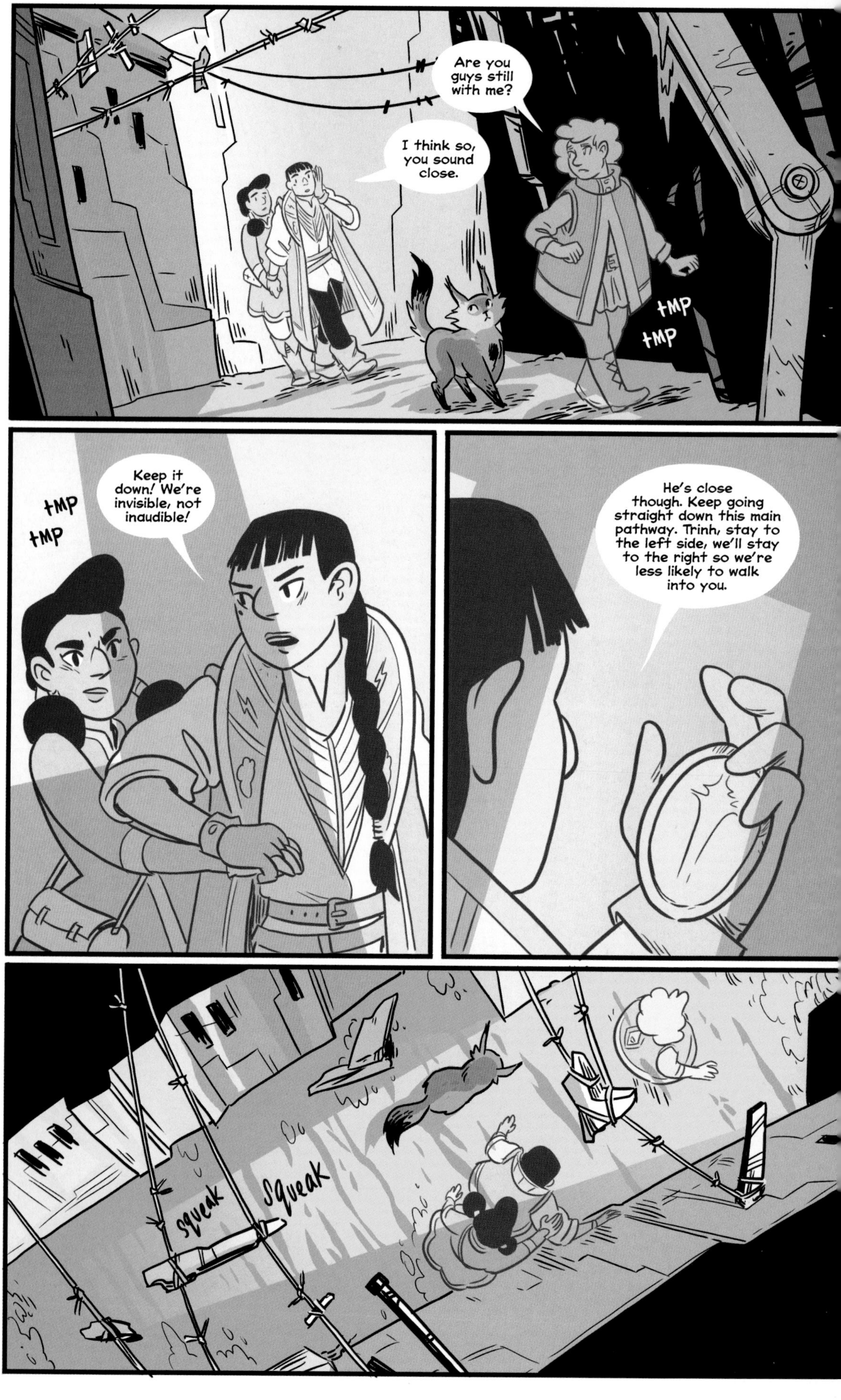
Are you guys still with me?
I think so, you sound close.
tmp
tmp
Keep it down! We're invisible, not inaudible!
tmp
tmp
He's close though. Keep going straight down this main pathway. Trinh, stay to the left side, we'll stay to the right so we're less likely to walk into you.
squeak
squeak

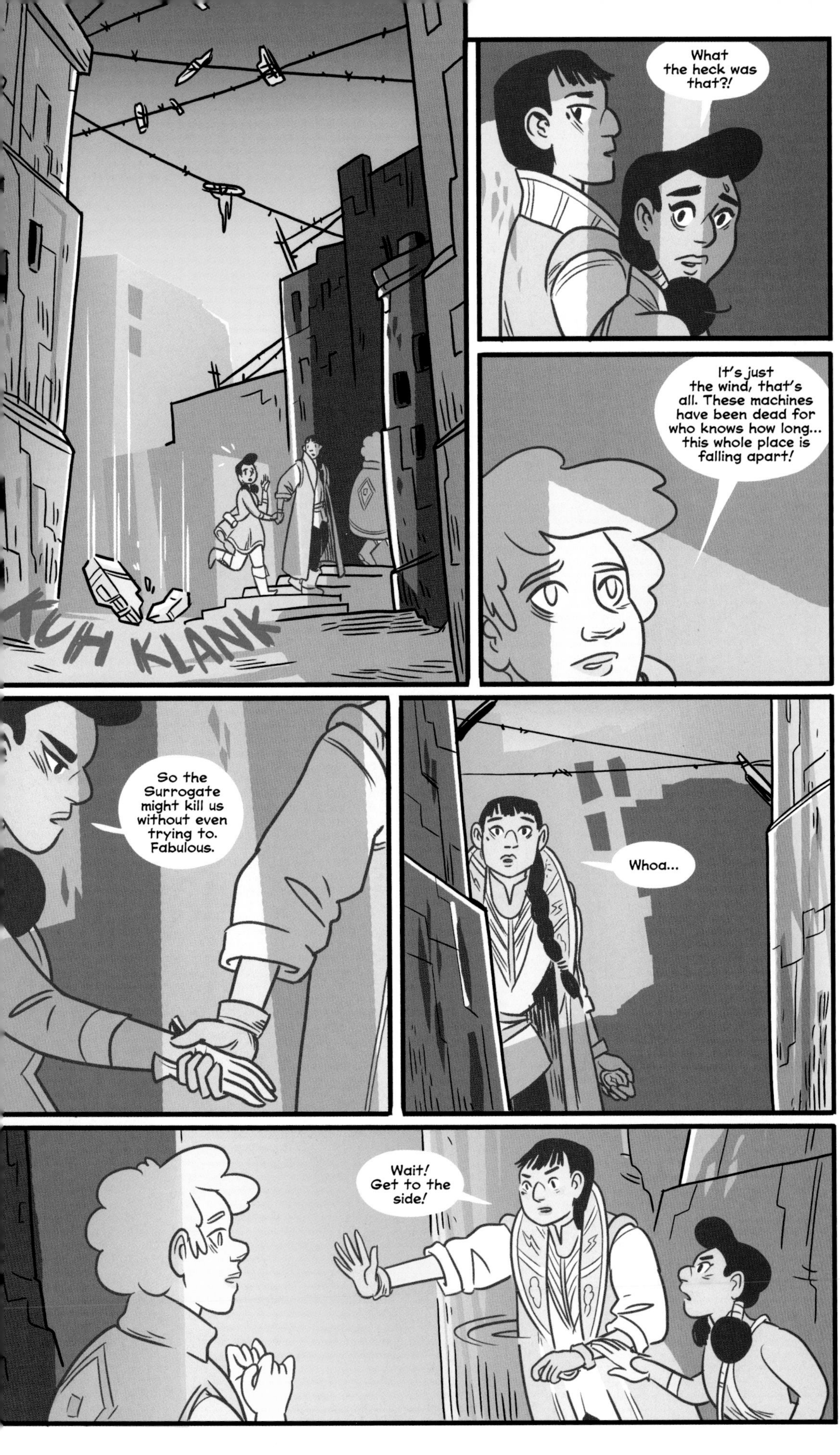
KUH KLANK
What the heck was that?!
It's just the wind, that's all. These machines have been dead for who knows how long... this whole place is falling apart!
So the Surrogate might kill us without even trying to. Fabulous.
Whoa...
Wait! Get to the side!

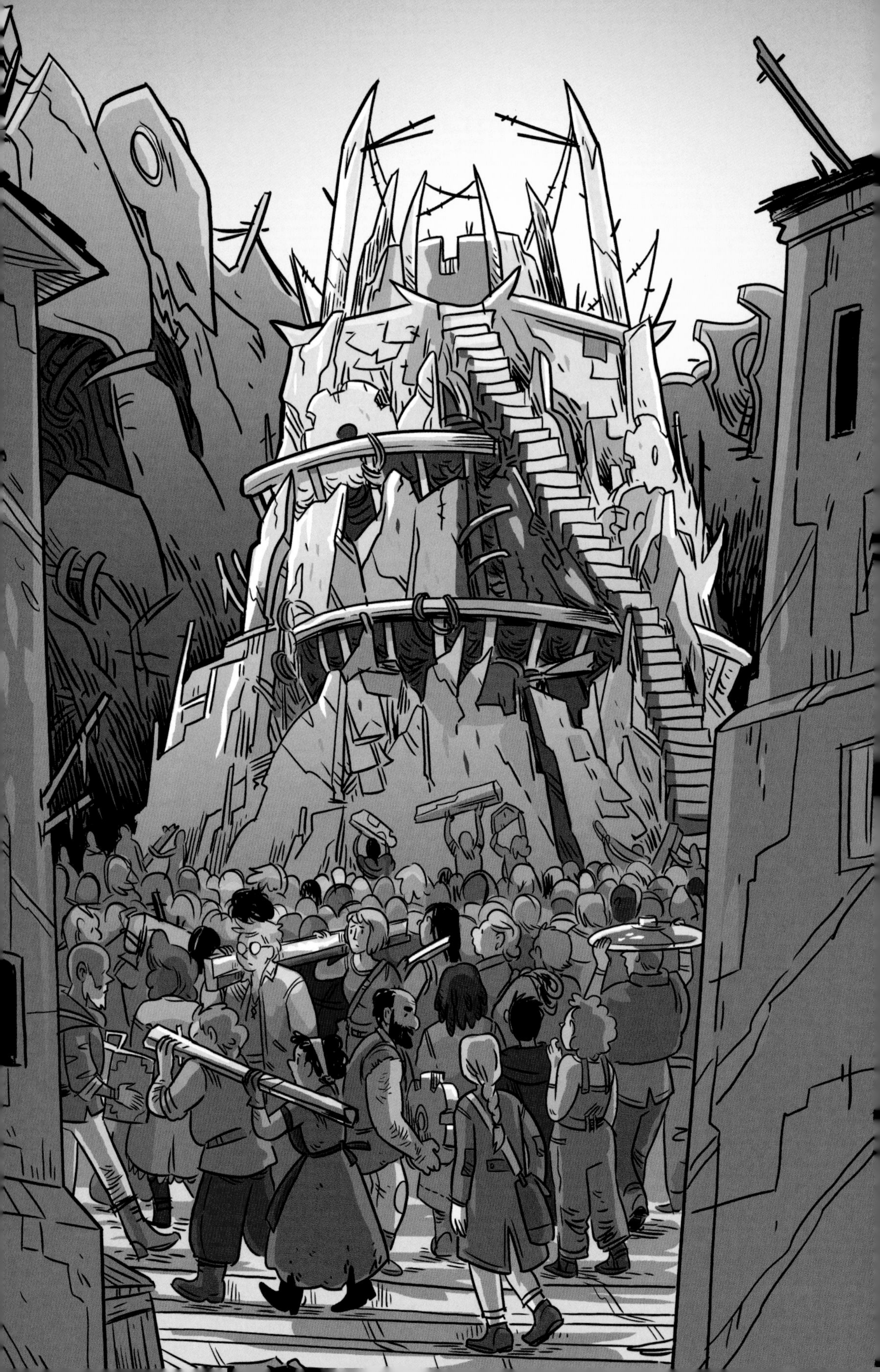

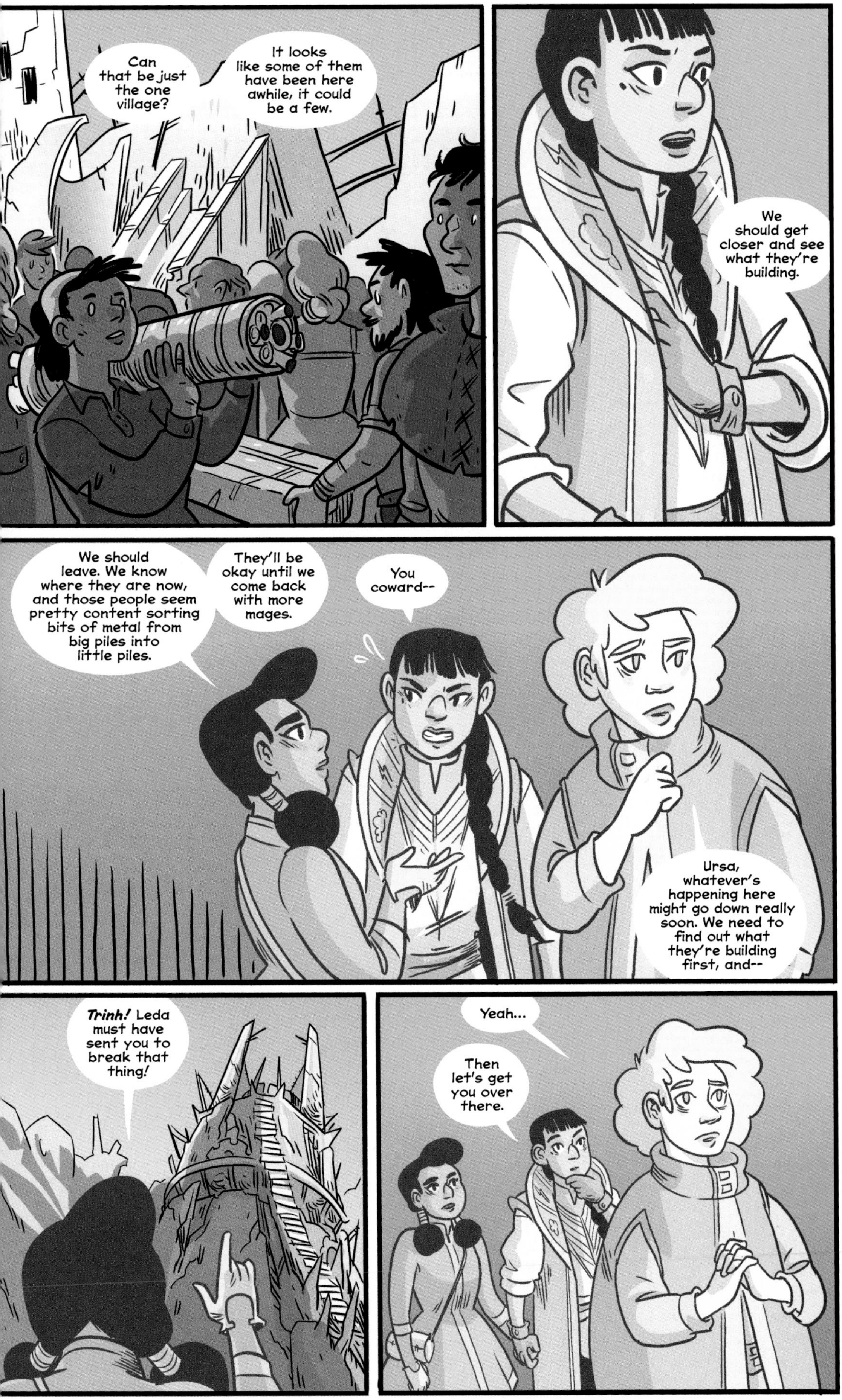
Can that be just the one village?
It looks like some of them have been here awhile, it could be a few.
We should get closer and see what they're building.
We should leave. We know where they are now, and those people seem pretty content sorting bits of metal from big piles into little piles.
They'll be okay until we come back with more mages.
You coward--
Ursa, whatever's happening here might go down really soon. We need to find out what they're building first, and--
Trinh! Leda must have sent you to break that thing!
Yeah...
Then let's get you over there.

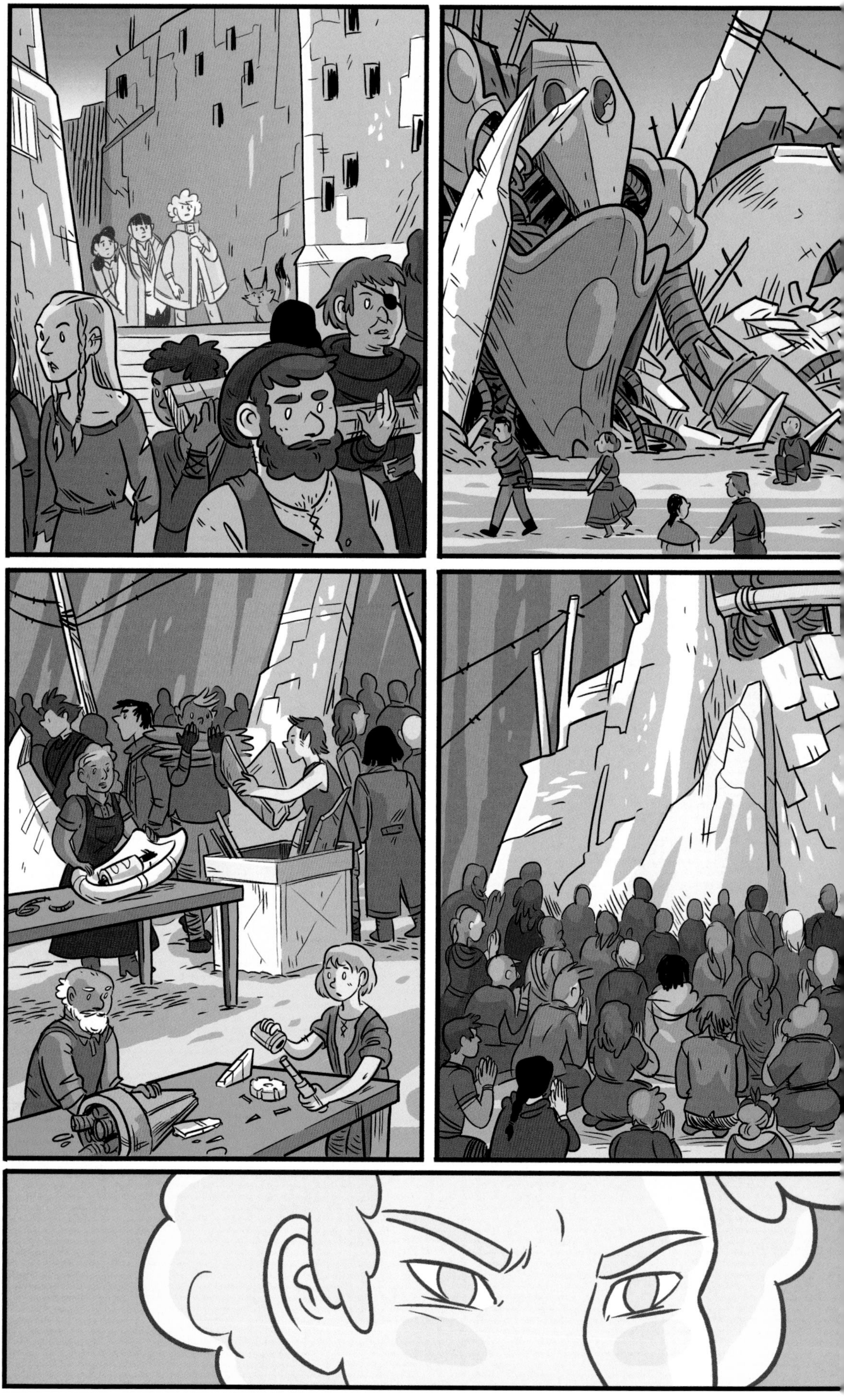

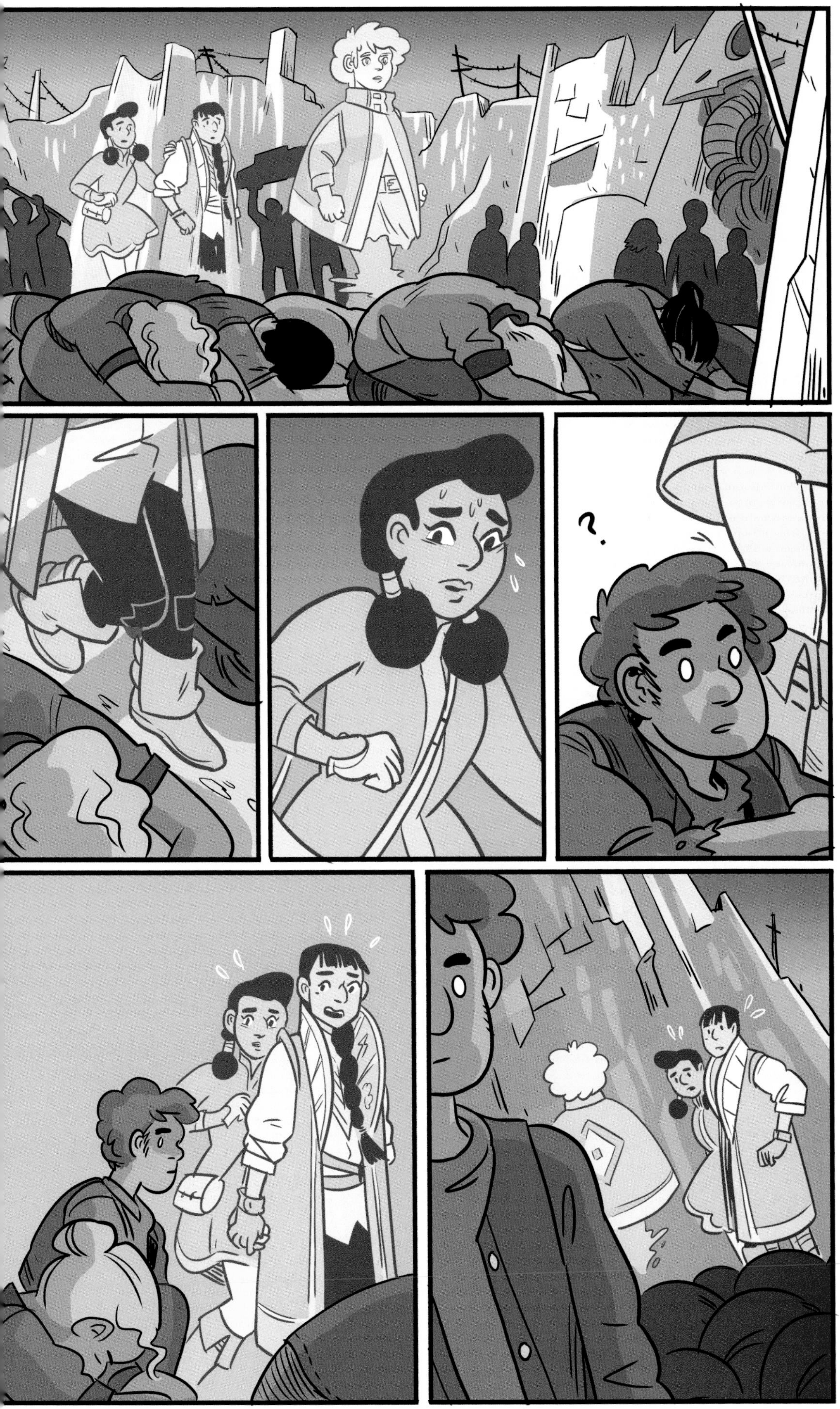
?

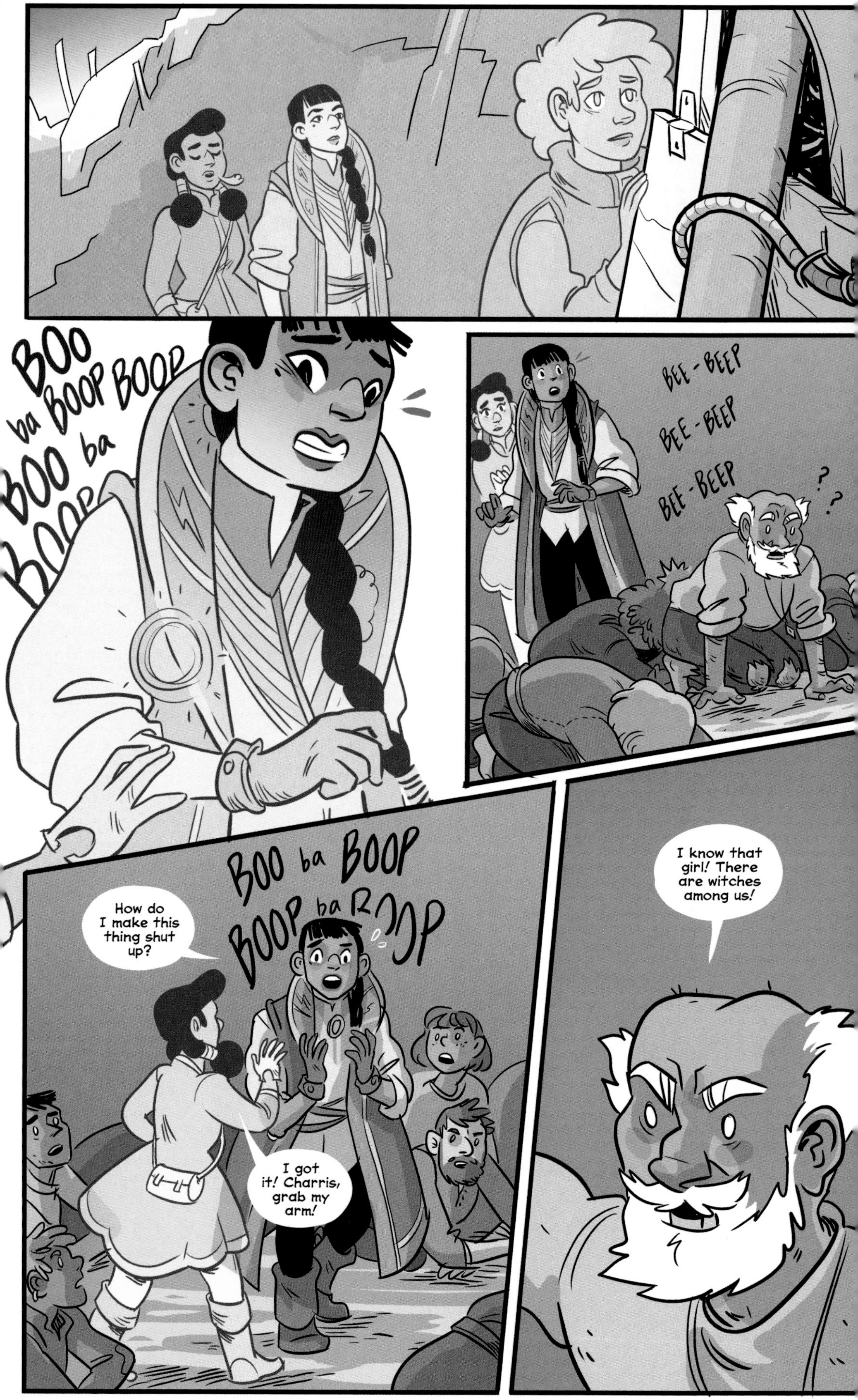
BOO ba BOOP BOOP BOO ba BOOP
BEE-BEEP BEE-BEEP BEE-BEEP
BOO ba BOOP BOOP ba BOOP
How do I make this thing shut up?
I got it! Charris, grab my arm!
I know that girl! There are witches among us!

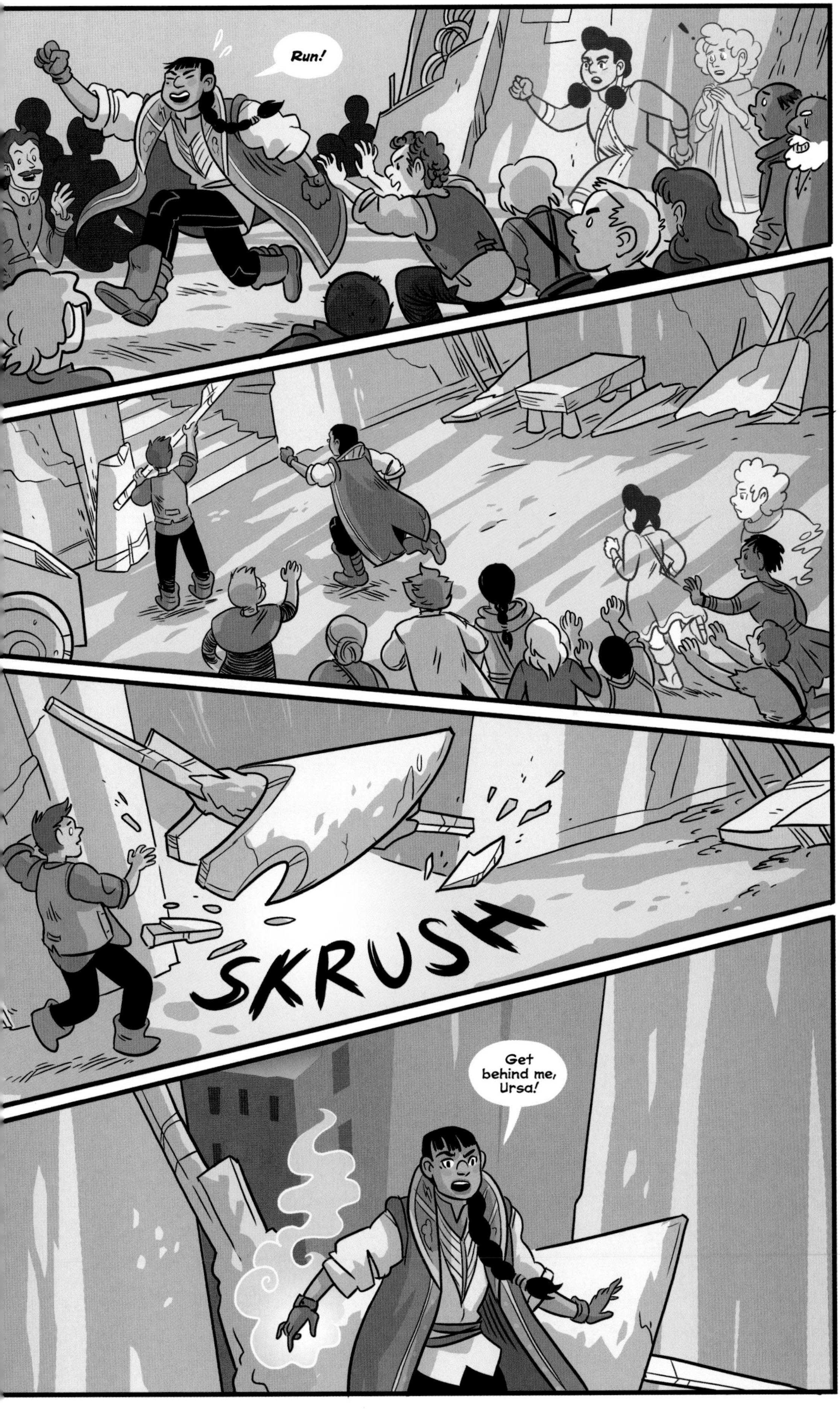
Run!
SKRUSH
Get behind me, Ursa!

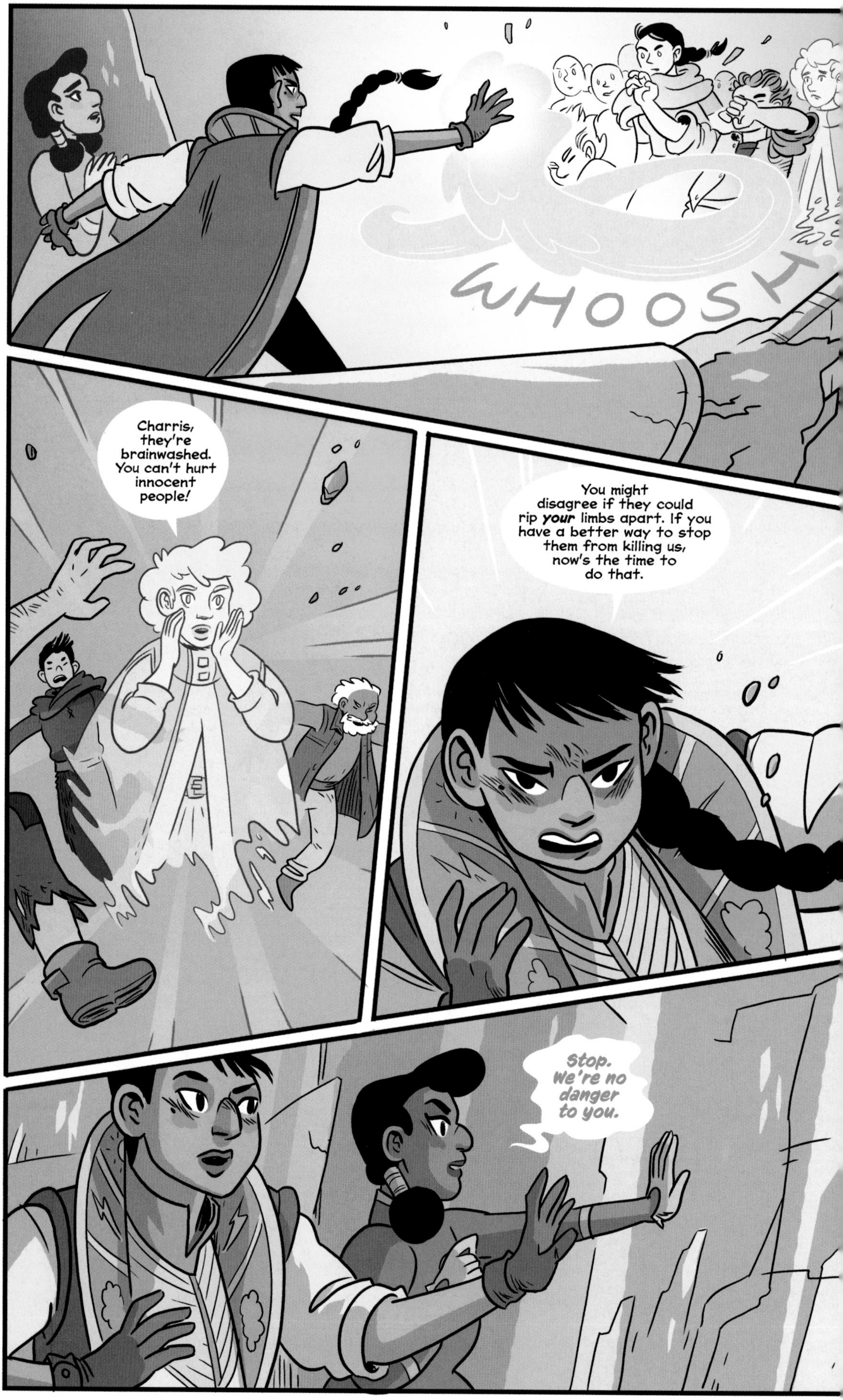
WHOOSH
Charris, they're brainwashed. You can't hurt innocent people!
You might disagree if they could rip *your* limbs apart. If you have a better way to stop them from killing us, now's the time to do that.
Stop. We're no danger to you.

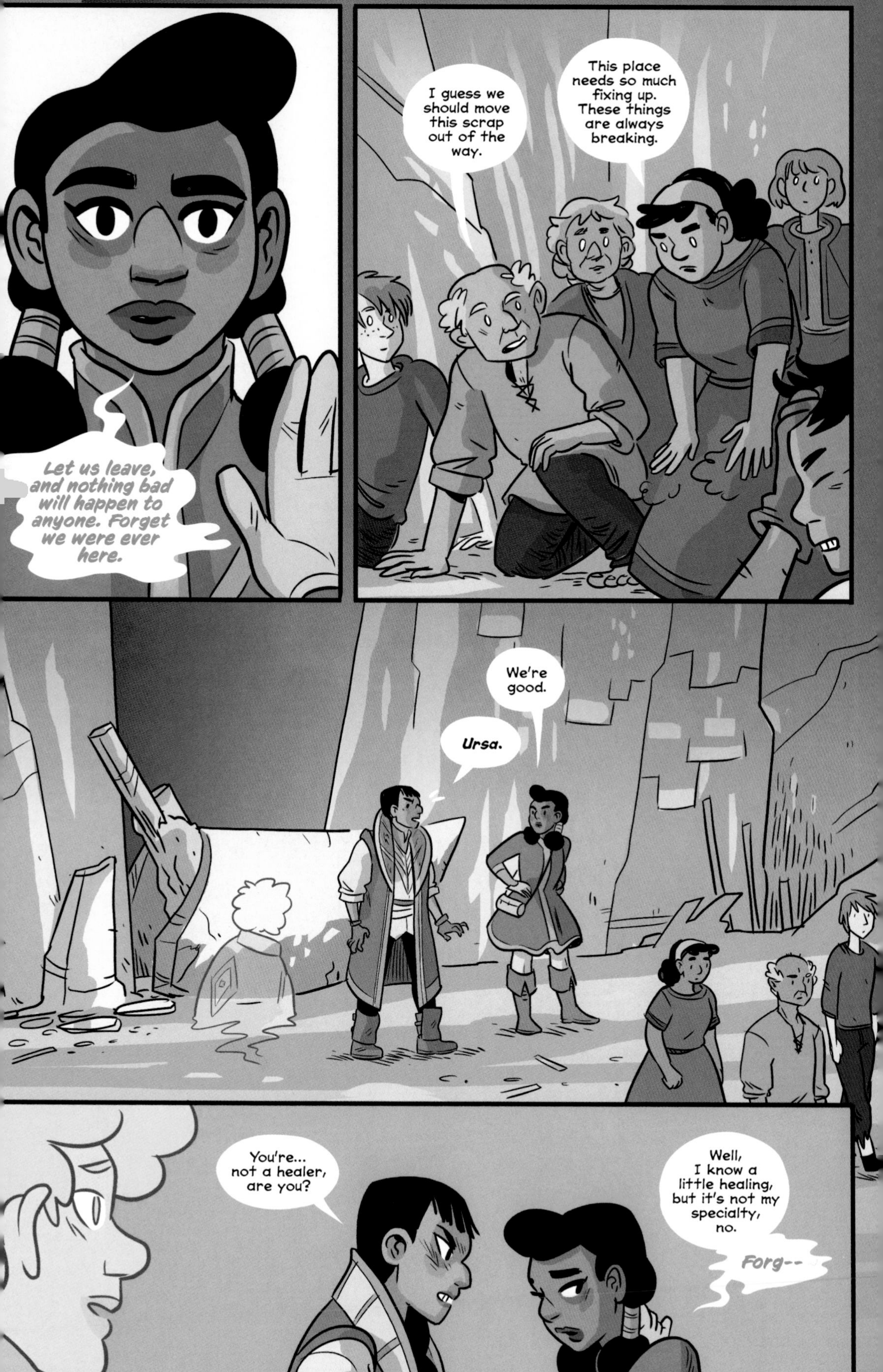
Let us leave, and nothing bad will happen to anyone. Forget we were ever here.
I guess we should move this scrap out of the way.
This place needs so much fixing up. These things are always breaking.
We're good.
Ursa.
You're... not a healer, are you?
Well, I know a little healing, but it's not my specialty, no.
Forg--

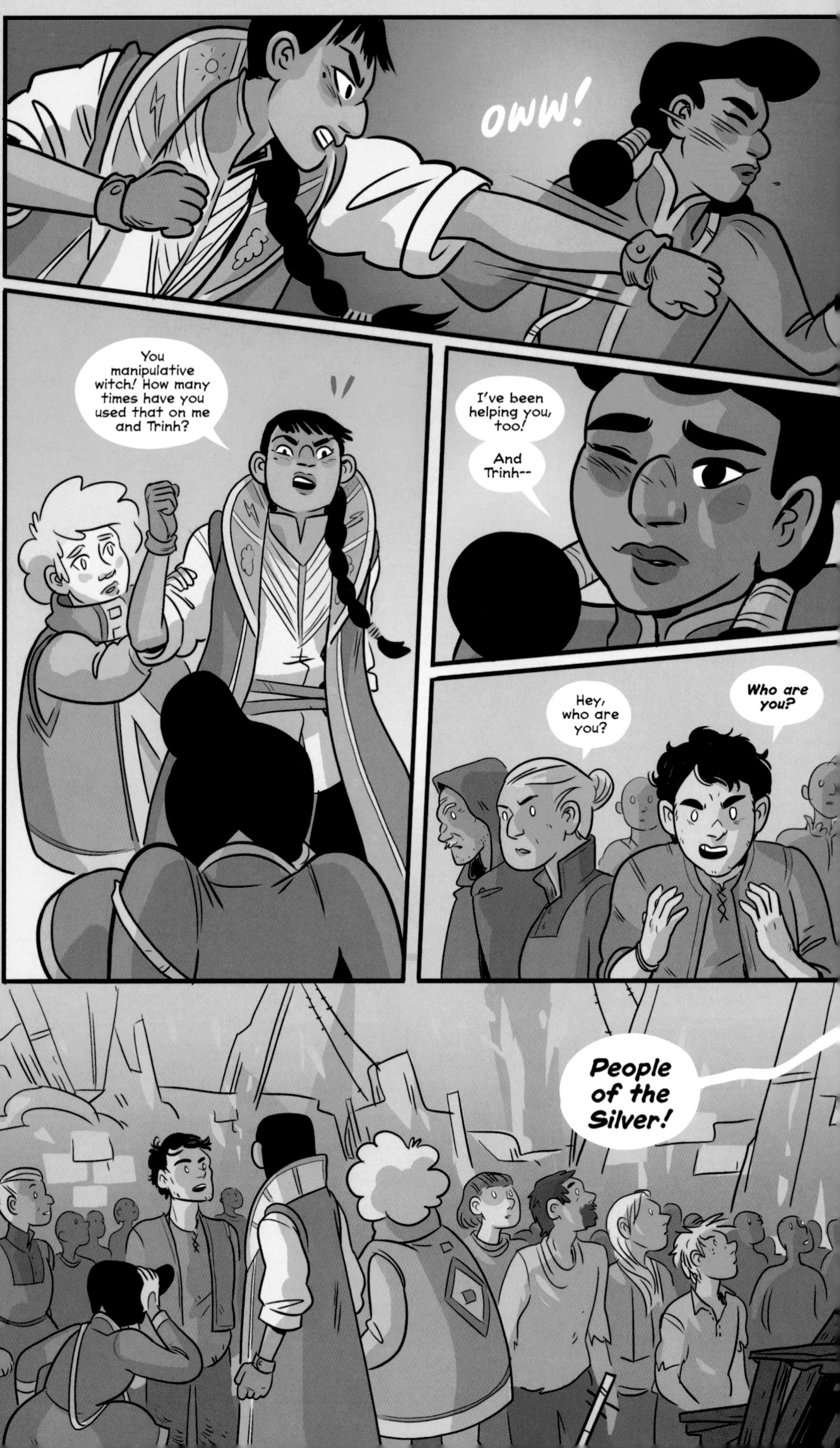
OWW!
You manipulative witch! How many times have you used that on me and Trinh?
I've been helping you, too!
And Trinh--
Hey, who are you?
Who are you?
People of the Silver!

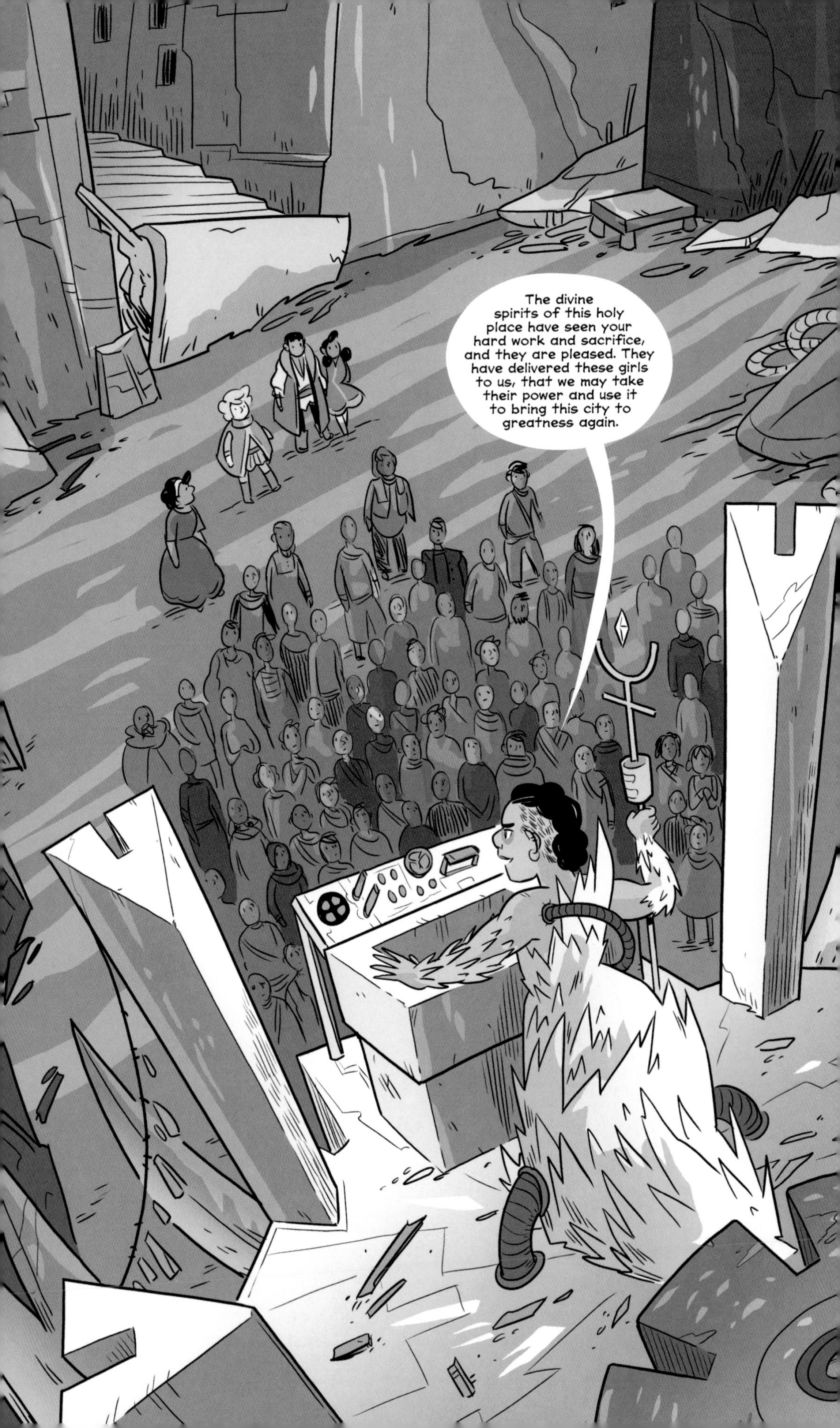
The divine spirits of this holy place have seen your hard work and sacrifice, and they are pleased. They have delivered these girls to us, that we may take their power and use it to bring this city to greatness again.

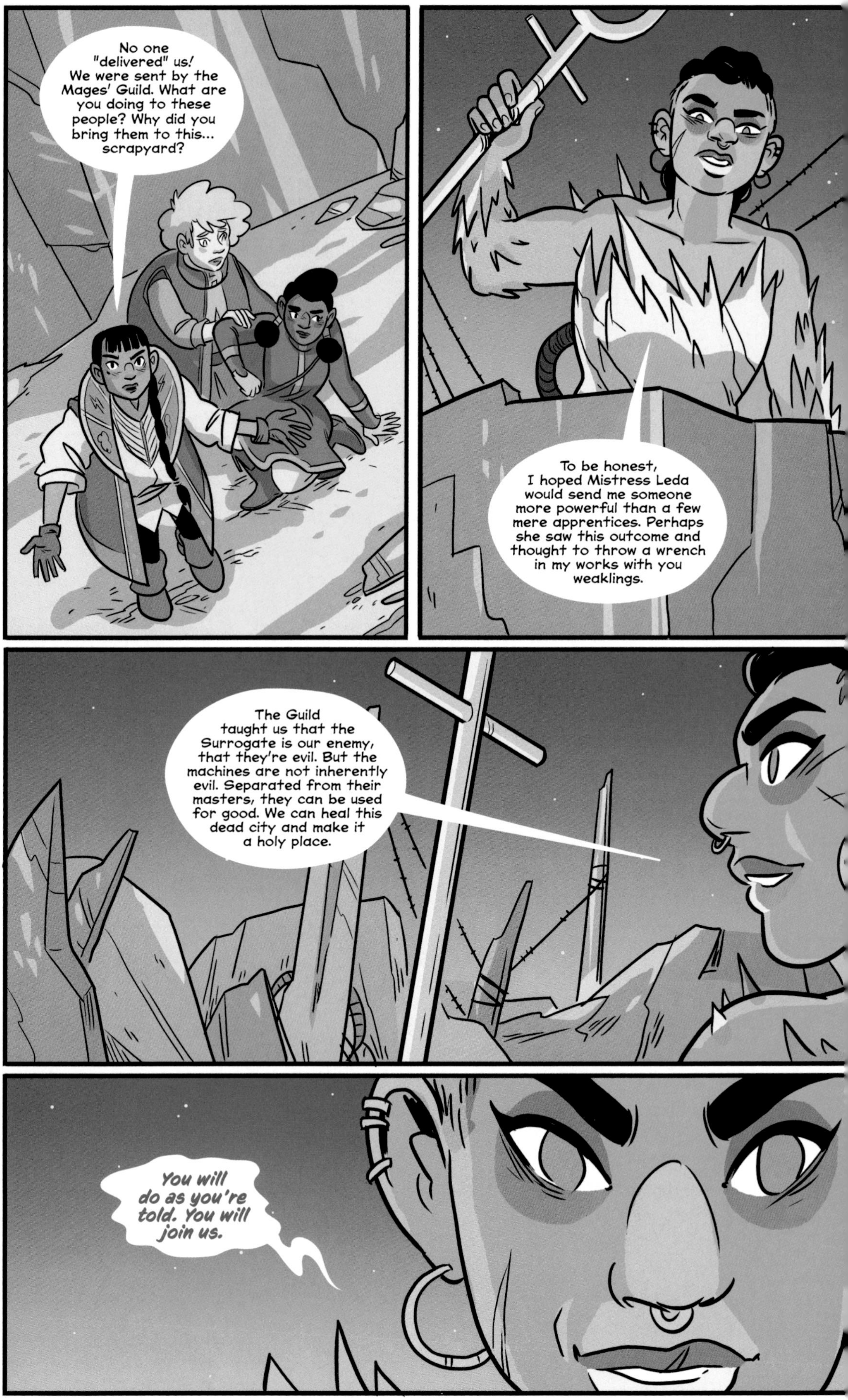
No one "delivered" us! We were sent by the Mages' Guild. What are you doing to these people? Why did you bring them to this... scrapyard?
To be honest, I hoped Mistress Leda would send me someone more powerful than a few mere apprentices. Perhaps she saw this outcome and thought to throw a wrench in my works with you weaklings.
The Guild taught us that the Surrogate is our enemy, that they're evil. But the machines are not inherently evil. Separated from their masters, they can be used for good. We can heal this dead city and make it a holy place.
You will do as you're told. You will join us.

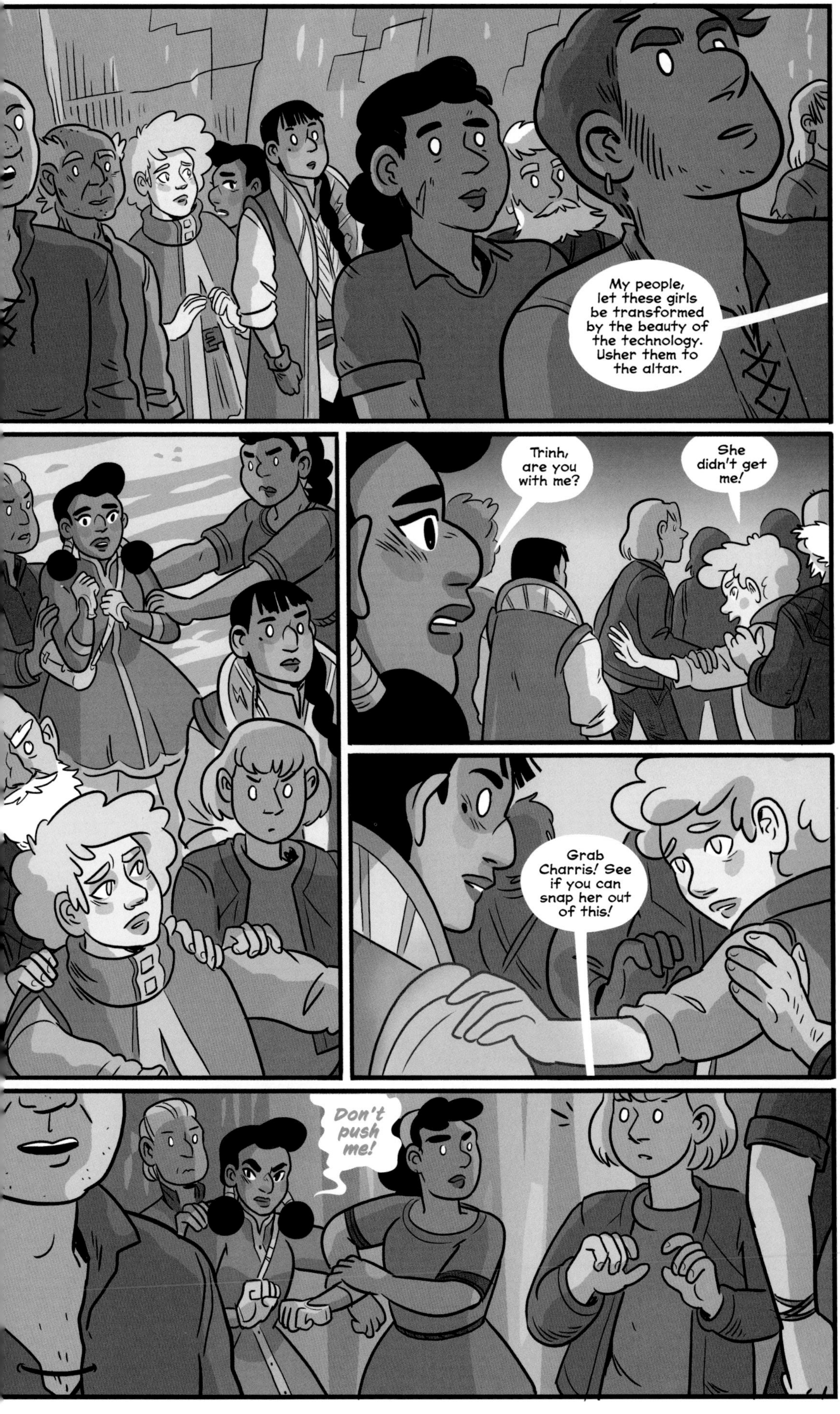
My people, let these girls be transformed by the beauty of the technology. Usher them to the altar.
Trinh, are you with me?
She didn't get me!
Grab Charris! See if you can snap her out of this!
Don't push me!

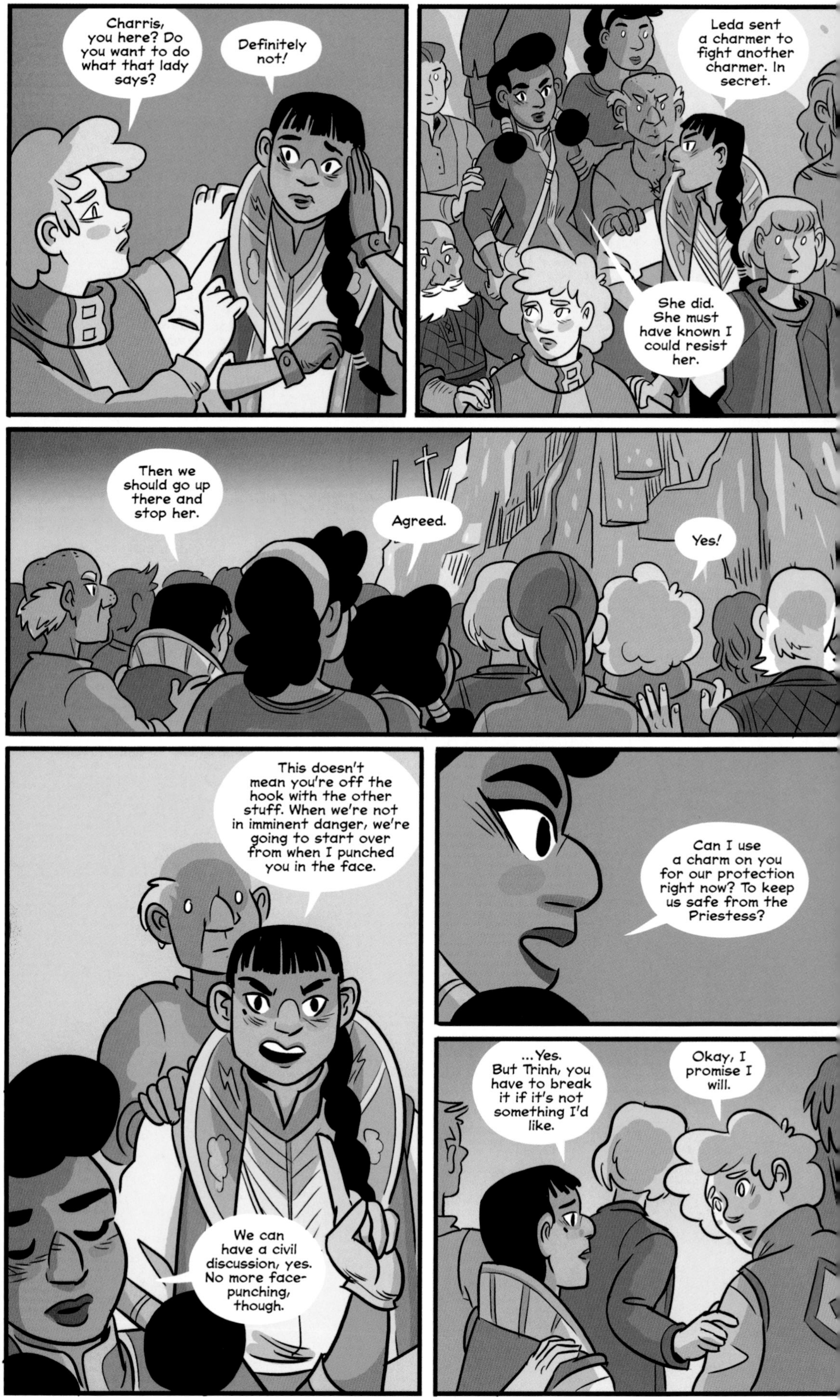

Charris, you here? Do you want to do what that lady says?
Definitely not!
Leda sent a charmer to fight another charmer. In secret.
She did. She must have known I could resist her.
Then we should go up there and stop her.
Agreed.
Yes!
This doesn't mean you're off the hook with the other stuff. When we're not in imminent danger, we're going to start over from when I punched you in the face.
We can have a civil discussion, yes. No more face-punching, though.
Can I use a charm on you for our protection right now? To keep us safe from the Priestess?
...Yes. But Trinh, you have to break it if it's not something I'd like.
Okay, I promise I will.

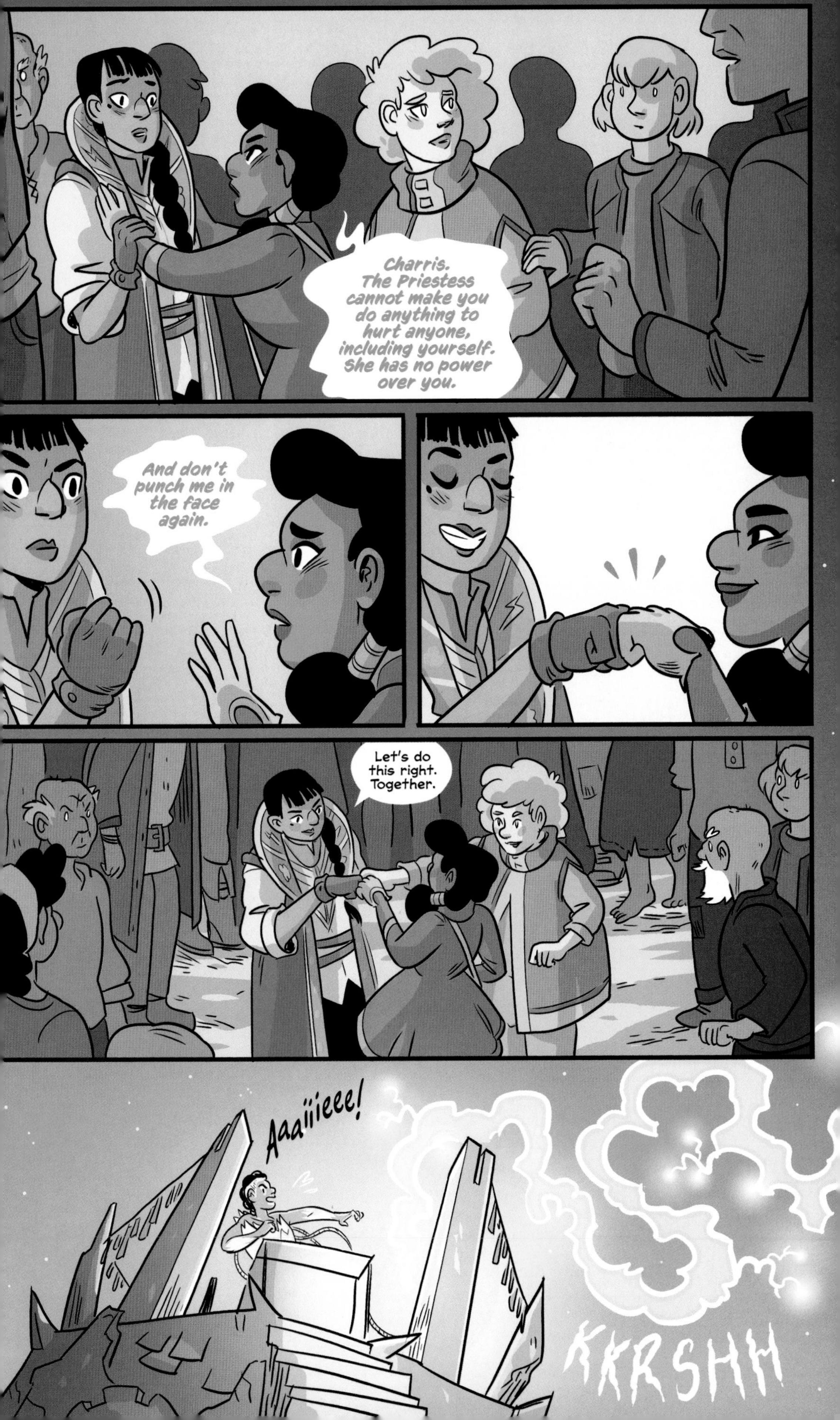
Charris. The Priestess cannot make you do anything to hurt anyone, including yourself. She has no power over you.
And don't punch me in the face again.
Let's do this right. Together.
Aaaiiieee!
KKRSHH

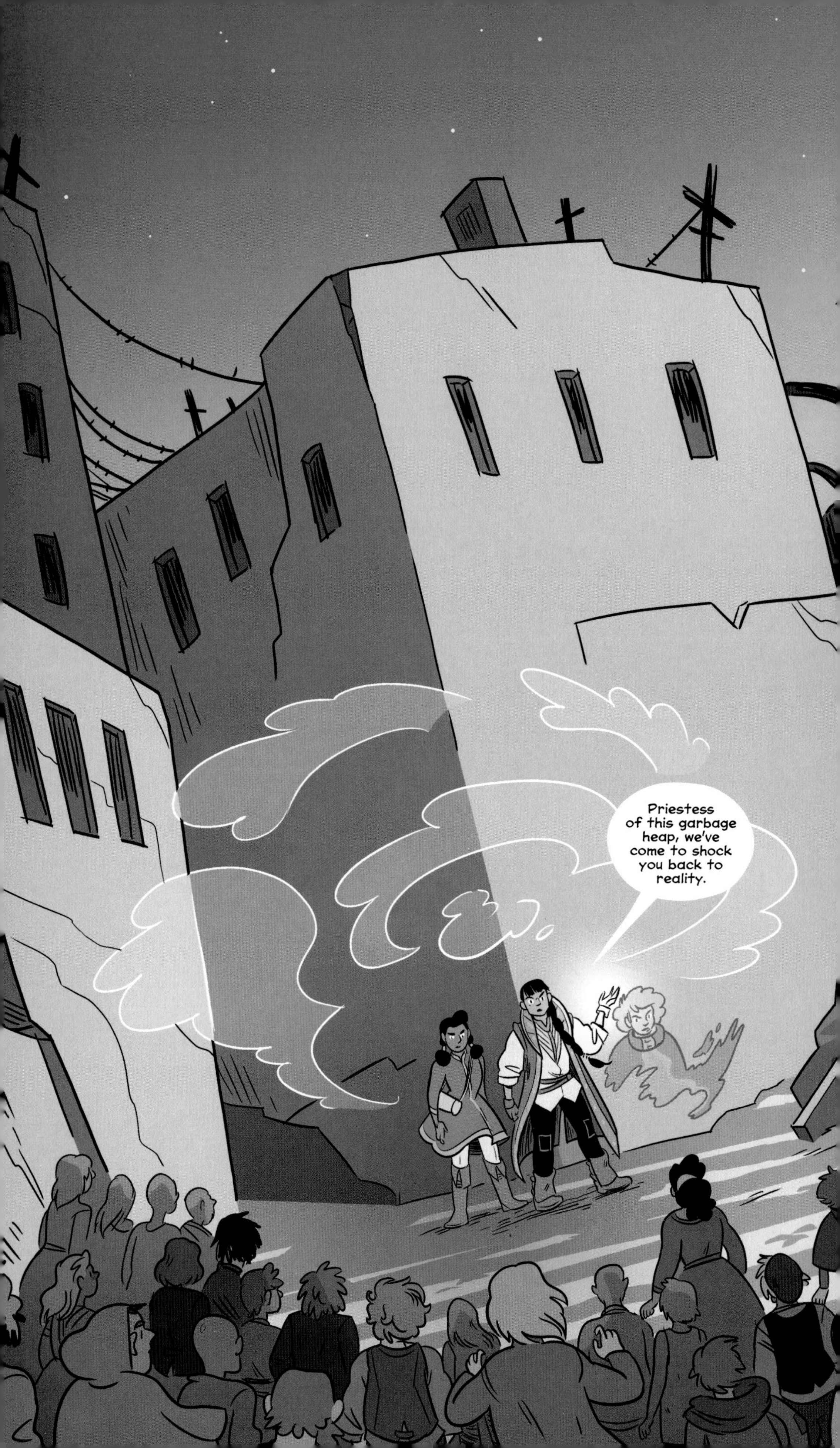
Priestess of this garbage heap, we've come to shock you back to reality.

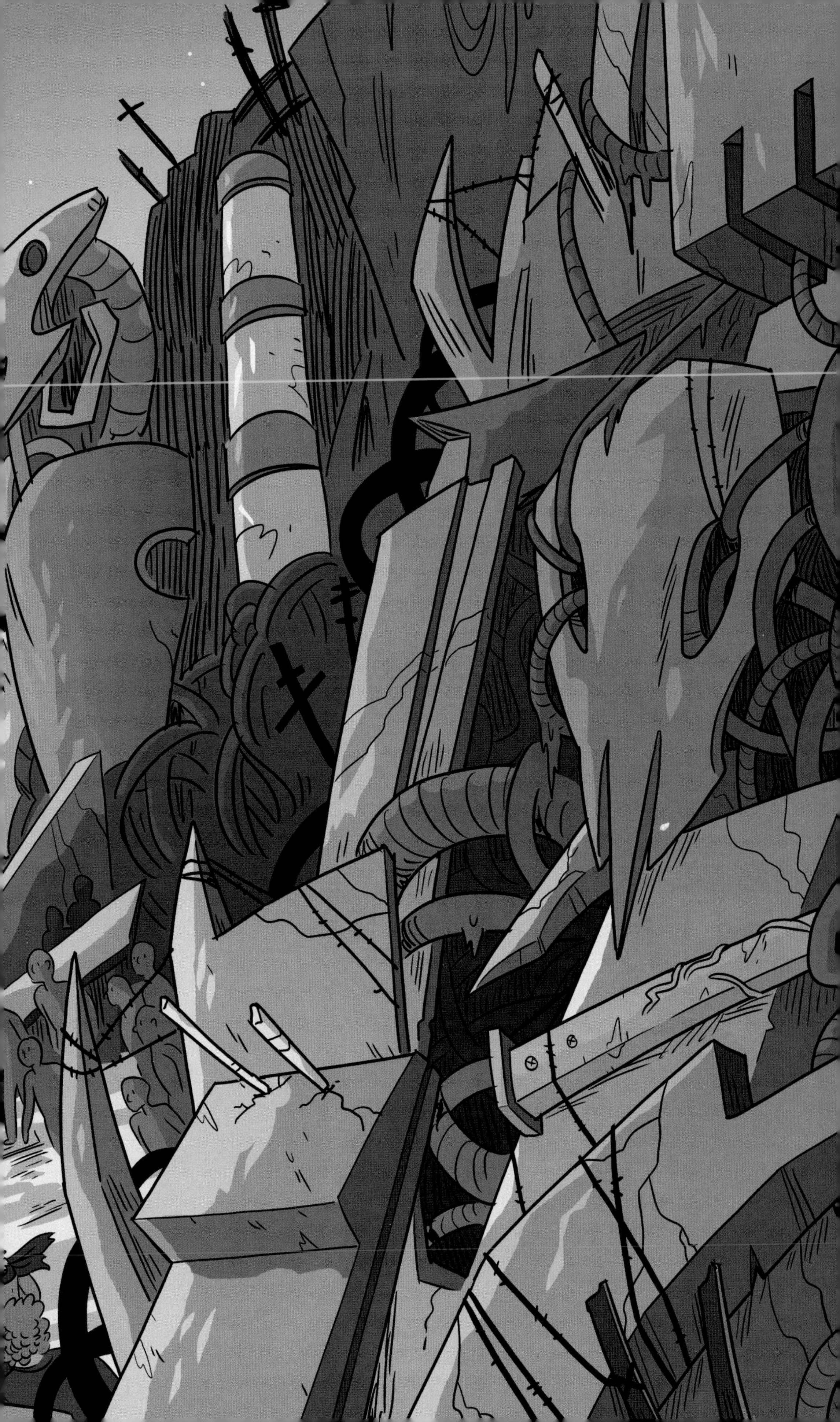

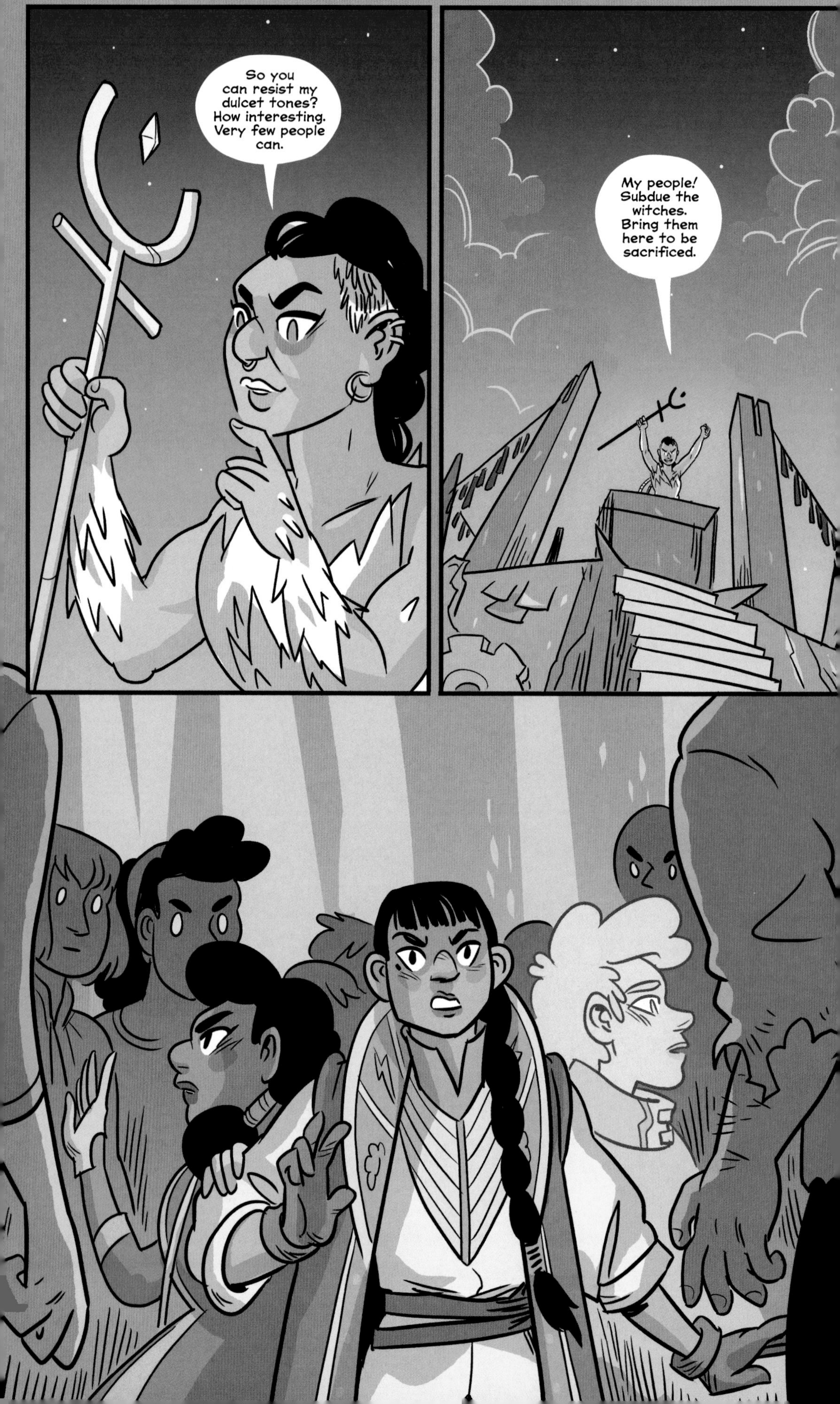
So you can resist my dulcet tones? How interesting. Very few people can.
My people! Subdue the witches. Bring them here to be sacrificed.

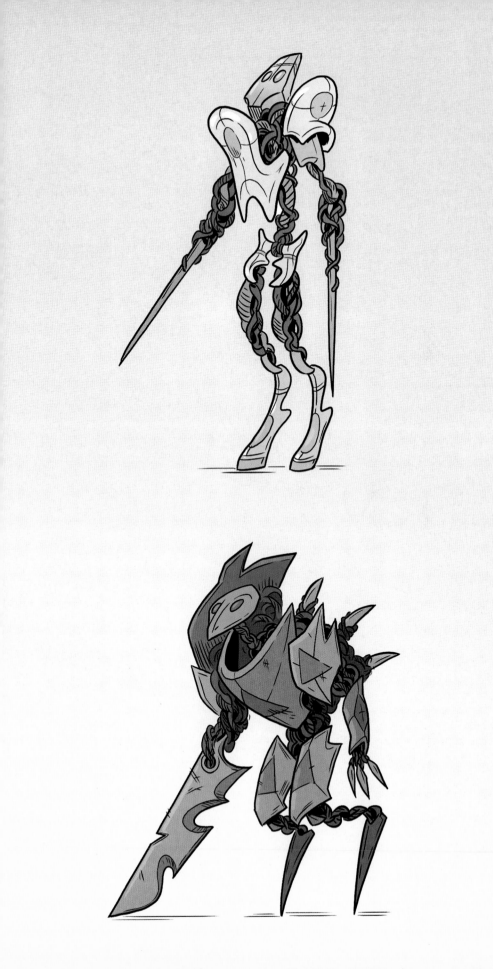

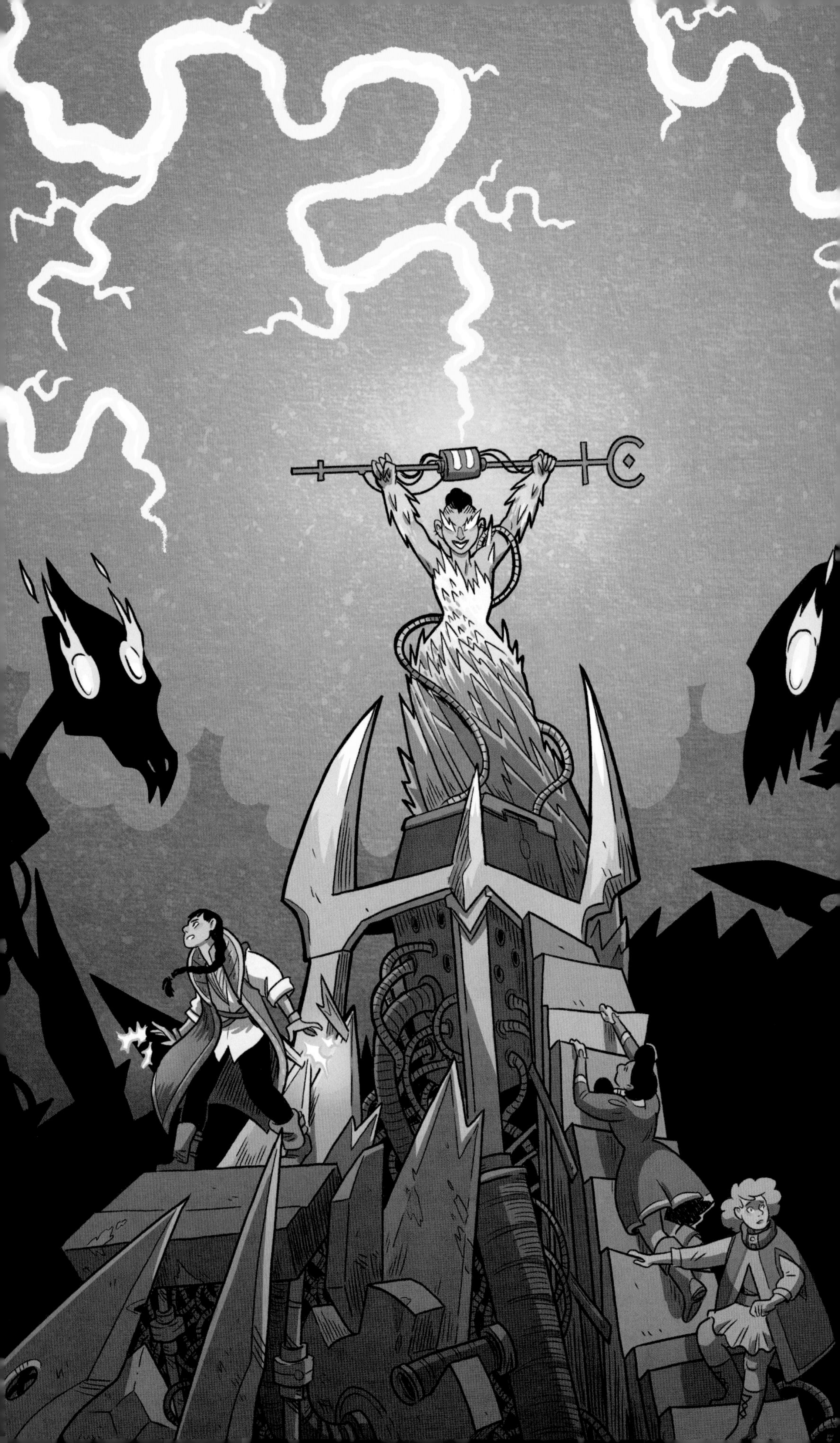

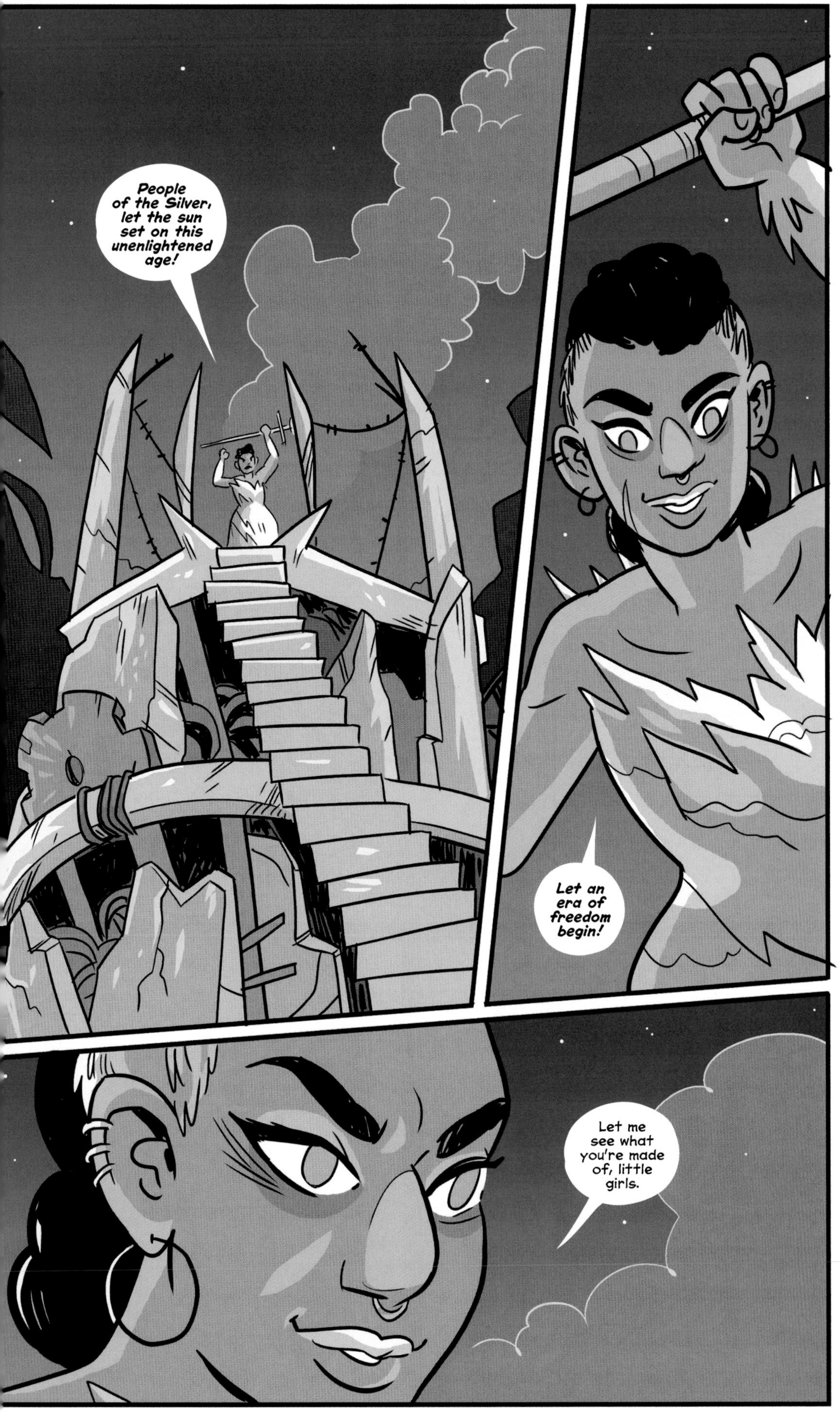
People of the Silver, let the sun set on this unenlightened age!
Let an era of freedom begin!
Let me see what you're made of, little girls.

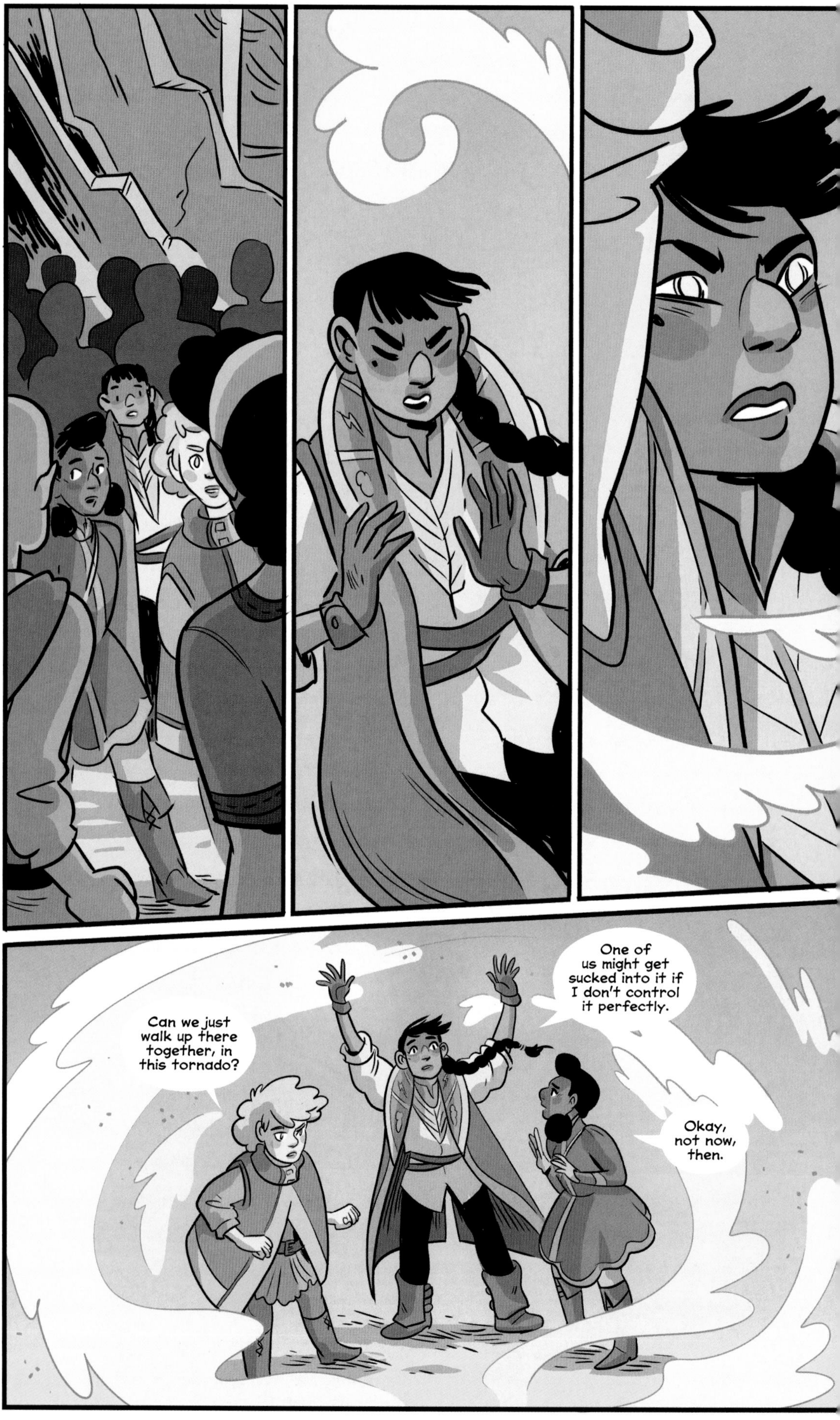
Can we just walk up there together, in this tornado?
One of us might get sucked into it if I don't control it perfectly.
Okay, not now, then.

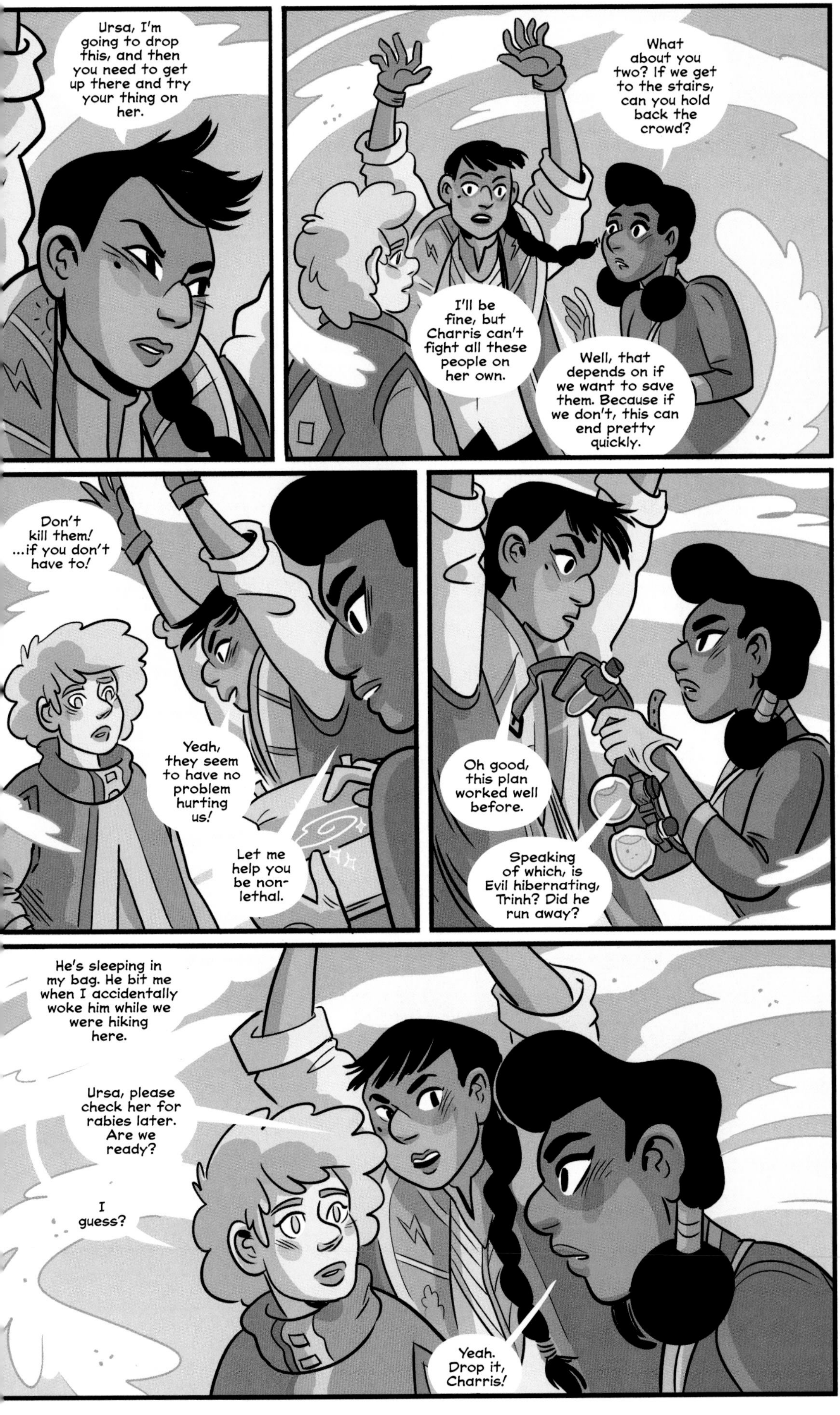

Ursa, I'm going to drop this, and then you need to get up there and try your thing on her.
What about you two? If we get to the stairs, can you hold back the crowd?
I'll be fine, but Charris can't fight all these people on her own.
Well, that depends on if we want to save them. Because if we don't, this can end pretty quickly.
Don't kill them! ...if you don't have to!
Yeah, they seem to have no problem hurting us!
Let me help you be non-lethal.
Oh good, this plan worked well before.
Speaking of which, is Evil hibernating, Trinh? Did he run away?
He's sleeping in my bag. He bit me when I accidentally woke him while we were hiking here.
Ursa, please check her for rabies later. Are we ready?
I guess?
Yeah. Drop it, Charris!

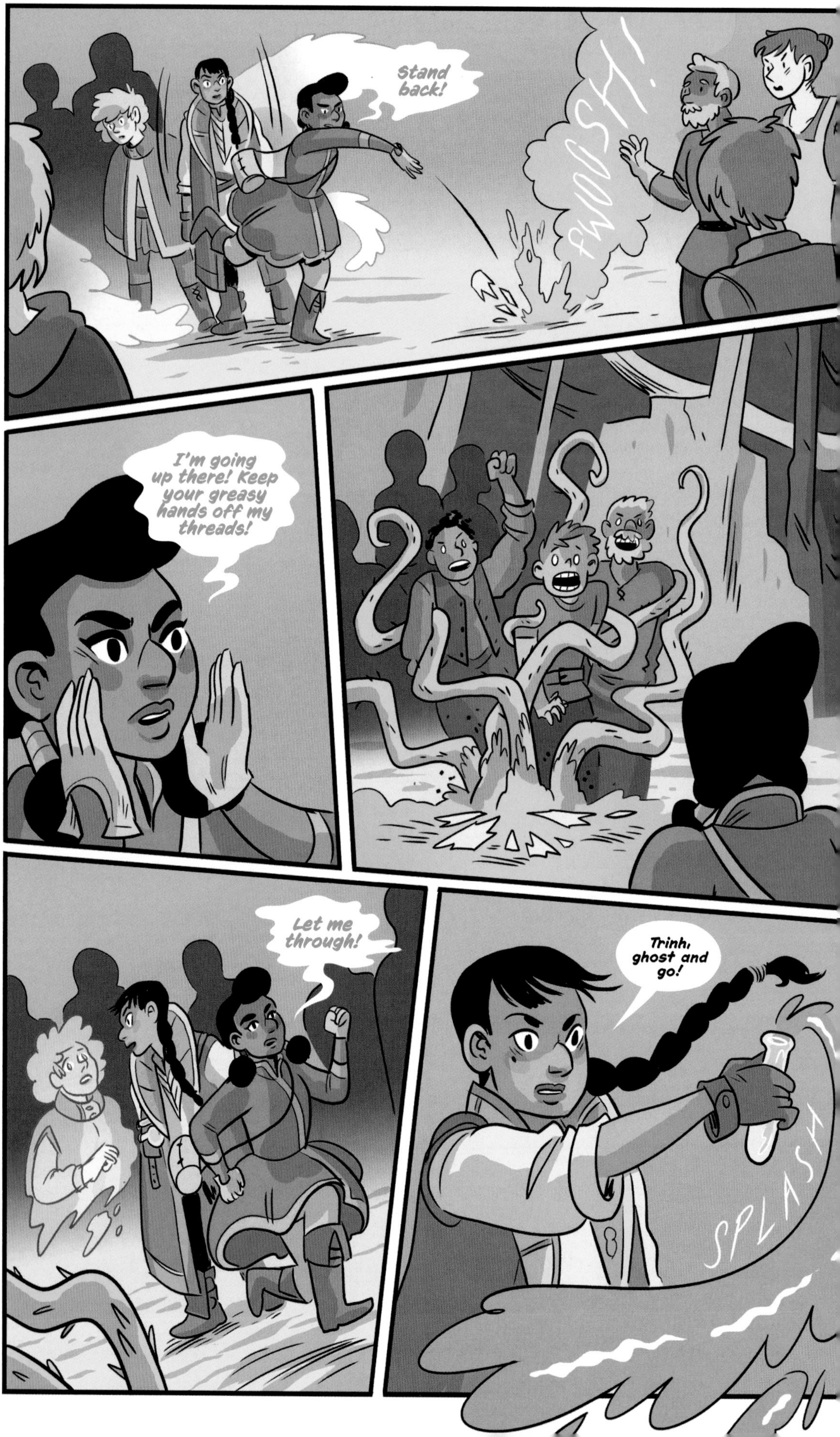

Stand back!
FWOOSH!
I'm going up there! Keep your greasy hands off my threads!
Let me through!
Trinh, ghost and go!
SPLASH

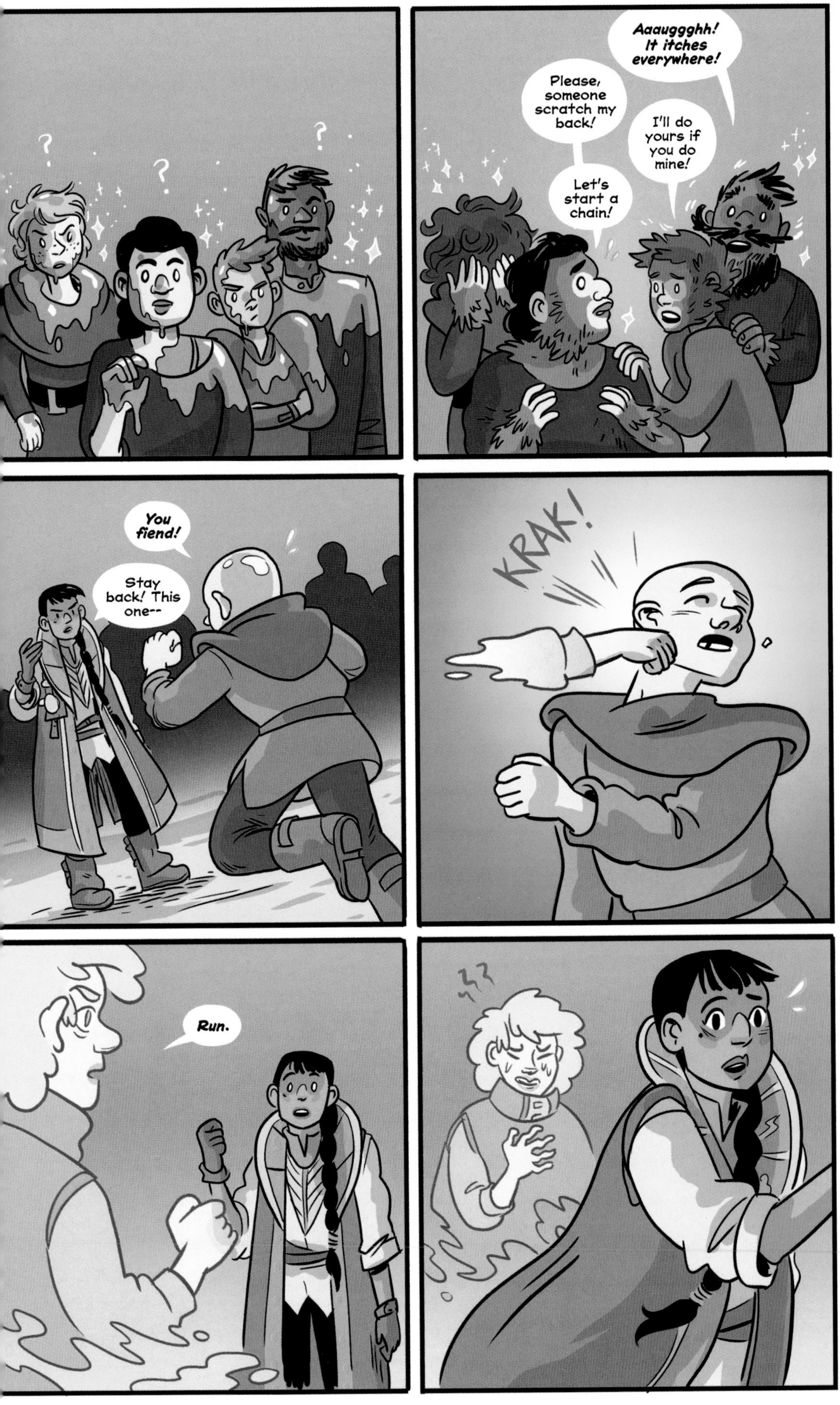
?
?
?
Aaauggghh! It itches everywhere!
Please, someone scratch my back!
I'll do yours if you do mine!
Let's start a chain!
You fiend!
Stay back! This one--
KRAK!
Run.

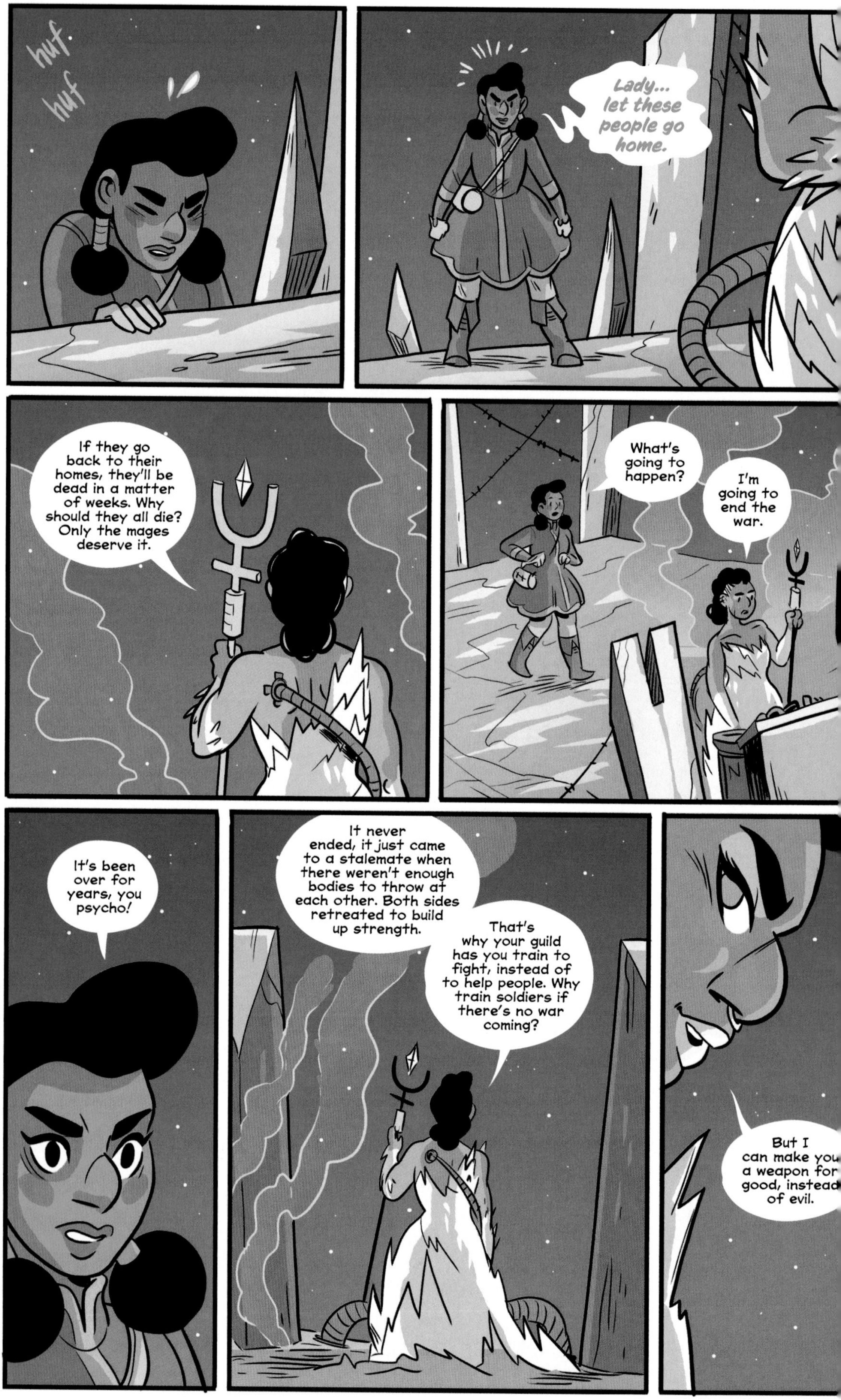
huf huf
Lady... let these people go home.
If they go back to their homes, they'll be dead in a matter of weeks. Why should they all die? Only the mages deserve it.
What's going to happen?
I'm going to end the war.
It's been over for years, you psycho!
It never ended, it just came to a stalemate when there weren't enough bodies to throw at each other. Both sides retreated to build up strength.
That's why your guild has you train to fight, instead of to help people. Why train soldiers if there's no war coming?
But I can make you a weapon for good, instead of evil.

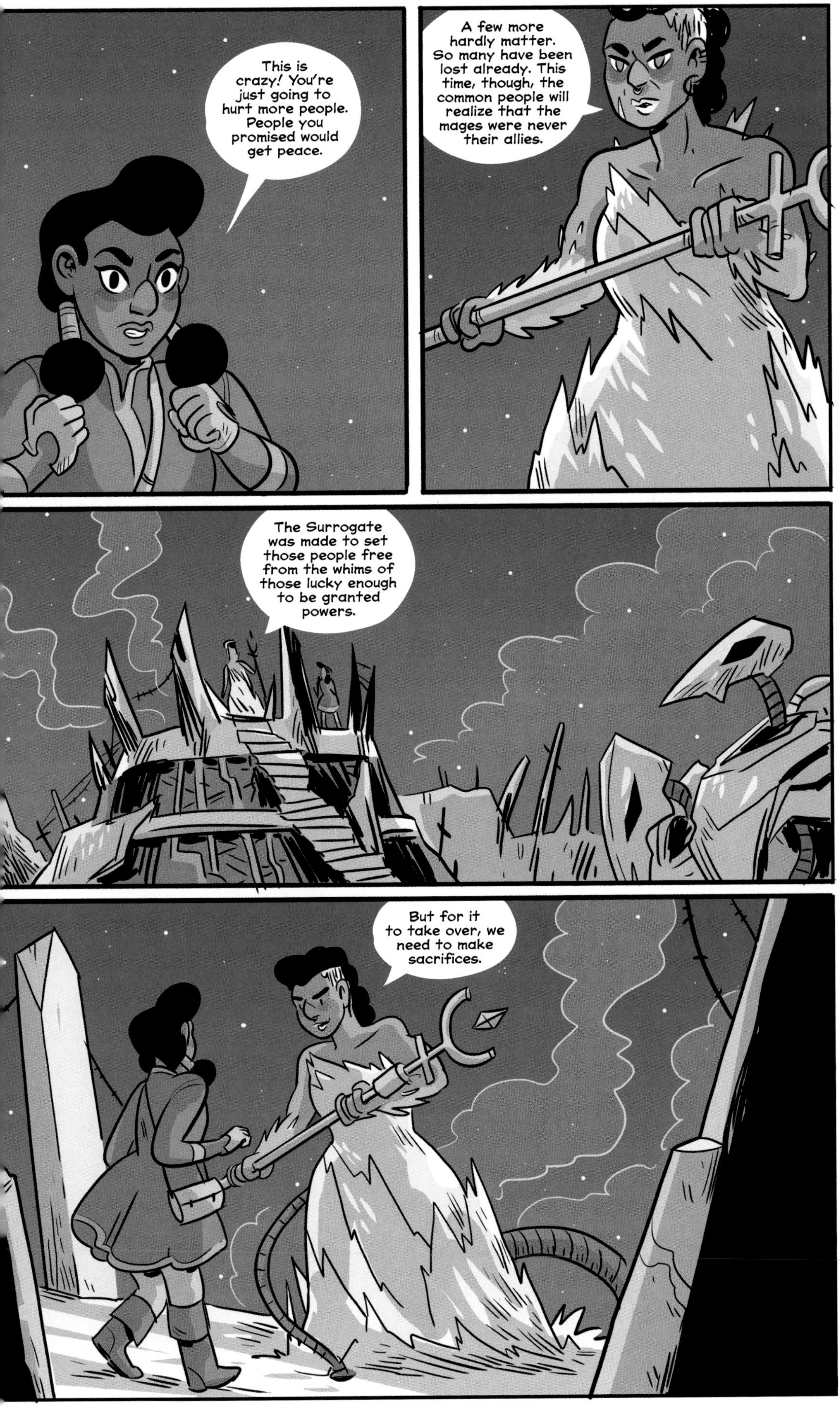
This is crazy! You're just going to hurt more people. People you promised would get peace.
A few more hardly matter. So many have been lost already. This time, though, the common people will realize that the mages were never their allies.
The Surrogate was made to set those people free from the whims of those lucky enough to be granted powers.
But for it to take over, we need to make sacrifices.

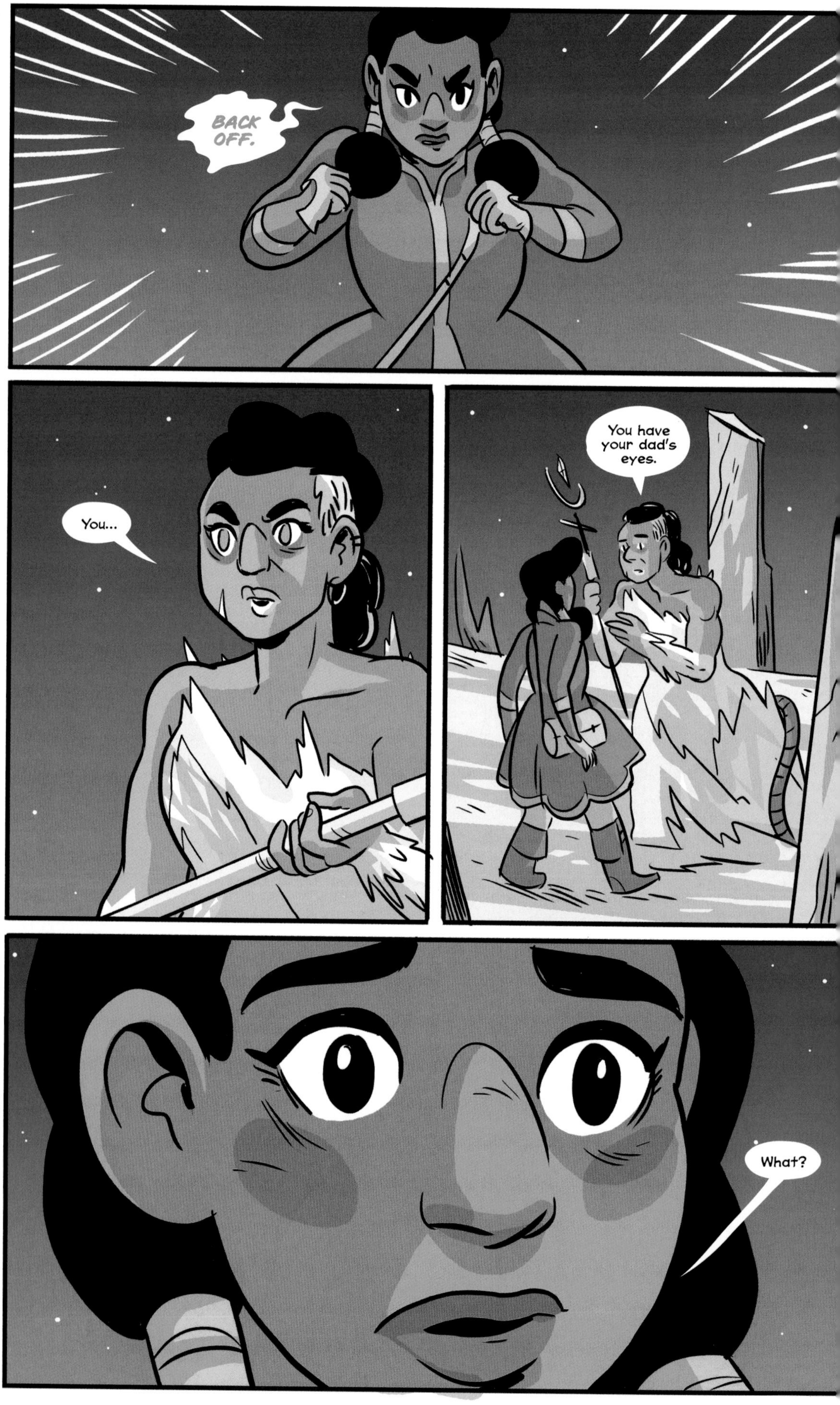
BACK OFF.
You...
You have your dad's eyes.
What?

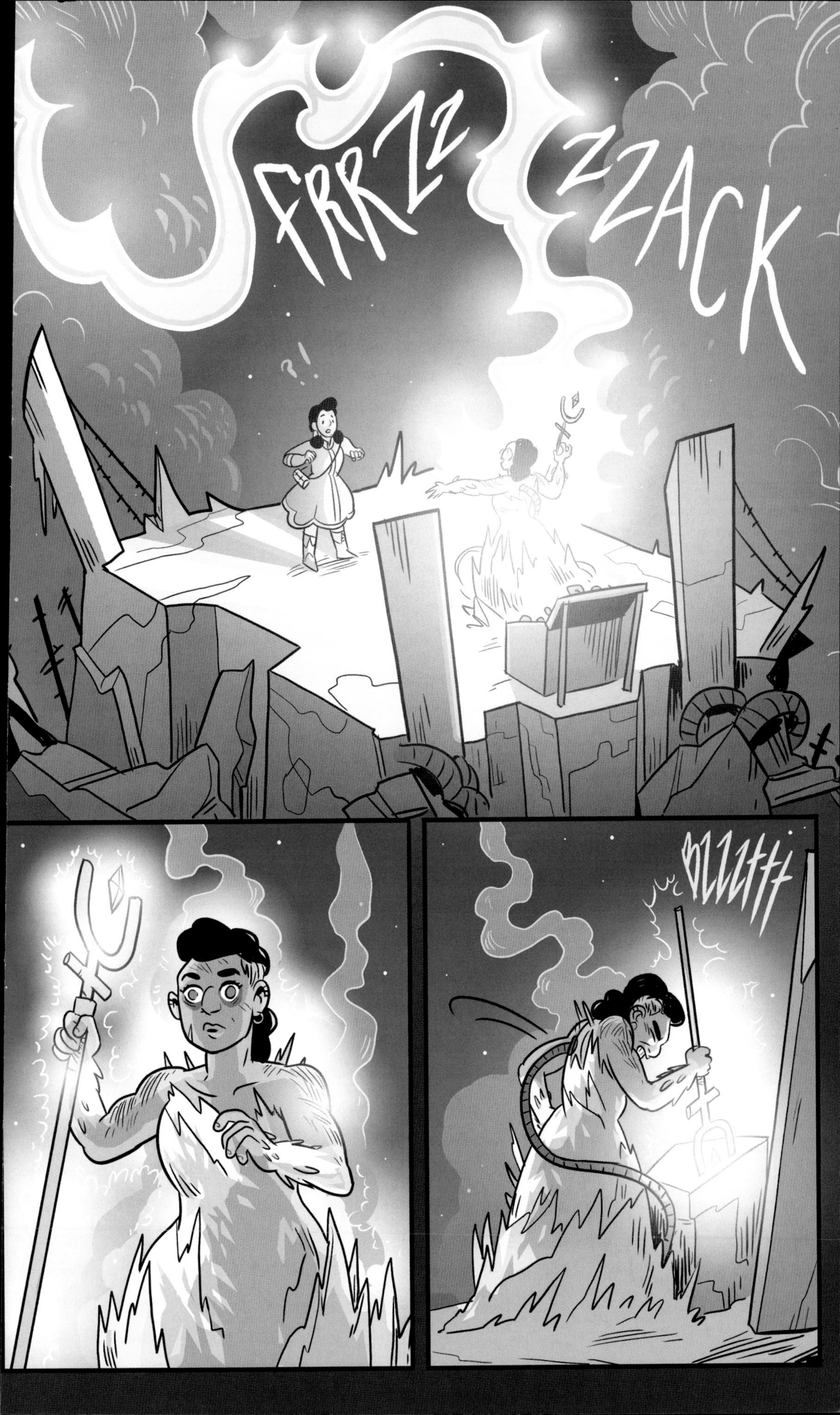
FRRZZZ
ZZZACK
?!
BZZZTTT

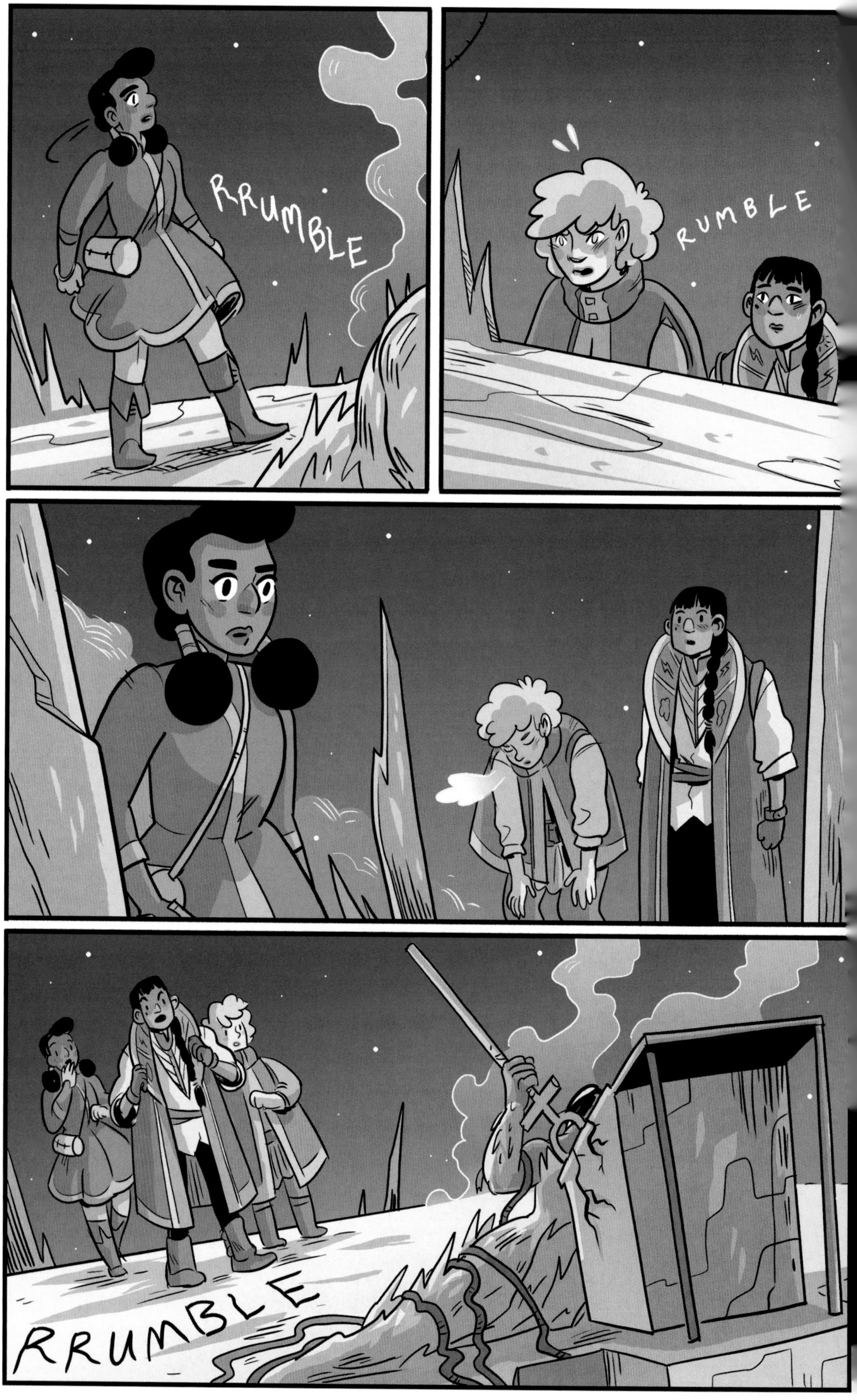
RRUMBLE
RUMBLE
RRUMBLE

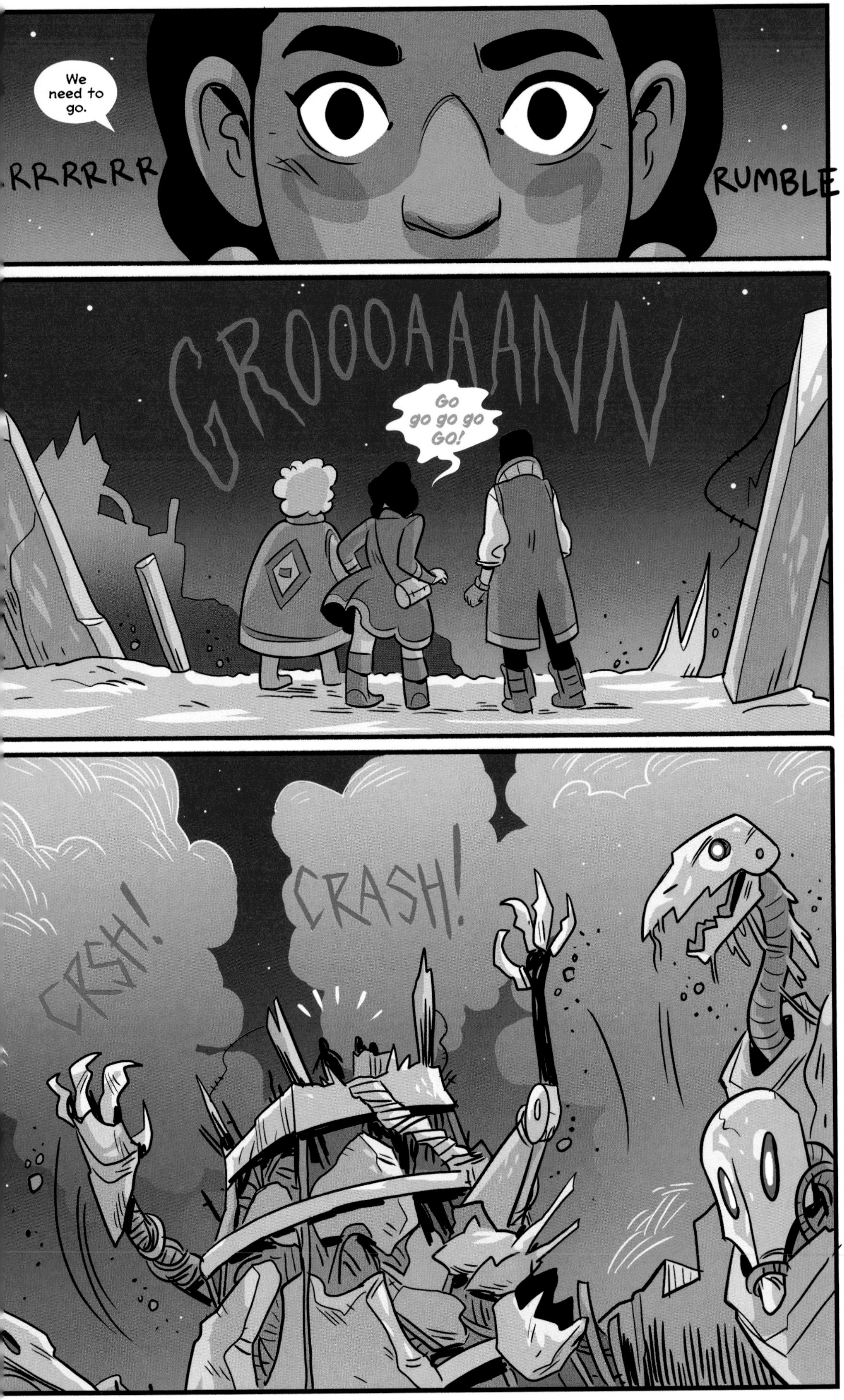
We need to go.
RRRRRR
RUMBLE
GROOOAAANN
Go go go go GO!
CRSH!
CRASH!

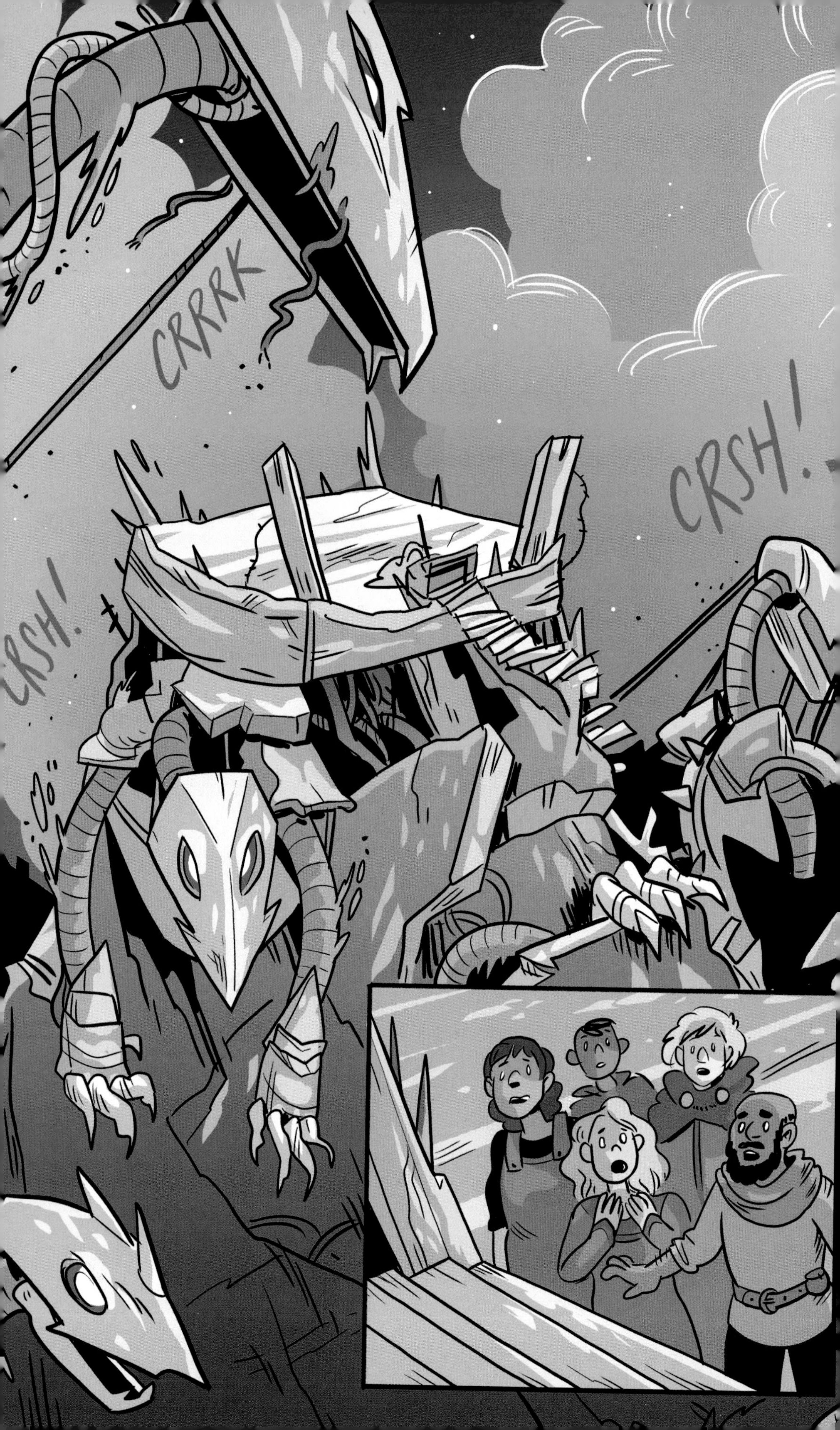
CRRRK
CRSH!
CRSH!

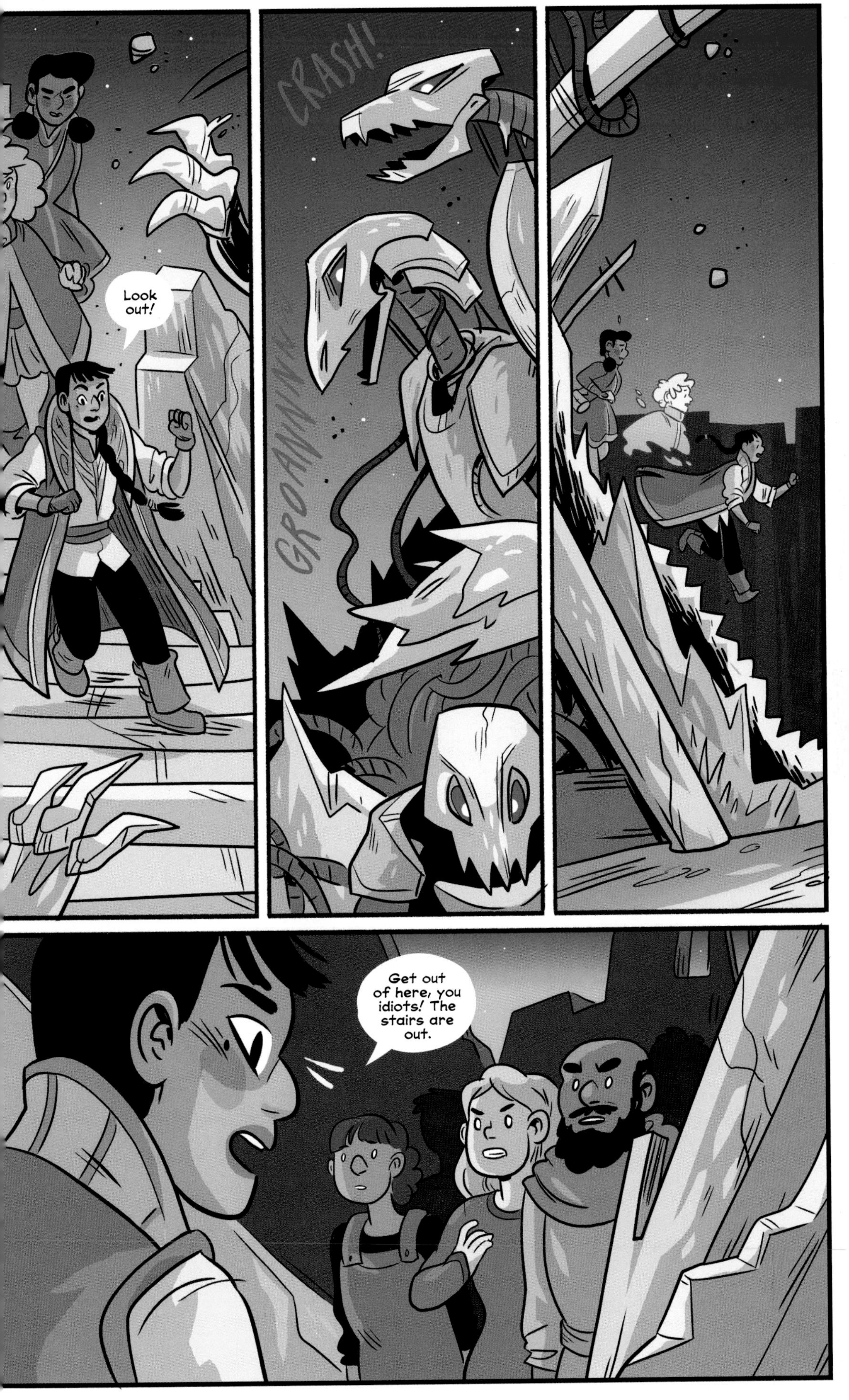
Look out!
CRASH!
GROANNNN
Get out of here, you idiots! The stairs are out.

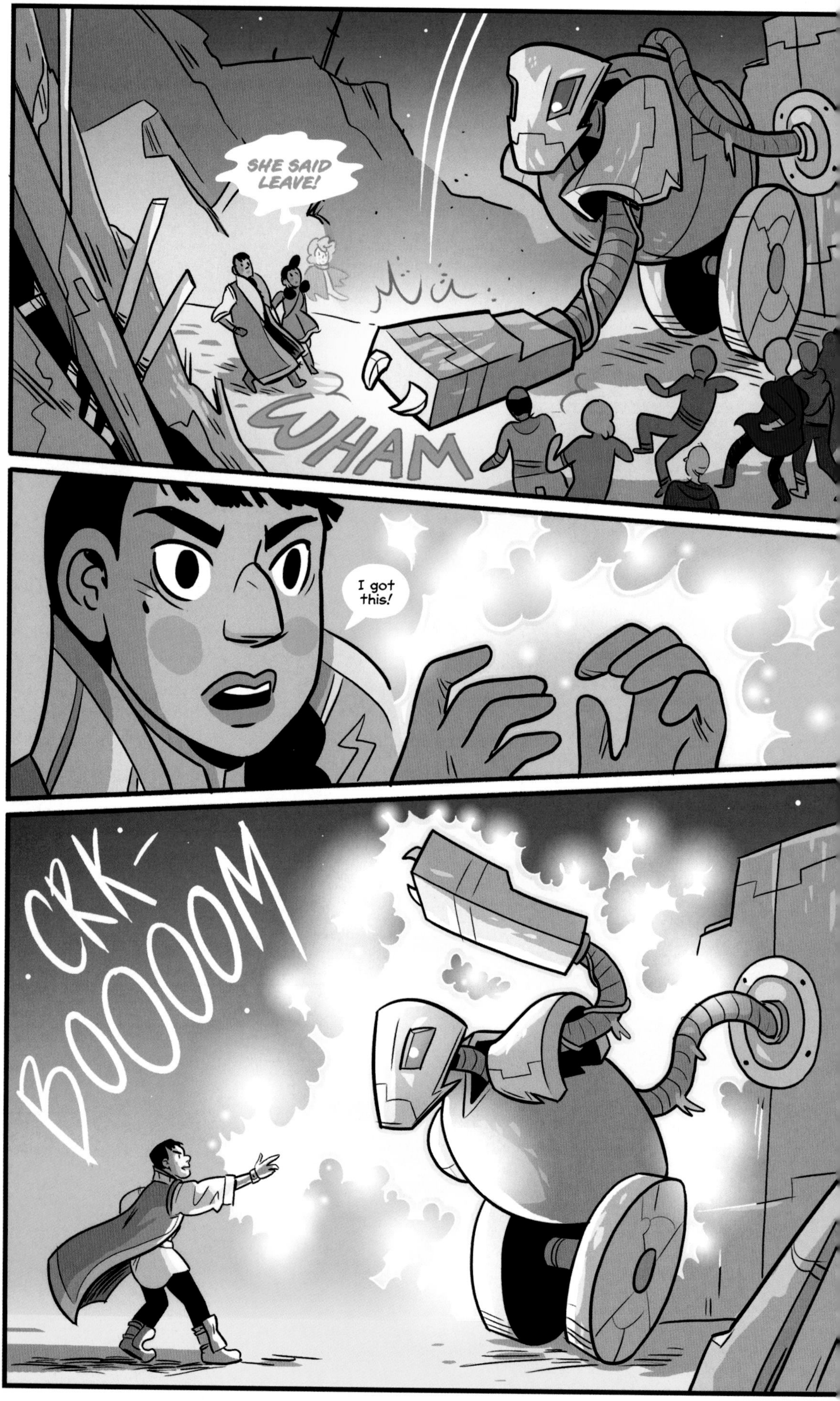
SHE SAID LEAVE!
WHAM
I got this!
CRK-
BOOOOOM

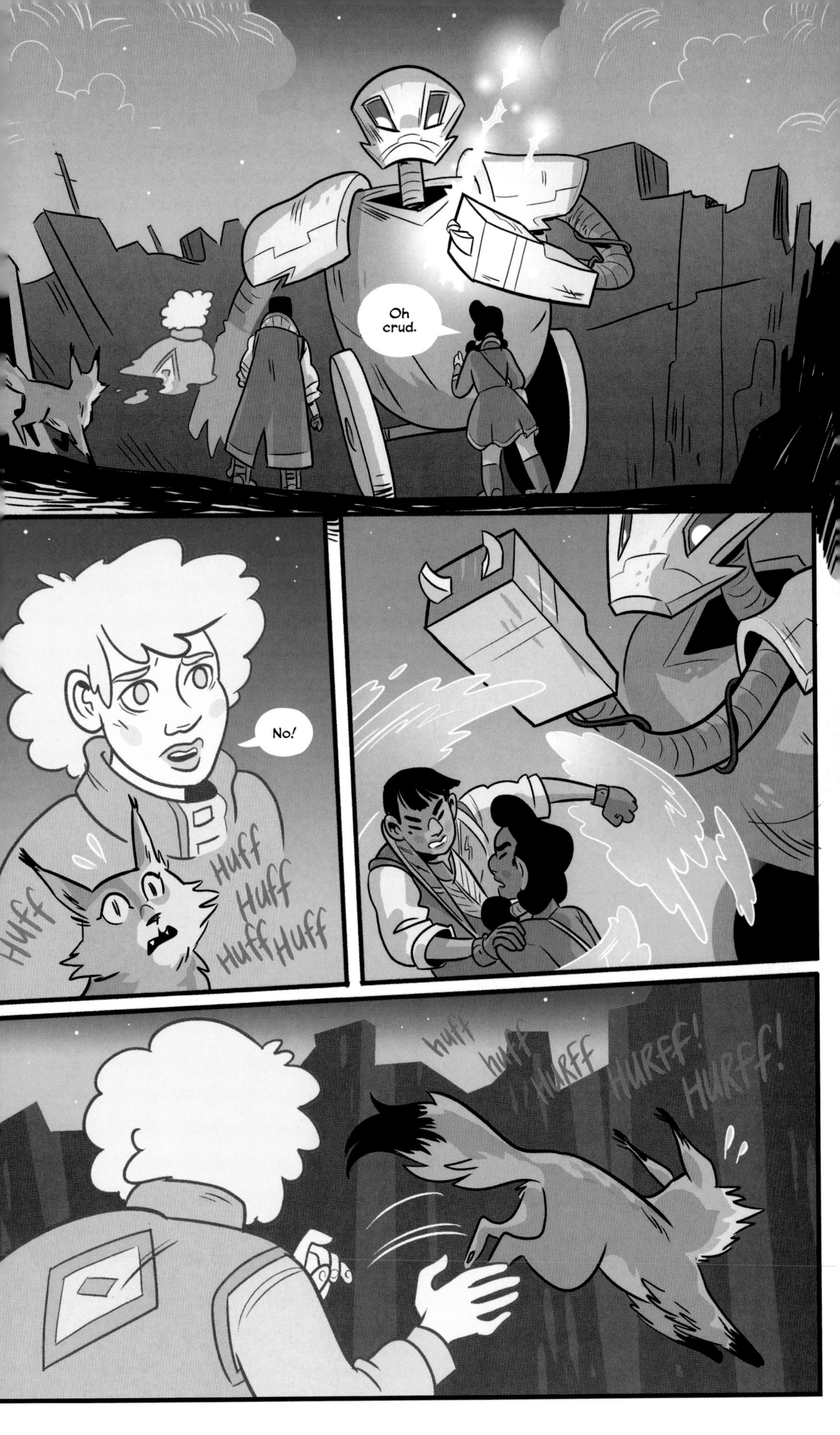
Oh crud.
No!
Huff
Huff
Huff
Huff
Huff
huff
huff
HURFF
HURFF!
HURFF!

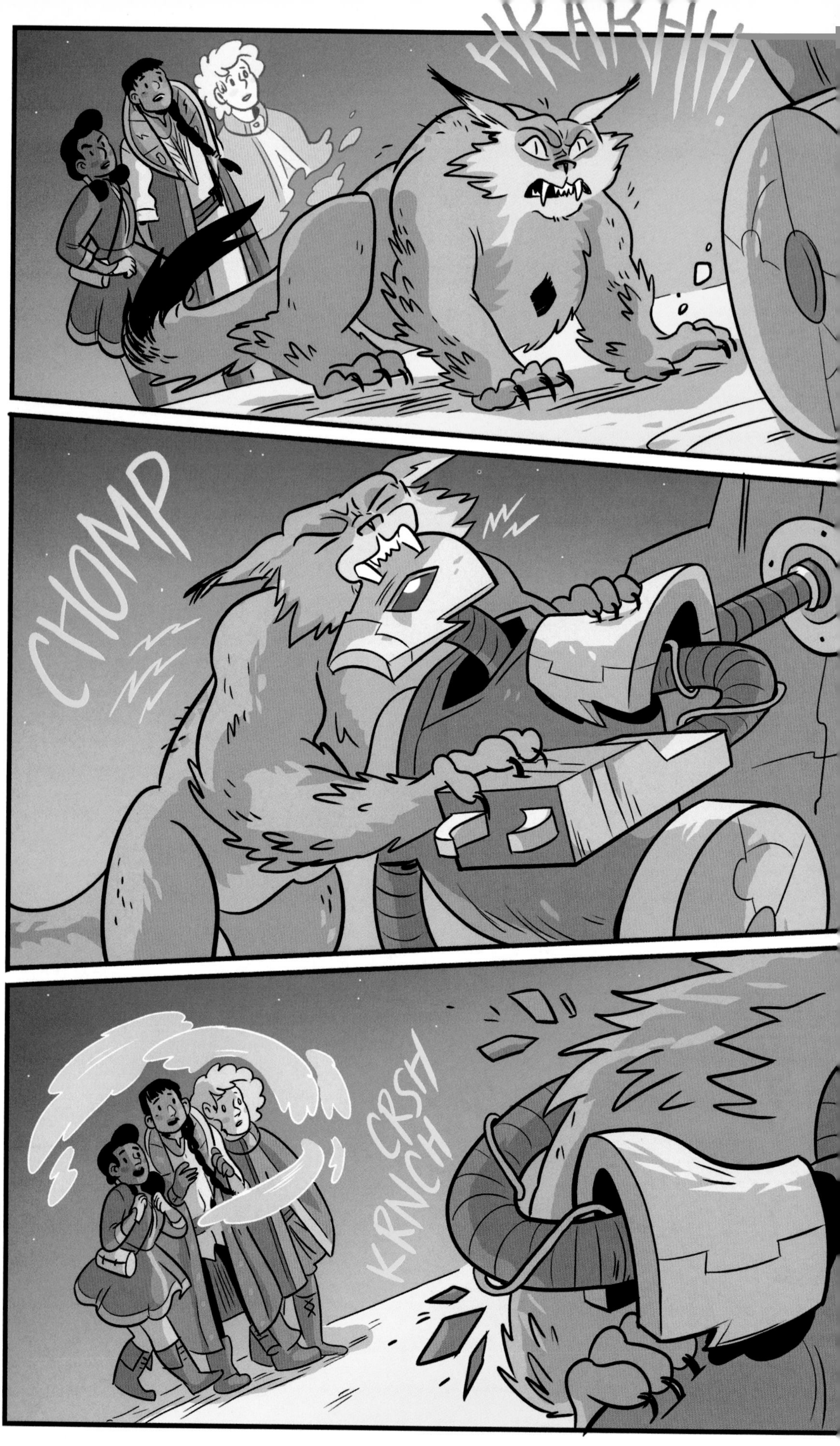
HRAKHH!
CHOMP
CRSH
KRNCH

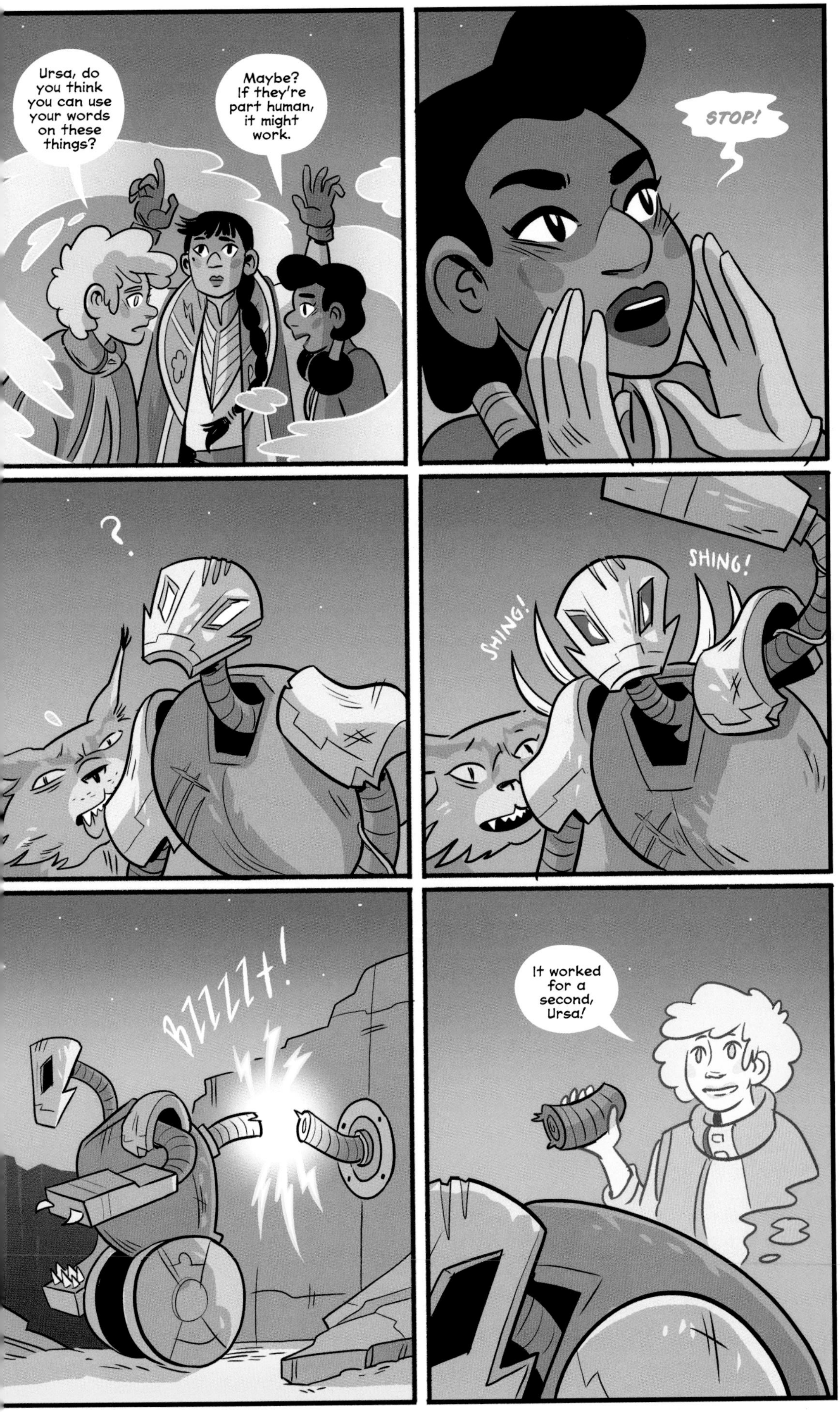
Ursa, do you think you can use your words on these things?
Maybe? If they're part human, it might work.
STOP!
?
SHING!
SHING!
BZZZZT!
It worked for a second, Ursa!

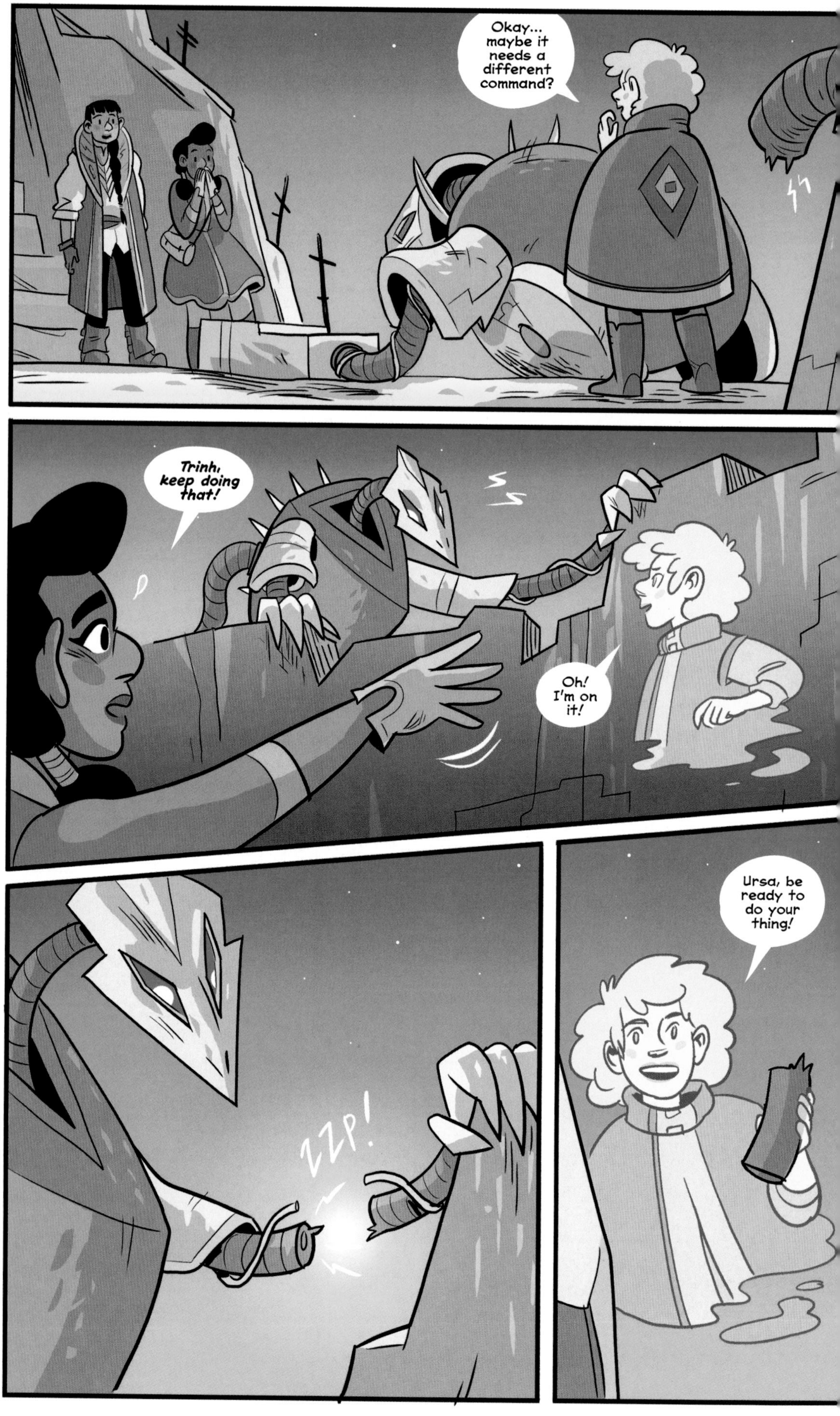
Okay... maybe it needs a different command?
Trinh, keep doing that!
Oh! I'm on it!
ZZP!
Ursa, be ready to do your thing!

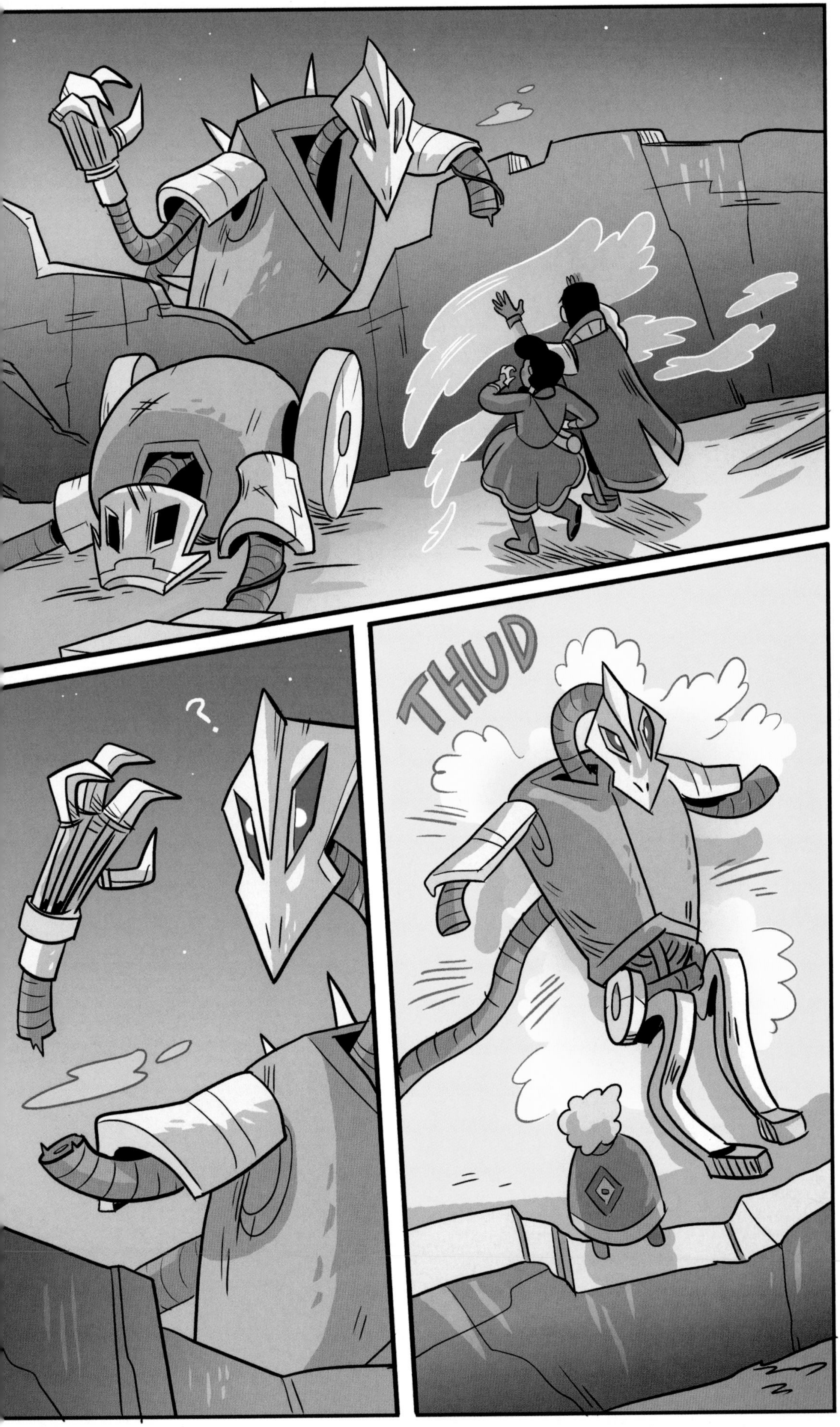
?
THUD

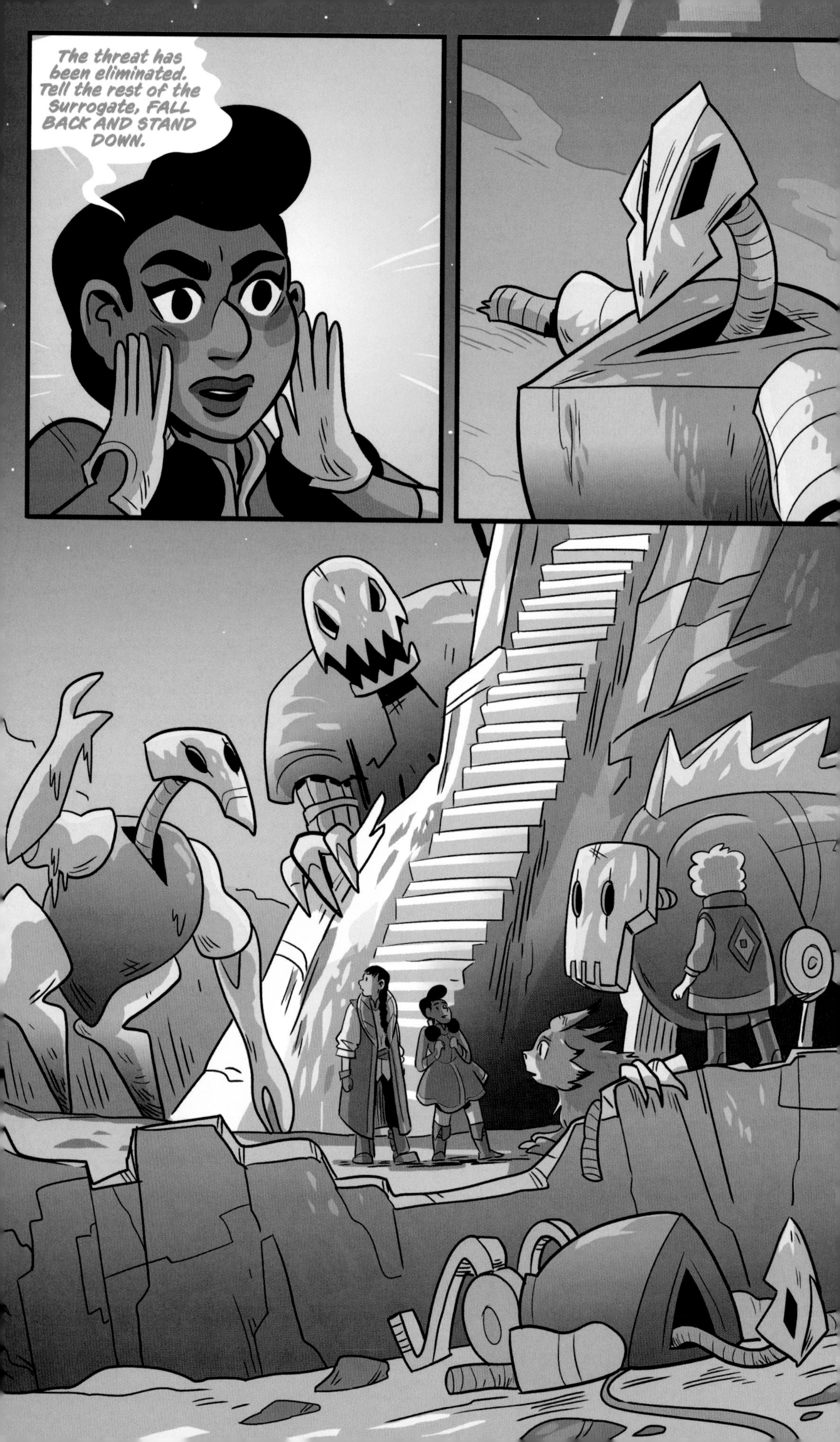
The threat has been eliminated. Tell the rest of the Surrogate, FALL BACK AND STAND DOWN.

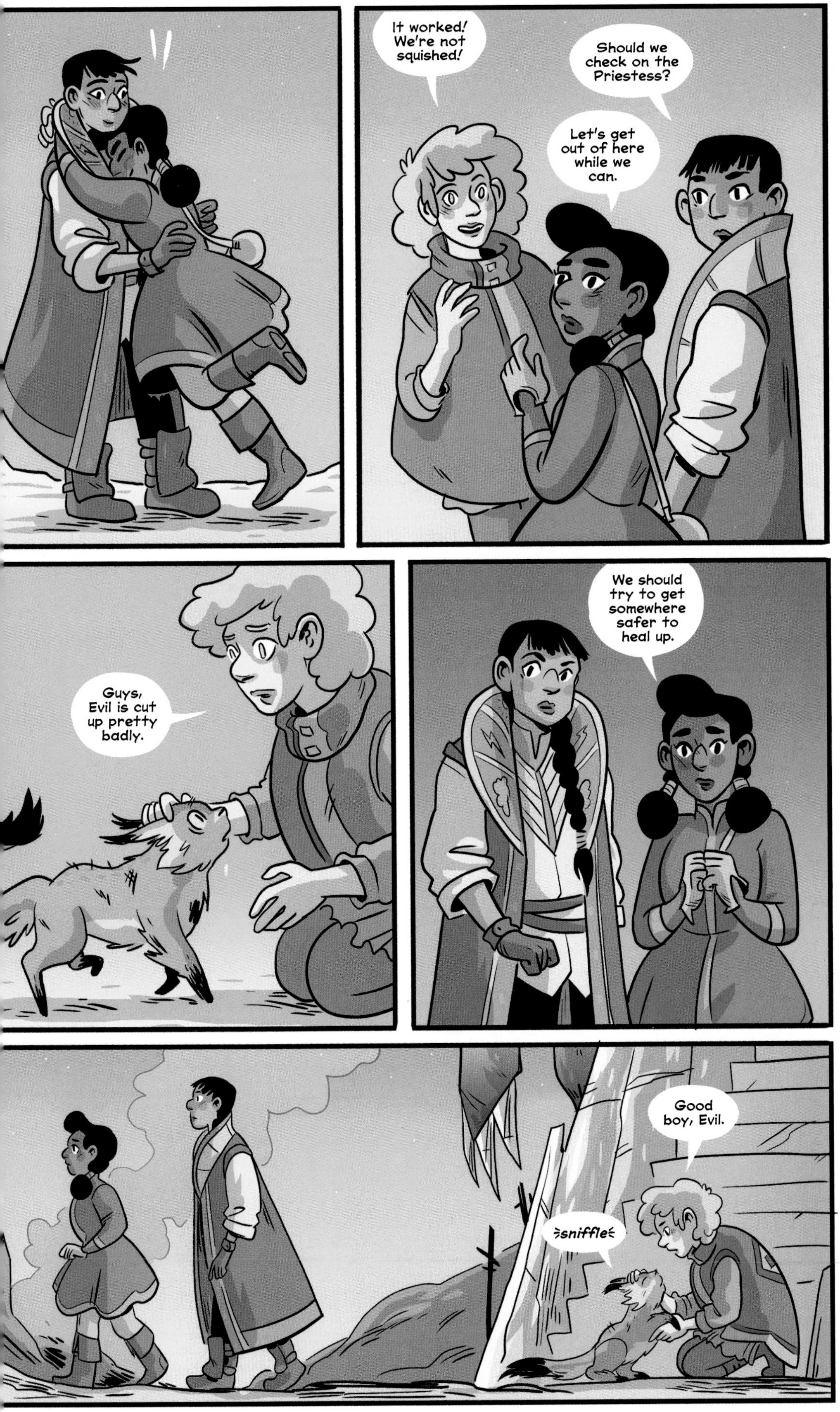
It worked! We're not squished!
Should we check on the Priestess?
Let's get out of here while we can.
Guys, Evil is cut up pretty badly.
We should try to get somewhere safer to heal up.
Good boy, Evil.
sniffle

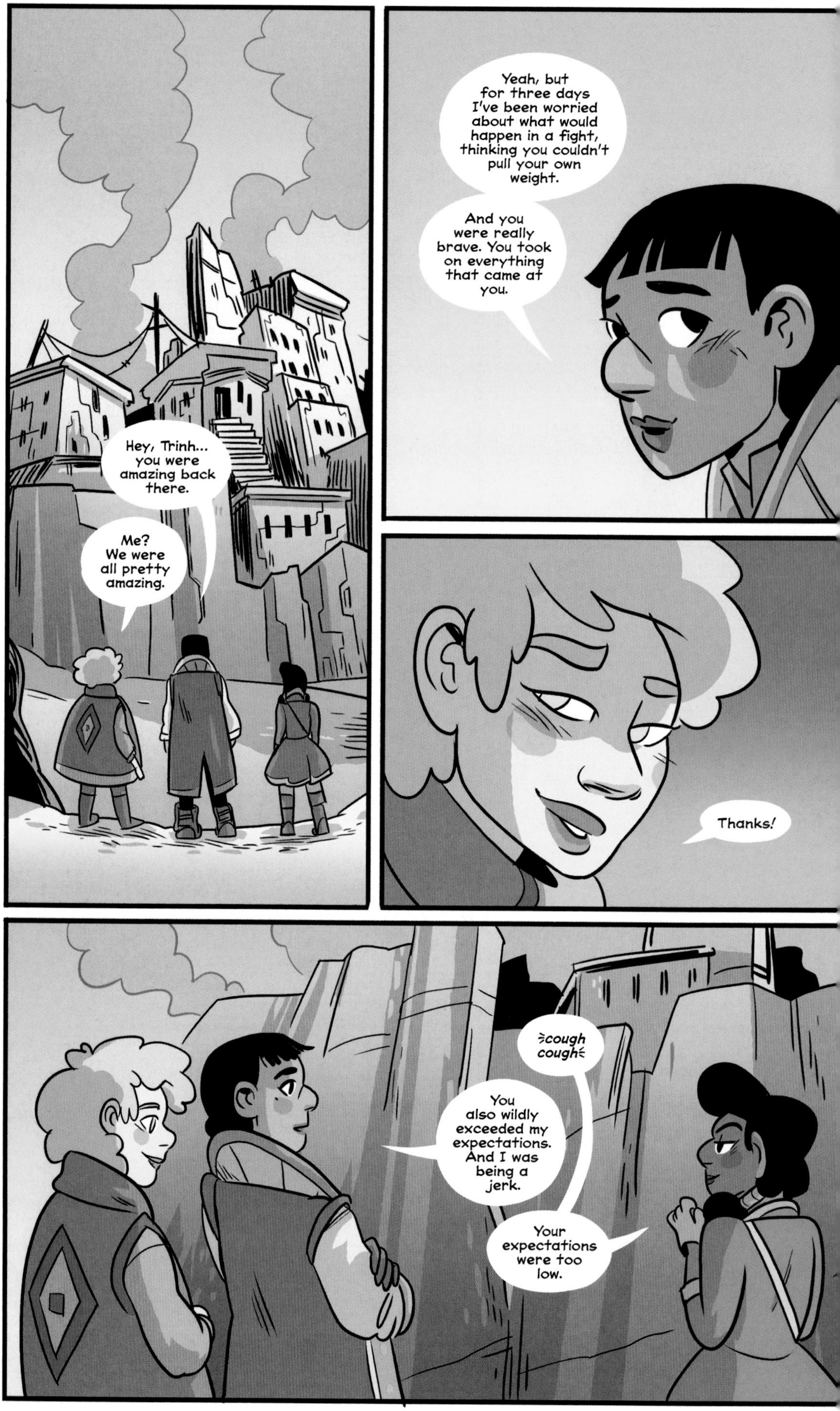
Hey, Trinh... you were amazing back there.
Me? We were all pretty amazing.
Yeah, but for three days I've been worried about what would happen in a fight, thinking you couldn't pull your own weight.
And you were really brave. You took on everything that came at you.
Thanks!
cough cough
You also wildly exceeded my expectations. And I was being a jerk.
Your expectations were too low.

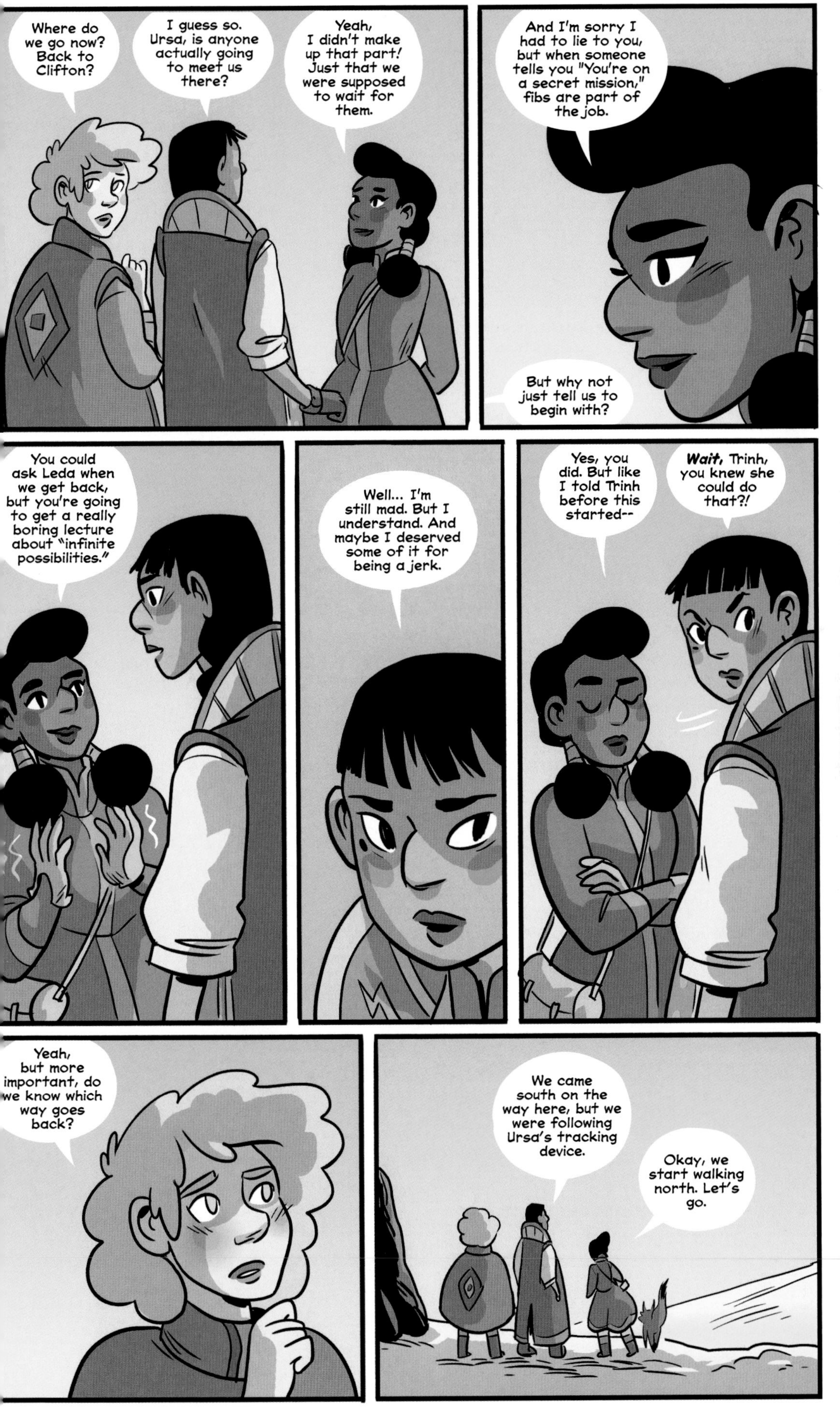
Where do we go now? Back to Clifton?
I guess so. Ursa, is anyone actually going to meet us there?
Yeah, I didn't make up that part! Just that we were supposed to wait for them.
And I'm sorry I had to lie to you, but when someone tells you "You're on a secret mission," fibs are part of the job.
But why not just tell us to begin with?
You could ask Leda when we get back, but you're going to get a really boring lecture about "infinite possibilities."
Well... I'm still mad. But I understand. And maybe I deserved some of it for being a jerk.
Yes, you did. But like I told Trinh before this started--
Wait, Trinh, you knew she could do that?!
Yeah, but more important, do we know which way goes back?
We came south on the way here, but we were following Ursa's tracking device.
Okay, we start walking north. Let's go.

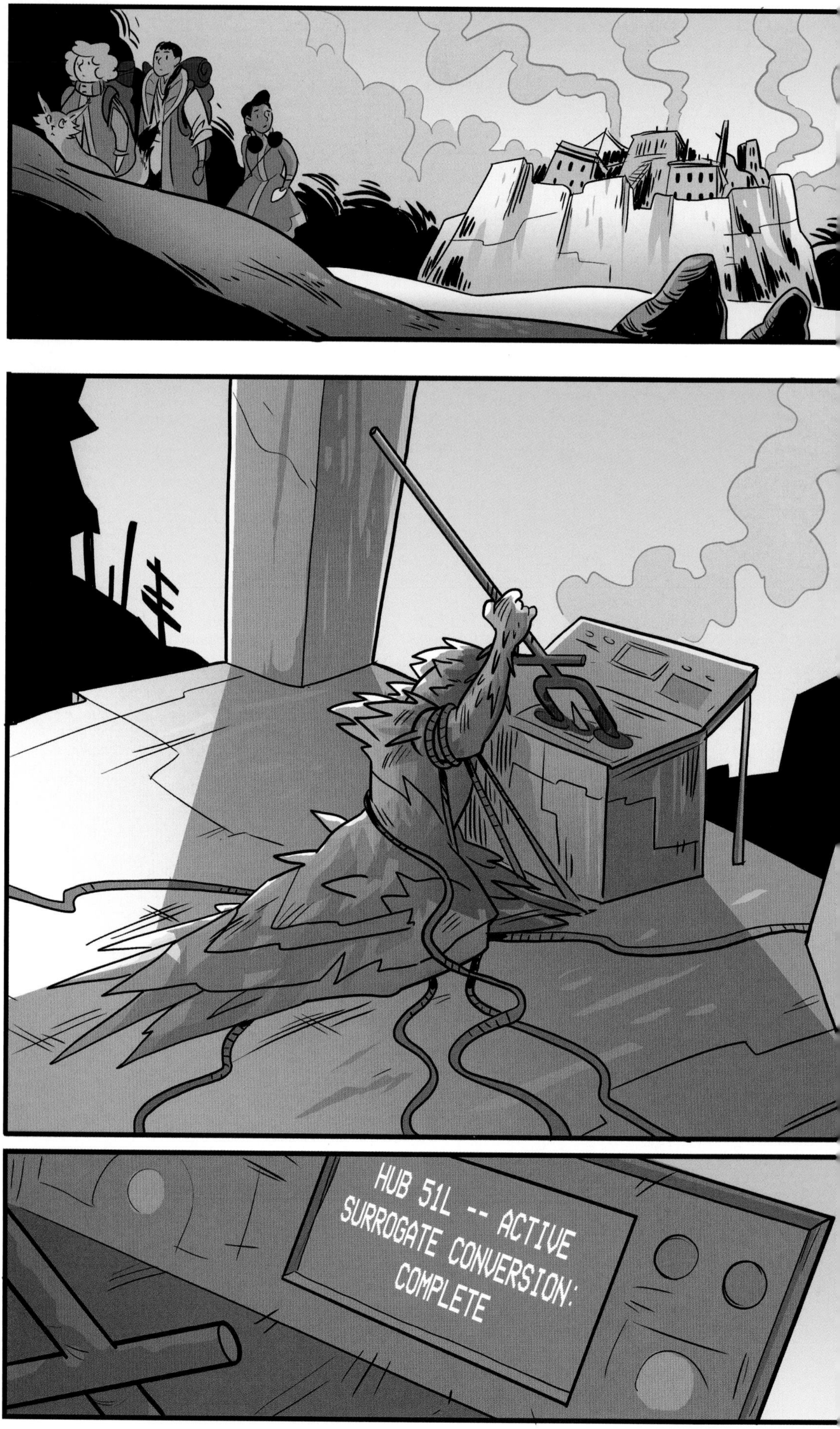
HUB 51L -- ACTIVE
SURROGATE CONVERSION:
COMPLETE

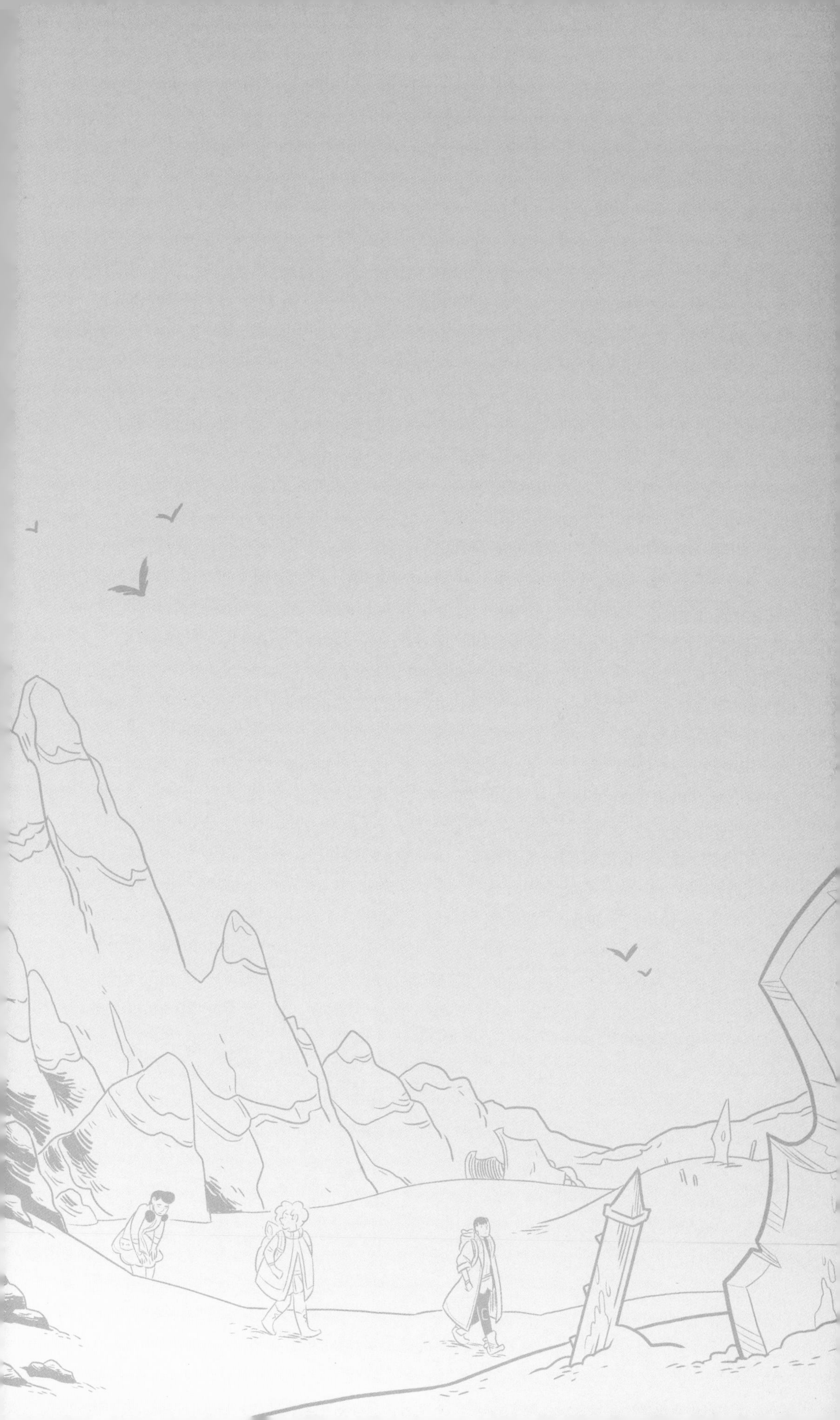

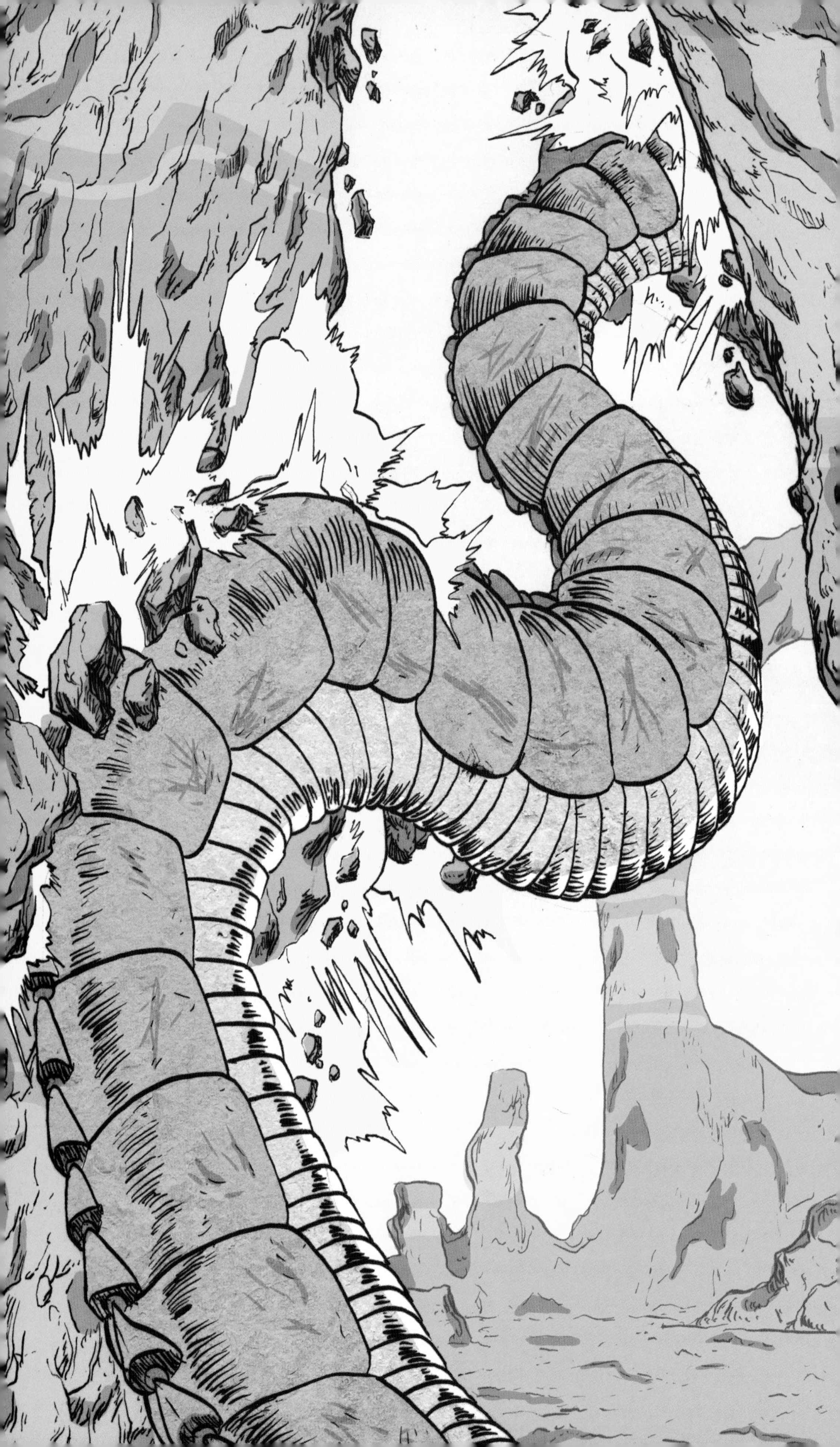

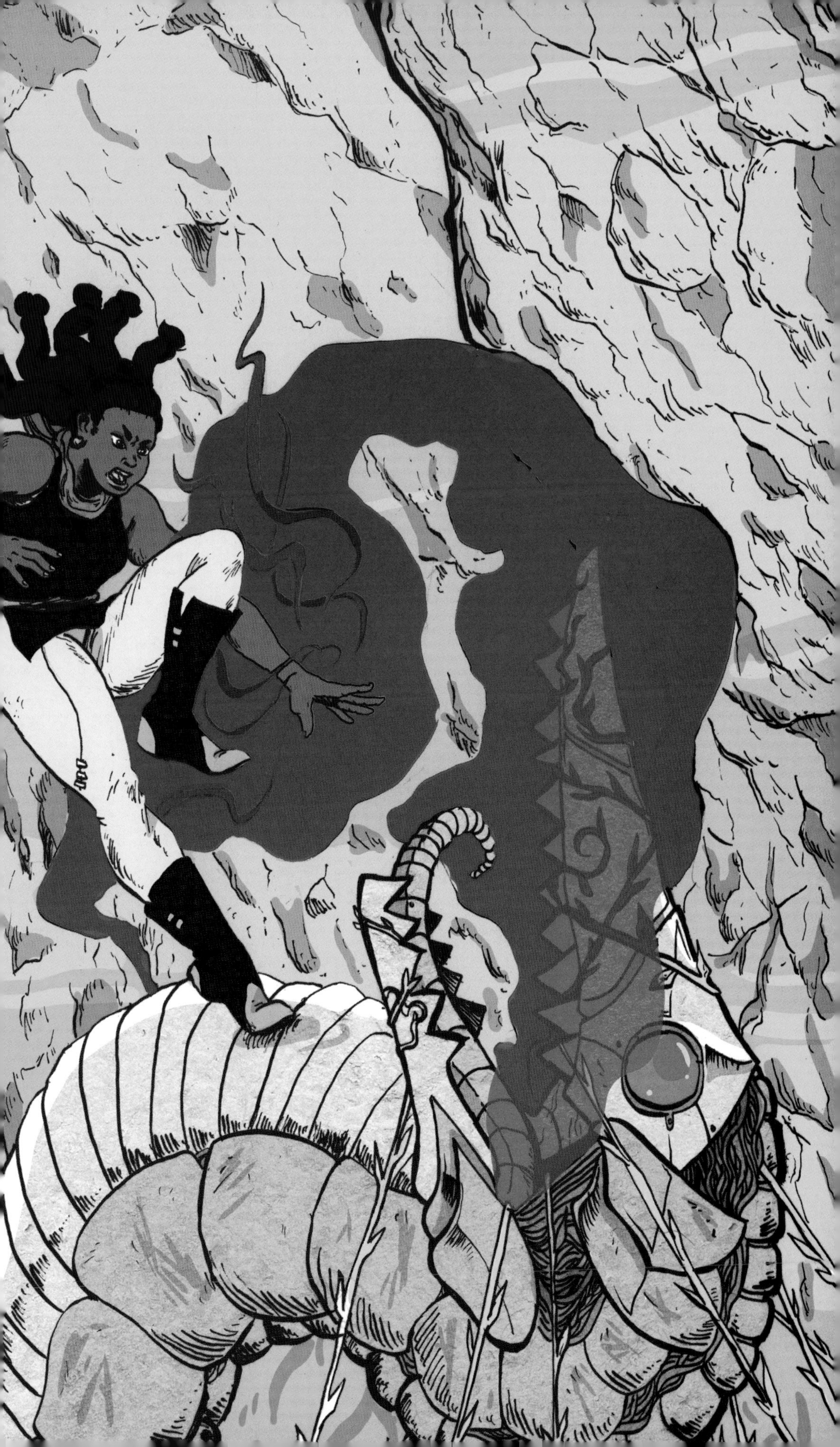

MK REED

is the author of the graphic novels *Americus*, *The Cute Girl Network*, *Palefire*, and *Science Comics: Dinosaurs*. She also writes and draws the web comic *About A Bull*. Her work has appeared in anthologies like *Papercutter*, *Chainmail Bikini*, *The Big Feminist But*, and the Swedish magazine *Galago*. *Americus* was the winner of NAIBA's 2012 Carla Cohen Free Speech Award, and was a 2011 American Booksellers for Children's New Voices title. MK lives in Portland, Oregon, with her very tall husband.

BRIAN "SMITTY" SMITH

is a former Marvel Comics editor, and the co-creator of the *New York Times* bestselling graphic novel *The Stuff of Legend*. He is the writer and artist of the all-ages comic *The Intrepid EscapeGoat*, and the illustrator of *The Adventures of Daniel Boom AKA Loud Boy* series of younger reader graphic novels. He is also the artist of *Madballs* from Roar Comics.

MOLLY KNOX OSTERTAG

is the co-creator and artist of the webcomic *Strong Female Protagonist*. She illustrated the graphic novel *Shattered Warrior* by Sharon Shinn, and her own graphic novel *The Witch Boy* will be released by Scholastic in 2018. She currently lives in Los Angeles and works as a designer on the Disney show *Star Vs. the Forces of Evil*.

WYETH YATES

lives in Brooklyn, NY, with his cat, Switch. He likes skeleton keys, the smell of old books, and has a lot of stories left to draw.

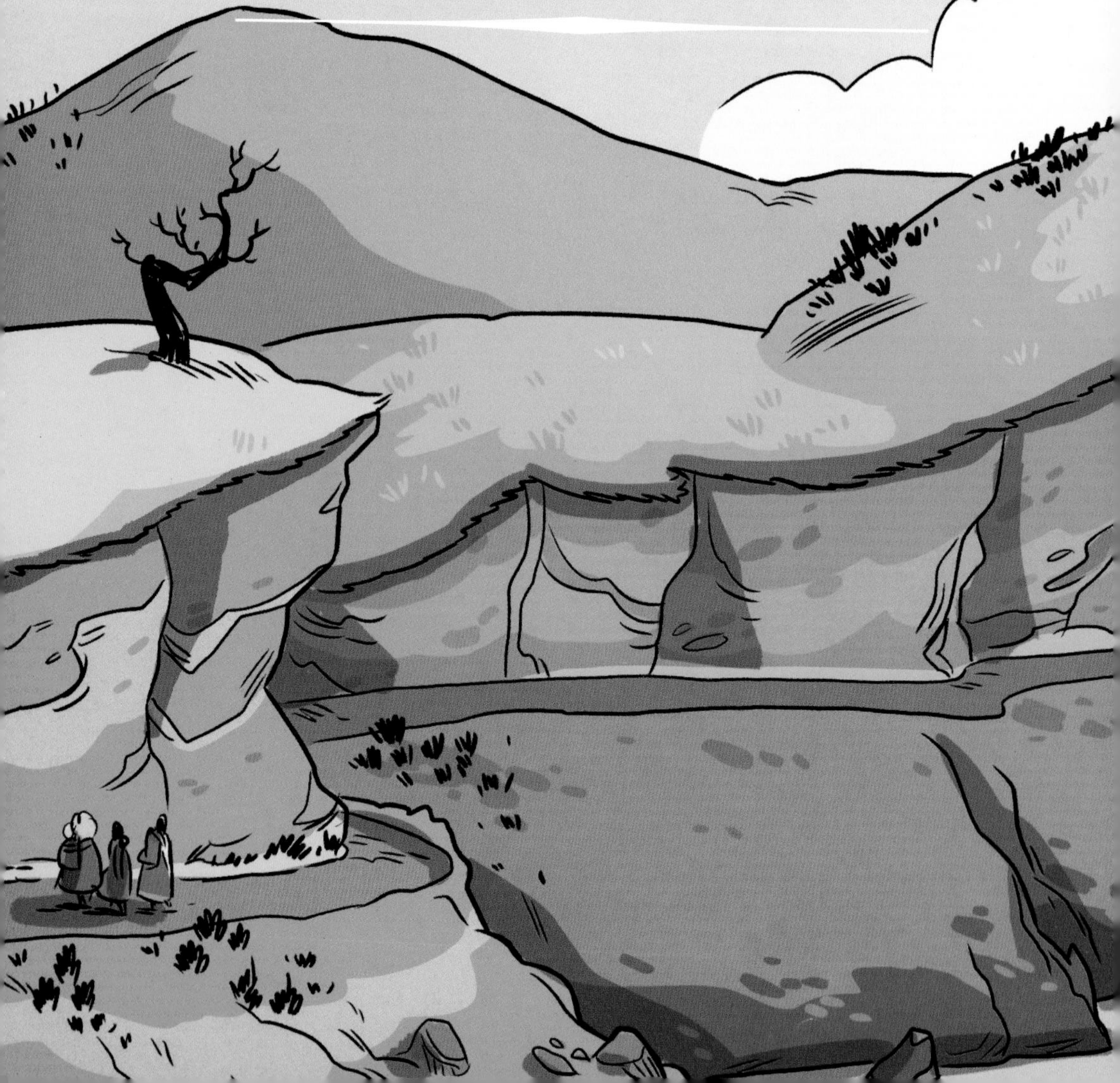